D0743217

In the Mind's Eye

Elizabeth Dodd

In the Mind's Eye

Essays across the Animate World

UNIVERSITY OF NEBRASKA PRESS

LINCOLN AND LONDON

Acknowledgments for previously published materials appear on p. ix, which constitutes an extension of the copyright page.

© 2008 by the Board of Regents of the University of Nebraska

All rights reserved

Manufactured in the United States of America

♾

Library of Congress Cataloging-in-Publication Data

Dodd, Elizabeth Caroline, 1962–
In the mind's eye : essays across the animate world / Elizabeth Dodd.
p. cm.
Includes bibliographical references.
ISBN 978-0-8032-1566-5 (cloth : alk. paper)
I. Title.
PS3554.O317715 2008
814'.54—dc22
2008004132

Set in Quadraat by Kim Essman.

Designed by Ray Boeche.

The natural object is always the adequate symbol.
Ezra Pound

Contents

Acknowledgments

I wish to thank the many editors who published versions of these essays in the following journals or books:

"Setting Forth in Their Footprints" in *The Southern Review*.

"Memory's Hills," which appeared as "Hills of Memory," in *Columbia Journal*.

"Walden, Woods" in *The Laurel Review*.

"Cañonicity" and "Here the Animal" in *Southwest Review*.

"Fragments" in *The Georgia Review* and *Landscapes with Figures: The Nonfiction of Place*, edited by Robert Root. Reprinted by permission of University of Nebraska Press.

"The Shannon Creek Eagles" in the *Flint Hills Review*.

"Bones of Fear" and "The Artists of La Grotte Chauvet" (portion of "La Descente") in *Notre Dame Magazine*.

"In Such a Homecoming" in *Good Roots: Writers Reflect on Growing Up in Ohio*, edited by Lisa Watts. Reprinted by permission of Ohio University Press, Athens, Ohio (www.ohioswallow.com).

"The Scribe in the Woods" originally appeared in *Fourth Genre*, published by Michigan State University Press.

I gratefully acknowledge the various agencies and persons who assisted me in my research:

Kansas State University's Office of Research and Sponsored Programs, for small research grant support; The Center for the Understanding of Origins at Kansas State University and my department head, Linda Brigham, for summer fellowship support; Jean Clottes, Yanik Le Guillou, and Dominique Baffier from the French Ministry of Culture; Steve Paul of the *Kansas City Star*; Michael R. Grauer of the Panhandle-Plains Historical Museum; Eumie Stroukoff and Barbara Lynes of the Georgia O'Keeffe Research Center; Roger Adams of Kansas State University Library's Special Collections; Claire Dehon of Kansas State University's Modern Languages Department; John Spence, Mark Anderson, and Jesse Granete from the Glen Canyon National Recreation Area; Ray Matlack from West Texas A&M University.

The Jim Ehleringer Labs at University of Utah; the Maturango Museum and the China Lake Naval Weapons Research Station, of Ridgecrest, California; James Q. Jacobs.

The University of Utah Special Collections; Brian McNulty from Ohio University.

Dan Mulhern, from the U.S. Fish and Wildlife Service; Tillie Autry, from the Otero Museum in La Junta, Colorado; Martin Lockley, of the University of Denver; Pat Momich from the National Forest Service in Asheville, North Carolina; Katrina Schultes from the Wayne National Forest Office; the Beinecke Rare Book and Manuscript Library, Yale University; and Yaddo.

To the friends and family who were fellow travelers, hosts, or otherwise supporters of these forays and essays, I owe special thanks:

Hudson Dodd and Dawn Gauthier
Wayne Dodd and Joyce Barlow Dodd
Gina Becker
Beth Rosenberg
John and Betty Rintoul
Roger Mitchell and Dorian Gossy
Rosemarie King and Robert Grindy

Moira Wedekind and Laddie Derenchuk
Ellen Welti
Cynthia Buel
Ana and Paul Hooker
Laurie Pieper and the Morning Star Bed and Breakfast Book Club members: Nadine Brazda, Linda Guthrie, Connie Hamilton, Susan Metzger, and Susan Shultis

And, most especially, to Dave Rintoul go my love and appreciation.

Setting Forth in Their Footprints

Walking realizes motion, and some biologists feel that motion planning is a form of intelligence.

Teresa Zielinska

On the long, hairpinned climb from the Valley of the Gods, heading north from the town of Mexican Hat, I meet only one other vehicle on the road, a pickup headed south. So in midafternoon, when I see the guy with his thumb out and a hopeful look on his face heading north along Cedar Mesa, I think it must be up to me, although I vowed years ago to never, ever, not-even-once stop again for another hitchhiker. I slow the car.

This traveler's a young man, wearing a Marines t-shirt and magnificent sunglasses, with a pack on his back indicating that he's just climbed up from one of the canyons that transect and drain the mesa—eight hundred, maybe a thousand feet. There's a different code of ethical behavior in the wilderness, and he's still crusted with its dust and dried mud, but I remain a little wary, wondering if this is the smartest thing I've ever done.

"What's your story?" I ask without opening the door. He's already smiling broadly, dropping his pack to the ground by his feet. He says he's finished three days of backpacking in Grand Gulch, from Kane's Creek to Bullet Canyon, and is headed back to the ranger station along Route 261.

"So your loop includes a long hike on asphalt?" I ask him.

"They told me someone would surely pick me up," he says. "But you're the first car I've seen. Thanks for stopping; you've saved me hours of walking."

I clear out the passenger seat, he crams his pack on top of my already dusty gear in the back, and we continue north. I learn that his name is Aaron, and he's not a Marine; that's his younger brother's shirt. In fact, he's just out of the Peace Corps, his wife is in Salt Lake visiting relatives, and in the fall he's starting a master's program in education at the University of Chicago. Then he tells me excitedly about his hike—bitterly cold the first night. "Nineteen degrees," he says with the precision of someone to whom each calibrated drop in temperature was significant. After that, beautiful weather. And he reached several Ancestral Pueblo ruins, even though his route came nowhere near to completing the sixty-mile length of the primitive area boxed in attractive green on the map. He's still elated, uplifted from the trip, and I recognize both the place names he describes—Turkey Pen ruin, Jailhouse ruin—and the near-rush of narration, the delight in telling someone who's interested— me, in this case—what he's seen. I'm planning to day-hike in, still uncertain an old foot injury will let me pack the excessive weight of my too-roomy, two-person tent. He sells me his map for half of what he paid for it—"I believe in karma," he says— and unfolds it on his lap, pointing out where he camped, where the water was clear rather than runoff muddy. In the parking lot, we shake hands, wish each other luck, and prepare to go our different ways.

That night I sleep on BLM land just up the road, overlooking Lyman Canyon, marked on the map as an intermittent stream a few hundred feet below the rim. There I pitch the tent on a few inches of soil above sandstone, hardly enough to hold the stakes in place. A high mesa to the east changes color as I sit watching, cooling in the evening; a tiny bit of snow clings to its upper reaches, but the rock glows various shades of vermilion, rufus, ocher, and I recognize for a moment the perfect shade of a stone I picked up days ago, grinding from it a few experimental grains as if to approximate paint. Then, briefly, the rock seems to shine from within, the way the dying heart of a campfire would have if I'd kindled one, just in the last moments before it would be time to scatter the coals, douse them with water, and listen to the hiss of ash-scented steam. Instead, I listen to the current in the canyon below, an allegro of motion, of flow, the world in its exquisite movement into spring.

The next morning, I'm on the trail before 8:00, a day-use permit tucked beneath the bug-splashed windshield in the unpaved parking lot. This is Kane Gulch, heading southwest; the water here is muddy, cold, and seems in a tremendous hurry to pass through the landscape, leaving everything behind to the dry heat of the coming summer. Almost immediately I begin the sinuous trek back and forth across this meltwater current, as the slope of the wash itself deepens toward actual canyon. Before 9:00, a red-tailed hawk startles from where it has landed to drink, and it lifts heavily, legs dangling their angled talons.

By 11:00, I've given up keeping my feet dry and no longer even try to cross the current; I slosh right through. Occasionally, mud sucks at my feet as they try to step free; other times the channel bed is slickrock sandstone, smooth and mostly level except for the downstream tilt that lets the water hurry away. And once, I slip and splash and get wet to the waist, worrying briefly that I've dipped the pack, but no, it's only me, my shorts, and of course my shoes that are soaked from the clumsy dunking. So around noon, I find a dry cottonwood log to sit on, un-lace the boots, and let my pale feet warm in the sunlight, wool socks dangling wetly, heavily, from a yucca spike. I take off my shorts, too, since no one is around, and sit in my underwear, drying off. Eating a peanut-butter-and-banana sandwich, I con-sider skeptically the ring of mud that rims each boot, the silty film that stains my legs, the faint dirty tinge that has darkened my spiffy blue orthotics, also set out to dry in the sun. In the sandy dust, the orthotics look like robot footprints, fleshless, toeless, futuristic in their shadow-cast of ball and arch, waiting for me to step into them again and move along.

For days, I've been thinking about the footprints that fleck the rock art of the American Southwest. Full sized, miniature. Sin-gle tracks or a series, left, right, left, indicating the route, the path, the journey—maybe even time (seven prints here, only four here). In Nevada, at Atlatl Rock, I saw what I want to call a classic footprint: the carved perfection of the idealized hu-man form, toes down, a narrow heel like my own, but no appar-ent arch. Another footprint, equally well pecked, showed much less symmetry: the second toe was far longer than all the oth-ers (indicating it may be female; my own second toe is the lon-gest on each foot). And that bonelike toe seemed damaged at its tip, bent, with the incised line interrupted as if in breakage. The foot pointed straight upward, heel aligned with earth and toes aligned toward sky, echoing the rock's monumental verticality. Rested from a night in a nearby, nearly empty campground, I stood awhile, considering. *Gawwwwd*, the composition seemed to me to say, *we walked nearly forever to get here. Just look what it's done to me!* In this it suggested something about the unidealized truth of the bipedal, perambulatory life. But who knows what specificity the artist meant in carving the foot's deformity on this pinnacle of stone in a broad, red, and very dry valley?

In Arizona, in Chevelon Canyon, I came across another perfect print, which seemed again to celebrate the beauty of our lives as wanderers, walkers across the world. It was a pale gray glyph on slightly less pale gray sandstone; a grisaille image without the paint. Here, the foot with all its perfect toes faced downward from the canyon rim to the cold meltwater rushing through the smooth, carved walls. *Go down to the water*, the print said to me. And, in sandals this time, I waded in the current, planting my feet along the sandstone bottom and its slow resistance to almost-as-slow abrasion. Above, on the mesa's rim, I'd stooped in the sunshine to study a flat rock, much weathered, that is believed by some to be a map of the canyon. A long meandering line seems to mimic particular bends between the canyon walls, and a spiral that terminates the image could suggest the permanent water hole in the stream below. The hole itself is a deep pool that stretches wall to wall to fill the canyon. There, the moving sun casts shadows on some portion of the water most of the day. The place is decorated on the upstream side with a panel of vertical, zigzag lines, some narrow and tightly angled, others wider, and one more curvilinear, like a series of ox bows; all are topped with a flourish of dots. *Go down to the water*, and here it is in vibrant glory.

Back on Cedar Mesa, along Highway 95, there's a rock that's thought by some to be a way marker, a kind of signal post to the traveler. It's a nearly rectangular boulder, perhaps twice a tall man's height, marked with a vertical, zigzag line a good yard long; human figures; another zigzag, on the horizontal plane. And sandal prints! Two of them, neatly side by side, each narrow heel and wider toe box looking like the yucca-fiber remains

I saw once in a museum display case. *Anasazi footwear.* Yucca is tough, called Spanish bayonet by European travelers through the western plains. It would stand up, I think, in an inadvertent pun, to rough treatment, but it would take a lot of work to process the sharp clumps of its leaves into something to protect the flesh. The single shoe in the museum display looked itchy, like a mat of burlap, with a few frayed hemp cords. How physical, how remarkable the artifact was, framed in glass and poised beneath a wall painted with replica petroglyphs. It would have been about my size, I realized.

In the midst of his otherwise astonishingly dense syntax, which feels a little like trying to gaze through a pane of conglomerate rock instead of glass, Heidegger writes a paragraph of utter clarity. He's explicating, suddenly, a painting by Van Gogh, conceiving of a pair of peasant's shoes as equipment for a certain kind of life, a truth the painting actualizes—"presences," he says—as it "unconceals" the otherwise ordinary objects of agrarian life:

From out of the dark opening of the well-worn insides of the shoes the toil of the worker's tread stares forth. In the crudely solid heaviness of the shoes accumulates the tenacity of the slow trudge through the far-stretching and ever-uniform furrows of the field swept by a raw wind. On the leather lies the dampness and richness of the soil. Under the soles slides the loneliness of the field path as evening falls. The shoes vibrate with the silent call of the earth, its ripening grain, its unexplained self-refusal in the wintry field. This equipment is pervaded by uncomplaining worry as to the certainty of bread, wordless joy at having once more withstood want, trembling before the impending birth, and shivering at the surrounding menace of death.

And so, Heidegger decides, through his essay's canyonland of branched and eddied sentences, through prose that pools and muddies and, to my mind, almost never holds a clear, bright mirror to the reflected sky: "World is never an object that stands before us and can be looked at. World is that always-nonobjectual to which we are subject as long as the paths of birth and death, blessing and curse, keep us transported into being." That is, he explains, "*World worlds*"—and, one recognizes in the gasp of unexpected alliteration, that the power of perception, especially that of the aesthetic, inheres in verbs, in the motion of becoming—"setting forth," he says later.

Canyonland is my term, rising from the landscape and its mapped representation that I've been traveling through. *Holzwege* is Heidegger's word, literally "Timber Tracks" or "Forest Paths"—rendered in the translation I trudged through as "Off the Beaten Track." There is something perverse in keeping intellectual company with a twentieth-century European phenomenologist while walking alone in the American Southwest. I realize this. But it's Heidegger's insistence on what he calls "the thingliness" of things, their nounitude, as it were, exaggerated until it makes the Doppler shift into verbitude, that cheers me as I think about these images in stone. Sandstone, mostly, that substrate's substance set against the shadow shapes that are the petroglyphs. My map, like every guidebook I've consulted, reminds in block letters, DON'T TOUCH THE ROCK ART— this is a ubiquitous caution to aesthetic pilgrims in the desert Southwest. Oils from your hand can accelerate the weathering, the self-effacement, of the images. It seems counterintuitive, that the mere touch of flesh could slough off what's been "set in stone" to last—as it has—for centuries, sometimes millennia. But that's part of the almost inexplicable joy of standing before rock art, heart pumping from the climb, or hike, or wade-through-water that brought you to this very instant when you pause, in the light and shadow of the day you're filling with the mortal exuberance of having arrived, and seen, and thought about the power of what seems like stasis—stone—but really is transitory, monumental but momentary.

"Art is, then," says Heidegger, "a becoming and happening of truth." And you feel it, even if you don't know what it means—the image on the rock, or the abstract noun that ends the sentence, there on the page.

No one is around when I veer away from the stream and follow the sand along the cliff's eroded curve. I met a few other small groups of hikers earlier this afternoon—couples, mostly, and a solitary man who sped past me with the taut, wiry musculature of the athletically elite, but for now I'm alone, and the path I've taken over the sand has been untrampled since the most recent rain.

Suddenly, the stream has hairpinned back to meet the canyon wall, and I'm standing, unexpectedly, before a panel of Ancestral Puebloan art. Right here, on the rock, just where my own arms could reach out and touch them, are a flurry of palm prints, dozens of them—nearly a hundred. They seem, as I abruptly stop and stare, to rise up, a show of hands. Some are painted red; others are slightly reddish-brown. Mostly in pairs. A few are larger than the hand I lift in greeting or comparison, but most are my own size, my slender fingers and unimpressive nails.

No one else is around, so I exclaim quietly to myself and try to make out patterns in the galaxy of hands. All the red-paint prints are pairs and are clustered toward the left of the panel; but the browner tints predominate, and among these are the largest palm prints, too. The occasional odd hand could be an anomaly, its mate erased by weather, by time. Perhaps a person who, some seven hundred years ago, most likely, besmeared herself with paint and leaned against the height of stone, right here, pushed a little harder with one arm than the other. Perhaps the pigment adhered imperfectly to the sandstone surface, even under her weight. Perhaps a trick of weather, some chaotic eddy of wind or sun-warmed, airborne sand erased one of the pair of hands. But most record the posture of the body—both hands up, in front of the face, thumbs inches apart—the un-stylized, un-improved-upon signature of the person, standing where today I stand, impressing on impassive stone the flesh print of an individual.

I love these hand prints, every one of them. I think of my friends who hang in their homes and offices the palm prints made by their young children, painted brightly in primary colors, molded into plaster of Paris. I think of the image of my father in the driveway as my car pulls away, lifting his steady, generous hand in farewell. I think of the night, in tears, I grasped a friend's hand and he grasped back, a blood-warmed grip of compassion, and of promised care.

I love the hand prints, but I keep returning to the image of the foot. Back home, on my desk, I study a photograph from Southern California, a remarkable canyon in the Coso Mountains, where the petroglyphs trace back through thousands of years; some were likely carved in the nineteenth century, while others date to more than sixteen thousand years ago. My snapshot offers up a lovely foot, a smooth pale shape on pale, water-polished rock. It is the toes that seem deeply, intimately perfect: the big toe is rounded exactly as in life, the others descending in length, one after another, with a delicacy that makes one think, for a moment, that it's not a carving at all, but the imprint left on a firm, wet beach, just moments ago. But as I gaze, I realize the print—the petroglyph, I mean—is static, with no hint of rolling from the heel, through the spring of the arch, to the toes' final curl before they release their friction with the resistant, solid earth. This foot is not in motion; the body language simulated by the artist's hand implies nothing of the press and swing and lift of gait.

This makes me wonder. I've never seen a "real" footprint, laid on deliberately in paint or mud, the way the hand prints mark the body's contact with the world. Nor, come to think of it, have I ever seen a pictograph foot, that is, a painted "footprint" rendered through abstraction or design. They're always petroglyphs, pecked and incised into stone. However elaborate the panels of hand prints, however symbolic their intent, they strike me as the lyric impulse, registering through paint on stone. The sense of physical spontaneity, the mortal press of once-living flesh, seems more directly accessed through these isolated vertical compositions of paint and mud. Both kinds of images could be construed essentially as metonymy, the *part* that implies, symbolically, the *whole*, but there's a different pitch or tone or timbre to the formal studies that these feet present. Two different meanings, I think, of "becoming." To my mind, the footprints register more fully in the realm of oratory, story. They lend themselves more easily to the narrative of journey—then we came this way; then we rose up; then we dropped down; then we traveled a long and difficult way to get here; I tell you, we walked until we felt our legs and feet had turned to stone.

Paleontologists tell us we stood up to walk long before we were ourselves, before we stepped into the chamber of language and art, the great clearing where our minds explored their abstract potential like a bright new habitat, bristling with richness and difference. For a few million years, we didn't stride out into the open of the imagination; we stayed near actual shadows of the trees. *Australopithecus afarensis*, the tiny hominid who lived in Africa 3.5 million years ago, was a more efficient walker, in terms of expended energy, than we are today, though she likely couldn't run very well. The famous trail of footprints at Laetoli records a pair who walked together, side by side, so close they may have been holding hands. It might have been a couple—a not-yet-man and a smaller not-yet-woman. It might have been a parent and a juvenile. And the pair may have been followed by a third, who stepped into the taller one's footprints, ever so slightly blurring the tracks. I've studied a photograph of one of these footprints, which, cast in the African dust and ash of another geologic world, looks remarkably like the footprints carved in Great Basin sandstone. The arch isn't high enough to register a narrowness of form; the outline is precise, a little boxy, but without the neat perfection of the toes that I love from some renditions. The bones of *afarensis* were like ours, where the thigh slopes back to meet the knee; this is called the valgus angle and permits the kind of swinging balance we need to stride from leg to leg as we move forward. Since they were smaller, they likely had less back trouble—one of the ills that accompany the bipedal life—and they were keenly athletic, excellent climbers as well as walkers.

Much later, about 1.9 million years ago, *Homo ergaster* ("the workman") headed out of Africa, spreading into Indonesia, China, the Caucasus of Europe. These beings lived for almost 2 million years, only disappearing from Asia about 50,000 years ago—well after other *Homo* lineages had stepped into something like the languaged life we know today. And of course, *Homo erectus*, *H. ergaster*'s descendent, who traveled, over generations, some 6,000 miles out of Africa and throughout Europe. The pattern of the journey, of the long walk, comes to us from way before our own deep time, from before the emergence of symbol and speech. Long before art. But the pattern, through time, becomes story, one of our oldest, and it's ritualized in its fine formality, like the handsome print that's sitting, yet another facsimile of paper and pigment, courtesy of the grocery store's film drop-off, on my desk this morning. And though the story of the journey has often taken its form through the masculine experience—the young man, for example, setting forth to meet some physical and psychological challenge, to slay beasts both within and without—primatologists suggest that it's the females in our distant ancestors who most often left the group and struck out for the unknown. For social beings living in small bands, what's called dispersal is essential to prevent inbreeding. And among chimps, our closest primate relatives, it's the females who leave the bosom of their families and move through the forest to find some other chimpanzee group to make their home. The journey is not, I believe, an exclusively male archetypal component of our deepest sense of self.

I think of this when I'm out walking, for I feel so fully alive, so exuberant in movement, *so presencing*, pack on my back, stick in my hand, heading up or down trail. Purposeful motion may very well be a form of intelligence; for me, it is certainly a form of joy. It is a part of living well and living wholly. Whole, I mean, and wholly present. Partially, it is the rhythm of the walk, the swing of being in concert with oneself—lungs and legs, arms and heart. Some scientists theorize that song was inherently part of the earliest rise of hominid language: unlike other primates, human beings are more deeply rhythmic, with a control of breathing and voice that allow coordinated, formal, and, perhaps importantly, *shared* participation in the song. The emotional reach of music, the way it unleashes feelings that seem free from language, is, when you think about it, remarkable—we are so usually shaped by speech that the wordless response to music, even a capella voices in a language we don't know, seems to stir deep portions of our psyche, what I want to call the body's mind.

What is bipedalism good for? Why did we stand and walk? Some say we needed to see above the tallgrass of the African plains, as the climate dried in the wake of the Himalayas' uplift. Some say we needed more efficient ways to move between increasingly distant food sources. Some say that as the African continent dried and heated up, we needed better ways to cool the body, presenting only our heads directly to the sun, instead of the broad panel of the horizontal back. Whatever the pressures of selection, we are their inheritors; and even today, it feels good to stand, and stretch, and walk. It feels so good to the body and, as I say, to the body's mind. Sometimes the journey is a walking away, a turning the back on what must be left behind, in order to carry on. Sometimes it's travel toward what beckons, full of hints and mystery, from just beyond the known horizon.

I'm hiking alone in White Canyon, thrashing my way through a tiny thicket of Gambel's oaks, when I come across a couple at the streambed. I stumble down the bank, calling a greeting, and the man begins talking at once, asking about the number of stream crossings still ahead. His wife is leaning on a pair of trekker poles, and she looks a little tired, though she's smiling.

But I interrupt him. "We know each other!" I exclaim. For, though we're dressed in different hats—for sun, today, not snow—I recognize their faces and search a moment for their names.

"You're Elizabeth," the woman beats me to it. It's Ken and Anita, a retired couple I met in an April snowstorm last week, two hundred miles away, on Skeleton Mesa, waiting for the guided hike to Betatakin Ruin. Ken's face opens wide in delighted astonishment.

"Well," he sputters. "Great minds think alike"—and he gestures mutely at the canyon walls, the landscape. Clearly, a *great* place to be. So I describe the stream crossings that await them—easy—and they ask whether, in the intervening days, I'd reached the other canyon full of petroglyphs that I'd planned to see. We're all pleased with this unexpected, social moment. Then we move off, they at their pace, and I at mine. They're headed for Sipapu Bridge, the landform to our north and east that spans this handsome canyon. I have a different goal; I'm going to Kachina Bridge, where Armstrong Canyon joins the White. I want to find the strange, stick-figure petroglyphs, like slender dancers with wild hair, carved into the southwestern edge of the stream-eroded arch. It's late in the afternoon, already, but the weather is fine. There's food in my pack and a bottle of clean water, too. There's a jacket in case of rain. And before me there are options. I could take the trail that loops back up, along the mesa, through pine and juniper, as it's pictured on the map; or retracing my steps the way I've come, I could return to see each rock face, each sandbar, from a different angle, in recognition and variation, rhythm and syncopation. Each foot's rise and fall, a journey of becoming.

Memory's Hills

All throughout my images of childhood the hills rise and fall sharply. From Grosvenor Street, it was a one-block drop to Franklin, with the connecting roads and alleys so steep you slid and skittered on icy mornings, the brick so slick that it seemed glazed with perversity under your already-scuffed school shoes. Above, Fort Street curved along the steepest hill, where decades before—nearly a century!—there had been a narrow-gauge train track for mining the clay, and a brick factory was in operation somewhere near where the National Guard Armory now stands. Those hills were red clay, still slicker than wit when you lit out for the territory and built forts two-logs high under sumac and box elder, or scaled the honeysuckled slope behind the car lot, or ran plunging down the hill beneath the Thayers' house, down to Highland Park, until you fell full force and bled so badly from your knee you'd have to get stitches.

Did I mention the hike back uphill, after school? Up we'd walk, up from the flood-plain level of the kickball field, up the broken sidewalks and lumpy brick streets. And since Athens, Ohio, hadn't fully shrugged off its village ways, those of a small university town surrounded by unreclaimed Appalachia, there were walkways, flights of steps set into the clay and shifting topsoil. One of these led from Grosvenor, a few blocks up from my house, to the hilltop neighborhood where Lisa Quattrocki lived with her large family, in a newer house with a "rumpus room" set into the hill (a "walkout basement," not like our old foundation, which still held a closed-up cistern and a coal room, complete with a little metal door where once the deliveryman would have shoveled coal).

Did I mention that "you" is "me"—the *me* I can almost look at as someone separate from myself, as I watch these memories replay? I'm both within my own perspective and standing somewhere nearby, wrapped in the knowledge of what will happen later—which houses will be torn down, who will move away before we go to middle school, who will be the first from our high school class to die—by her own hand, from self-obliterating despair—and where are the places I'll someday travel, distant from the small terrain of southeastern Ohio streets and hills and surrounding woods.

We lived in town, and we could walk everywhere: to the neighborhood grocery, uptown to either of the two department stores or to the movie theater where there was a free summer film series for children on the single screen. (Most of these films were utterly forgettable, but once, I recall, I saw *My Side of the Mountain*, about a child who was living alone in the wilderness, sleeping in an enormous hollow tree and making acorn soup. I remember it because I loved it, of course.)

I had a skateboard, too, and I rode my bicycle, but some of the hills were bike-defeatingly steep, and depending on where you were going, it might just be better to walk. And in some of the neighborhoods, the hills meant that back porches sagged and driveways developed unshoveled glaciers for a few weeks in winter; in some, vacant lots had gone feral in a tangle of undergrowth, saplings, and returning woods. (I still sometimes dream myself back to one of these lots, which was really somebody's backyard with an ordered world of a perimeter hedge and carefully planted flower beds.) I recall one day when my younger brother, a neighbor girl, and I all watched with lung-emptying delight as a deer—poor, panicked thing—galloped through the used car lot and scrambled uphill into honeysuckle and sumac while we jumped up and down, pointing. Later, the adults didn't believe us and were sure we'd imagined it, which made us sulky with righteous indignation. But then, some years later, a deer actually crashed crazily through a window in a university building and somehow bounded, bleeding and broken-legged, into the language lab where, in college, I'd repeat endless French sentences, approximating the lilt and tilt of foreign inflections. When I recalled the tale of the Deer in the Car Lot, my father said, yes, you must've been right after all.

Here is a memory: Lisa and I are walking home from school. We've left the alleyway (what was it named? I know it had a name—Merkle! It was Merkle Street) and are about to climb the flight of steps. Unlike the stairway that rises from Fort Street, closer to my house—a solid, poured-cement construction with a sturdy handrail all the way and occasional landings where you can stop, turn around, and take a near-dizzying look back toward downtown, the courthouse, and the campus lying beyond—unlike that one, this stairway is a sprawling, eroding mess. It's built of stone slabs set into the hill unevenly with varying heights of what I'll someday learn to call "rise" between the steps. The stairs themselves are shaded by mulberry trees; sometimes in summer I come pick the berries. I like their peculiar mixture of crunchiness and shirt-staining juiciness, like celery masquerading as a fruit. There is a handrail, since I remember beating my palm against it—a hollow metal thing, made of iron pipe, I'm pretty sure; it would make a dull ringing sound. We've left my tier of neighborhood and not yet arrived at Lisa's, and the steep drop of the land means no one has tried to build anything. On either side of the stairway are deciduous woods; it's clearly a setting for archetypal stories.

But we're no longer walking. The neighborhood bully, Chris Howard, has followed us this far and is chasing us, both of us, up the hill. Or am I misremembering? It could have been his brother Mike, older by a year or two. Chris was a slouch and what my mother called a ne'er-do-well, but Mike was the more aggressive one, with greater personal initiative for his never-do-wellery. Oddly, Chris was the coward, though if you said his brother's name quickly, it came out My Coward. But then, if you just squished together Chris's first initial and his last name, you got the same rather satisfying result. Coward.

But he's a boy and a bully, and whichever brother he is, he's chasing us. We're running all the way up the steps, as fast as we can—we both are good runners. Even so, I can see Lisa seem to pull ahead of me just a little bit, lengthening her lead by maybe a step or two. That must mean I'm falling behind, and this is especially dangerous because we think he has a knife. He's a boy, and a bully, and his family are really country people even though they live in town. Unlike Lisa and me, who are transplants because our fathers teach at the university, all the Howards have a very strong Appalachian accent. Years later, at a professional dinner after I have given a talk, I'll be surprised to hear one of the guests, a linguist, say that he can hear traces, just traces, of that accent in my voice, and later still I'll sometimes embrace it, shifting into its vowel sounds and pacing in the middle of a sentence, just to root my comment in the clay dirt of my past. But now, in the world of memory, accent fences us off on opposite sides of a cultural divide, and the public schools I recall are filled with sometimes-violent skirmishes. So, we're pretty sure he has a knife, though I don't remember seeing it in his hand.

But like I say, we're both good runners and the Coward isn't—those kids all started smoking very early, and they cough—and Lisa and I make it to the top of the stairs and speed up when we hit the street, and soon burst tumbling into her house, which always smells of fabric softener and has somebody's homework or artwork spread out on the kitchen table.

But here's the peculiar thing. Several years later, Lisa and I recall that afternoon. Oh, he probably didn't have a knife, we both agree now. We're in college, headed already toward the careers we've positioned in our sights: a professor, a doctor. We realize that we must have imagined that heightening detail in the after-school drama, the self-induced frisson of excitement. But it turns out Lisa remembers me as just ahead of her on the steps, while she's the one behind, with nothing between her and the Howard boy who hounds our steps. And of course, I can *see*, in memory, Lisa in front of me, her dark, fine hair on her shoulders, too fine to bounce even though she's running as fast as she can, as fast as either of us can. I remember the feeling of fear in my lungs as I work hard to keep up.

But she's sure it was me, running ahead of her.

The actual events of that afternoon have left no physical trace, not anywhere in the world. But memory holds them in its cupped palms, or in a carved wooden box on its dresser, or somewhere in a jacket pocket—wherever memory can be imagined, in its individual persona as You, to have put these images for safekeeping. Look, you say, pulling it out of a patch pocket, your arms just thrust through memory's sleeves. I had forgotten all about this.

Some researchers like to speak of the *landscape* of the brain. To follow this figure of speech, memory is laid down through our neural network in a wrinkled topography of hills and basins.

These basins are called attractors, and, like rainwater, neural connectivity can be imagined to collect and pool here, easily sliding downward as if following gravity's familiar pull. Sometimes, in the effort of thinking or feeling, or in the grip of concentration that somehow combines the two, I can really feel *locations* within my own head, aching or expanding under the weather of my own attention. Still, I can't say I've ever felt a run-off of thought, the waters coursing over grass or rock, making the kind of neural glaze, like rainwater, that William Carlos Williams once glimpsed upon some red wheelbarrow, perhaps upended in memory the way my own now stands in the backyard, empty but available. I can't convince myself I've felt the downhill slip of memories converging into thought's impounded waters. Nope.

But here, in the near silence of evening, in the quiet of solitude, I still love the very image of it: little neural bursts brightening the inner cortex, calling on the texture of complexity to flesh out memory's presence. In the calm lamplight that almost warms my desk, I can imagine my brain's amygdala sleeping, like a kitten, maybe, with its head snugged down between its paws. It's the amygdala that may have somehow shaped my remembered images of that day near Merkle Street, the mind's recollection of Lisa's hurrying feet, the tingling feeling in my shoulders and along the back of my neck that I have to hurry, hurry, because, behind us, the Coward has a knife. (Perhaps the amygdala never sleeps, not even during the dreamless, deep-stage sleep we have most difficulty waking from.) Neurologists tell us that the amygdala colors memory with emotion. People with damage to this brain area still form new memories, but they are drab, gray things devoid of personal feeling, like our cold war imaginings of Soviet block housing, where

not even curtains saved from your childhood can warm the un-
friendly shape of the windows or the street scenes they look out
on. When researchers experimentally removed the amygdala in
monkeys, I have read, they found the animals seemed to have
lost their sense of fear.

But here, in my inner landscape, the limbic system has been
busy: sorting impressions, binding feelings to sensory details,
routing (through the channels of REM sleep, maybe, and its
steep-waved hills and valleys from the CAT scan's graph, had
anyone been measuring my brain's activity) the day's stored
catalogs of being present into long-term memories, folded under quilts, or wrinkles of the brain's pale lobes. My body has
been storing the electrical pointillism of its own impressions.
This, then, is the original Impressionism, I think, the points of
synaptic illumination that are the body trying, always trying, to
render the ineffable into flesh.

I'm focusing on the beauty of memory, the mind as a gallery
or palace of fine arts, holding these artifacts of our past life.
For memories are made: they're creations of the brain. I have no
picture in mind of the Coward's hand gripping a knife, no inner image of its handle or curved and pointed blade. The memory of that day combines visual details—the sprawling steps set
into the steep hillside, the mulberry trees alongside—with my
feeling, that flush or glow of belief: *we think he has a knife.* Where
did that thought come from?

Researchers tell us that the mind's splendid ability to learn
and categorize, which it employs in the storage of memory, has
a darker side as well. My mind, like yours, can easily recognize
people despite changes to their appearance and know they are
the same: they all belong to individual categories I label with
their proper names. I recognized Lisa when she first showed

up at school wearing braces and blue eyeshadow (that trashy fashion of the 1970s), and I'm sure I'd know her today if I saw her somewhere, unexpectedly. It might take a minute. Should I see her sitting, for example, in an airport, a place of dislocation, I'd likely pause and rifle through those mental files, since she'd be unexpected though familiar (and if my mind is like my office, there might be untidy piles of memories heaped in a corner). In fact, it wasn't Lisa, but Mary Seelhorst whom I recently ran into, quite unexpectedly. While sitting in a silk pantsuit and a brilliant feeling of delight on a white folding chair waiting for a friend's wedding ceremony to begin, I noticed the name of one of the musicians in the printed program. "Oh!" I said to the stranger next to me, with whom I'd been chatting. "I went to high school with a Mary Seelhorst." And there she was when I looked up, unmistakably that particular Mary (somehow conforming to the mental category I'd filed twenty-some years before). How utterly unlooked-for she was, in Michigan of all places, far from our Ohio childhoods; she wasn't even an acquaintance of the bride or groom, but there she was, playing the fiddle, and I recognized the way her body swayed and dipped while she was playing.

You noticed, maybe, as I told my story of Lisa, the Coward, and the Many Steps, that I had plenty of categories for Chris-or-Mike, whichever he was. He was a Bully and a Boy. And the Howard family wasn't like Lisa and me; we would have called them rednecks at the time. And so that categorization, dressed in its unwashed jeans of stereotype, helped shape my memory of the afternoon. In fact, there *was* conflict often in the public schools and on the street between university people—faculty brats or college students—and local people unrelated to the academic circles of the campus. A young man—a student—*was* knifed on the courthouse steps one Saturday night in what was called town-gown conflict. Boys in my high school *were* suspended for bringing knives to school. But researchers tell us that people unconsciously employ categorizations—stereotypes—in all sorts of ways, including laying down false memories. I was running, I was afraid. He was a bully, chasing us. This much is "true"; but I wonder, really, which one of us was in front and which behind, and had we said anything to egg the Coward on? We'd like to think the past is there, like sedimentary layers or little fossils of verifiability, if only we can remember back carefully enough, to access the preserved cache of fact, but I recognize that what I find may have been imperfectly transcribed, or somehow stained or damaged by the heaps of memory laid on top.

That's not the way the scholars I've read describe these confusions, or accidents, or conglomerates of recollections. They speak of "spurious memories," little jags in the landscape of hills and basins that are formed when one memory somehow is overlain with another. Only in my figurative world do the piles of files, the sedimentary layers of deposition and fossilization, take the lead as controlling metaphors. So now I wonder: is this a spurious memory, morphed in some dark hollow of my cerebral cortex, since there were knives and knivings in the Appalachian world where I grew up—did later memories leak into the inner knowledge of that day we raced from Grosvenor Street and leave the explanation for the Bully Boy's pursuit (he had a knife)? Or did the worry that he was armed originate on that fifth-grade day, and we falsely believed, both of us, that he had a knife because of our inner categories—subterranean caverns, maybe, echoing with our fears?

How clearly I can see it, decades later, and how sensory the experience becomes, as I sit at my desk trying to will it all back. I recall the deciduous smells of a landscape where I no longer live; I smile to think of the mulberry trees here, just down the street, where I have stopped throughout late summer these past few years to pick the fruit, stretching on my toes to reach them, in full sight of traffic, enjoying the body's indulgence in remembered sensations. Smell is so tightly bound up with memory, everyone knows. You brush against the corduroy nap of recollection, and it floods your skull's great basin: sumac. Honeysuckle. Home. From the amygdala's coloration of fact with feeling, memories pass to the hippocampus, another locus in the brain's perplexing map. Damage to the hippocampus means a person can't lay down new memories. While all the old ones remain intact, familiar cliffs and valleys, maybe, where we can't get lost, the new ones can't take root. This is the kind of amnesia that leaves one mostly in the perpetual present, alert, responsive, but with no way to retrace one's steps. I think it's tragically ironic: for people who live on the streets of their mind, homeless except for the immediate now, the distant past grows ever more important, like dogma that can't be added to or modified.

One scholar, George Christos, contends that spurious memories are vital to creativity and learning. He's a mathematician, so the examples he gives are combinations of grids and geometric forms that the ever-creative brain has overlaid, one atop the other, to create new and distinct forms, "memories" that are extraneous to those actually observed. I have a hard time turning the Howard boys into memories analogous to simple geometric forms, but I can see that this concept could pertain to the memory that Lisa and I have since discarded: that we were chased by someone with a knife. It's more difficult to regard the suspect memory—which one of us ran ahead and which behind—through the explanation of these discrete images recombined by the creative mind. And I've read so little about what research has revealed of the brain's inner functioning that I must be grasping here, without the wide expanse of understanding that might offer a clear view of my own mind's landscape.

Still, the fact of the brain's great creative capacities is stunning and delightful. Thirty years ago, Julian Jaynes described an historic turning point in the way people perceived their own powers of thought. In what he called "the breakdown of the bicameral mind," our forebears began to experience their own thoughts as something created by themselves as they developed full consciousness. We ceased, he says, to hear gods or ancestors whisper in our mind's inner ear, suggesting courses of action we should take, or ways of understanding what challenged us. This was an event in neurological evolution that took place only some three thousand years ago, so recently that its traces are clearly visible in written texts—the Homeric poems and the Hebrew Bible.

I remember reading Jaynes's book in college, at about the same time I was first studying The Iliad; astonishment gripped me for weeks, like the heightened adrenalin delight I also knew then as a distance runner. He cites the peculiar location of the brain's speech centers—Broca's area, Wernicke's area, and a patch called unimpressively the supplementary motor cortex—in only one of the brain's two hemispheres (the left, for the vast majority of people, who are also right-handed). Why, he wonders, can both sides of the brain understand language (a fact that has been amply demonstrated through various experiments), but only one can speak? Why wouldn't the brain evolve a symmetrical redundancy for this most essential element of human existence? In Jaynes's hypothesis, the areas of the nondominant, or right, hemisphere that correspond to the left's language centers could "think" in language and convey the right brain's insights across the corpus callosum, where they were experienced as auditory hallucinations—the voices of gods or ancestors. The right hemisphere is well adapted to conceive advice, or direction, or admonition (the kinds of things we might expect to hear from gods), since it is especially good at perceiving order, context, and "the whole picture." Thus, the Greeks appearing in heroic couplets would hear their gods speak to them, upbraiding them for their folly and offering them divine counsel when faced with stressful situations and challenges.

We still have the bicameral brain. It's the mind we've left behind, the way of perceiving our own thoughts. We now are conscious, says Jaynes, and so we do not experience the right brain's contribution to our decision making as hallucinated voices, or suddenly appearing angels, as a matter of course. Historical anomalies—like Joan of Arc—and those we classify as mentally ill—like schizophrenics—lack the kind of consciousness that is now socially prevalent, but even mainstream, rational people—ourselves and our neighbors—may still have vestigial moments when they are thinking with the old bicameral mind. And, indeed, throughout the world many people still find that they hear voices of angels, or God, or their departed parents, who startle them with sudden suggestions, speaking to them as from another realm of being. Insight and direction can still come to us as from outside our Selves.

I have no memory of voices from that day on the Merkle Street steps, but I can imagine my grade-school right brain assessing the situation, worrying that the Coward might have a knife. Could this kind of "insight" have crossed my corpus callosum as a whisper from my self to my Self, even as I pounded the stones with my narrow feet, so that now, years later, I realize that I never saw a knife in his hand but still felt certain he must have one?

What's most fascinating—and not a little troubling—about Jaynes's hypothesis of the bicameral mind is how he frames it in evolutionary terms. The bicameral mind is the latest stage in the evolution of language, a process that he places very late in the development of the human species. He imagines the development of nouns as variations on alarm calls, with inflected endings (which he calls vocal qualifiers) to designate different kinds of predatory threats. This kind of protolanguage he suggests would have persisted into the Pleistocene, until roughly 42,000 years ago. A subsequent development, the age of commands, would then have lasted until perhaps 27,000 years ago. The first neo-sentences, "with a noun subject and a predicative modifier," would have appeared, he suggests, somewhere between 25,000 and 15,000 B.C. The development of "nouns for things" would have corresponded to the development of pottery; the development of names for people—personal names— he places in the Mesolithic, perhaps 10,000 to 8000 B.C.

This comparatively late appearance of language is startling. Anatomically, our ancestors were recognizably "us" long before these dates. Based on archaeology, most researchers agree that modern humans walked out of Africa more than 100,000 years ago. Some put the event around 130,000 years ago, but skulls from *Homo sapiens sapiens* have been recently found in Ethiopia that are believed to be 160,000 years old. What Jaynes suggests would mean that, for up to five and a half times longer than we have been able to form the simplest sentences (those that a toddler's cognition bubbles out from enthusiastic linguistic springs), we—the species Us—walked wordlessly through our lives. Put another way, for 84 percent of the time that people with our bodies—and our skulls!—explored and expanded across the continents, they had minds so unlike ours as to be nearly unrecognizable.

And what caused human beings to leave behind this way of thinking and embrace consciousness as Jaynes describes it? Here he shifts from a discussion of evolutionary development, with the slow time scale of natural selection, and suggests that the breakdown of the bicameral mind wasn't an evolutionary event: it was a social one. We abandoned the practice of listening for "gods" within our heads because they failed us in a particular period of environmental and historical chaos, in the area of Mesopotamia. Further, the development of writing and trade allowed greater contemplation of others and otherness outside the inner realms of the bicameral mind, and led to the philosophical revolution that was modern consciousness. It was a social adaptation, not a biological one. Essentially, we chose to experience the life of the mind in a profoundly different way.

Much as I like the metaphor of inner-whispered insight as a personal god, I find it is most convincing as simile, but the direction of some of Jaynes's discussion is toward the literal, substituting "auditory hallucination" for "god." To my mind, the evolutionary aspects of Jaynes's argument fall short. First, in the years since he published, archaeological discovery has pushed back, not only the dates of our earliest anatomically human ancestors, but dates for very striking evidence of the symbolic and subjective nature of their inner lives. We now have artwork and fine tools that greatly extend the period of Paleolithic artistic production. Second, although Jaynes presents artistic evidence from Olmec and other New World peoples to suggest the universality of the bicameral mind, it's only in Mesopotamia—among the Sumerians, the Assyrians, and the relatively local historical and geologic events of around three thousand years ago—that he finds evidence for the "breakdown of the bicameral mind."

But what happened elsewhere? What, for example, went on in the other great concentration of city empires in the ancient world, in Mesoamerica and South America? On a rainy day in early October, I walk through the restored ruins of El Tajín, a cultural center and residential city that was first inhabited nearly two thousand years ago and reached the height of its influence from roughly 600 to 900 A.D., eventually being abandoned around 1200. Today, one enters from the south (as one would have throughout the city's history) and strolls into grassy ball courts and plazas set among the impressive stone buildings rising from the plain in pyramid form. The rain moves in from the nearby ridge, obscuring the banana trees and other jungle vegetation I have no names for, and a small flock of parrots flies brightly overhead. It is too wet for me to be taking many notes from our tour, so I whisper aloud as I stare at the written signs (presenting information in three languages—Spanish, English, and Totonaca), hoping I'll remember the dates and other particulars printed there. Then I gaze from under my wet hat brim at the gray stone murals carved along a grassy corridor where ballplayers would have walked to reach the courts. The imagery is crowded, framed at top and bottom with geometric borders suggestive of other realms, and indicating the heroic work of the ballplayers in maintaining the fecundity of the world, from dry season to wet. Today it's *very* wet, and I'm silently delighted that there are almost no other tourists out; our small group moves among the ruins in near isolation. Tajín, I read, is named for the thunderstorm or the hurricane, so it seems symbolically appropriate that we should slosh along the wet grass, stepping over stone-lined drainage channels and standing, in the periods of heaviest downpour, beneath a few trees at the plaza's edge.

Only a portion of the original city has been excavated. The density of tropical growth has overgrown the rest for centuries. The near hills stand in symmetrical profiles, holding their carved murals or steep stairsteps or calendrical niches—one for each day of the year—beneath the green disorder of perhaps eight hundred years' worth of leafing and decay. What would those niches once have stored, besides the people's need to count the procession of days, carving the ineffable into the built world of stone? They could have held sculptures, or icons, little mnemonic figurines to help make manifest their understanding of time's movement through the visible world. These courtyards and buildings had already been abandoned before Hernan Cortés convinced the local people, the Totonacs, to join him in overthrowing the ruling empire farther inland, the Aztecs at Tenochtitlan. Still, because I have been busily reading about that conquest, and just three days ago I walked the dry, cactus-speckled plain the Spaniards had to cross in their march to the Aztec capital, I stand by the famous Pyramid of Niches, each neatly shaped square facing outward to the open air and now utterly empty except for a thin veneer of rainwater, and try to put together these hints and glimpses of cultural realms that the landscape itself seems to be trying to forget.

It could be tempting to imagine the Spaniards' ease of conquest over the Aztec's empire, for example, to be due to Montezuma's inability to think like modern people—the conquest surely was one of mind over military might. And, indeed, Jaynes suggests this is what happened with the Incan empire, farther south. But there's not a small amount of condescension in this line of thinking—the New World inhabitants had primitive minds, and so the conquest was only natural, as success of the (culturally) fittest. Other scholars have noted the absence in Jaynes's argument of any treatment of the other early-literate cultures: those in China and India. "Parochial" is how one writer characterizes his emphasis on Greek and Assyrian texts, and I have to agree.

Besides, I'm more convinced by another scholar, Robbins Burling, who points out that the growth of the brain began two million years ago, from 600 cubic centimeters to modern humans' doubled capacity of at least 1,200 cubic centimeters—in culinary measurement, we have today about two and a half cups of brain in the curved bowl of our skull. As he notes, from its Australopithecine beginnings the hominid brain had very nearly reached our own modern size long before the archaeological record reflects great innovations in tool production. Our changing brains weren't littering the landscape with evidence of flourishing technological innovation. So what were we doing with those bigger, more complex neural capacities? Talking, he says. Our brains grew as both natural and sexual selection guided our species toward ever increasing capacities for language—both comprehension and speech. And unlike some earlier linguists who argue that language itself shapes the basic way we see and understand the world, Burling suggests just the opposite.

"Perhaps language confirms, rather than creates, a view of the world," he reasons. Syntax often reflects an iconic understanding of the relation among agents and goals (often through grammatical subjects and objects); our ability to perceive patterns and to "read" or "hear" the world precedes our induction into any specific language form. "We seem to understand the world around us as a collection of objects that act on each other in all sorts of ways," he says. "If our minds were constructed so as to let us interpret the world in this way, that would be quite enough to account for the structure of our sentences."

What I like about Burling's take is the suggestion that language, despite contemporary theory's emphasis on the distance between signifier and signified, has as its core the urge to bridge the gulf, to reach outward toward the world beyond the mind and to open the brain's sensory gates to allow synaptic sparks to cross that very gap. "Poets think they're pitchers, but they're really catchers," says the poet Charles Simic. Perhaps it's true of all word-wielders. We learn first to listen to language before we can speak it; surely, in our evolutionary history, we learned first to understand the world in certain ways before we tried to talk about it.

By the Upper Paleolithic, when we finally see the great painted caves and sculpted figurines of the Aurignacian culture and those that followed, the artwork suggests a level of mythic and symbolic thinking that could not have been possible without language. The images, I feel certain, point to narrative, and one cannot tell stories with only a rudimentary lexicon. And I love the fact that European writers favor the term *parietal art* for what Americans call "cave paintings." The roots of the word lie in classical Latin, referring to a "wall"—thus, art on the cave's walls. But we also refer to the parietal lobes of the brain, portions of the cerebral cortex that involve sensation and perception (those sparks across our metaphorical synaptic gap) and the integration and comprehension of visual perception—the images that our mind paints on the walls of our brain.

One day in late October a couple of years ago, I was driving alone across the southern tier of Ohio. I was in transit, on my way "home" to Kansas after a visit back "home" with my parents. Despite the lateness in the season, the day was mild, sun flooded, and I felt a leisurely sweep of time before me, so I headed north from the highway and drove through the forested hills toward Ohio Brush Creek, to see the Great Serpent Mound. Though I remember my mother taking me to see other Moundbuilder sites sometime in my childhood, I'd never been to this one. With no need to be anywhere specific by nightfall, it suddenly seemed like the perfect time. But when I arrived, I found the public park was closed that day, and a gate blocked the paved driveway to the hilltop site, so I parked in the grass beside the road and walked up. Only a handful of others were there, interlopers like me, strolling around in the sunlight and quiet.

The effigy mound itself is huge, probably the largest such structure in the world. Though only four or five feet high, the snake's figure is about a quarter of a mile long, and it stretches its length in a tidy, sinuous form that suggests, narratively, that it has been caught and suddenly stilled in the act of wiggling along the high ridge top. Stylized embellishments at either end suggest a coiled tail or rattle and a head with a large elliptical form that could approximate an enormous eye, or an egg being swallowed by the snake's wide mouth.

Carbon dating from the 1990s places the construction period just under a thousand years ago: 1070 A.D., during what is called the Fort Ancient culture. Some aspects of the figure's position on the land suggest that it may have been oriented with the summer solstice sunset and, less prominently, the winter solstice sunrise. It was the wrong time of year for me to glimpse any of this: my autumn afternoon was gloriously poised midway between the calendrical peak and valley of light in the northern hemisphere, but I still like thinking about these possibilities. I like thinking about the modulation of the solstices: each extremity is softened with its diurnal opposite—midwinter's dawn, midsummer's dusk. And I like thinking about the effigy's ritual role in conceptualizing the rhythms of the seasons. The mound becomes a physical place to keep watch for time's passage and to keep faith with the year's underlying patterns. It is, I suppose, a landscape artifact, a carefully built hill for memory, though it's not a personal memorial, since the mound contains no burials.

And so I spent some time in this particular spot in the world, on that precise day in my life. Unhurried, I stood near the snake's head, or eye, or the great egg of life it might have once been symbolized. I tried to look as far as the creek below, but the understory was too thick and the slope too steep, obscuring the narrow sinuous curve of flow. With no one to talk to, nothing impending to brand these memories brightly into the living tissue of memory's grasp, I was utterly free to loaf in the day's sunlight, smelling the aromatic scents of Ohio, that particular home.

One of the near-miracles of language, I think, is that it allows us to converse about the past, to share our recorded impressions of what happened, how it felt, and what, for the rest of our lives, we should clutch close to memory's chest, to keep something of those vanished actions warm, near our breath. And we can write about it all, too: as here, now, the screen of my laptop lifts its parietal image of a clean white page, and my fingers remember their way quickly across the keys, typing out thoughts, following the associational currents that have led to this essay. My father once told me, after his parents had both died, that the most powerful fact of such bereavement is that the loved ones who held your earliest self in the bosom of their minds—the ones who remembered with you, or for you, your formative times—those loved ones are gone from the world and, with them, the world they carried inside their minds. It's true for other losses as well. Whether they're dead or vanished, when people we loved have left us, we're left with only ourselves, the shaky shadows of memory ashen on the cold inner walls of the skull.

Cold Meditations

Hwapp! Unmistakable, the sound of a bird hitting the storm door's glass. And when I look out on the stoop, there it lies, a chickadee, flat on its back, stunned from impact, panting with what must be dismay. It makes no move to right itself, so I go for a towel, wrap it in soft, warm darkness, and lay it on the floor where I sit by the wood stove, reading. I think that its neck isn't broken; it only needs to rest out of the cold and pull itself together for the extended courage that is winter life outside. After half an hour, I peek under the towel, and it's still on its back, but the eye seems bright and focused, looking at me across the few feet of pale sunlight that falls between us. I sit back and continue reading, in the soft sounds of the fire and turning pages. Another twenty minutes and then when I lift a corner of the towel, the bird grasps the terry-cloth texture in its foot and ruffles its wings. Time to go back.

Towel open on the snow-brushed cement, the bird flutters to a low limb in the euonymus by the window, defecates, and blinks. I close the door and return to my reading. Later, glancing at the feeder, I watch a chickadee flit and flick its tail. What a tiny, spirited presence each bird is, its rapid breath and food-fueled inner fire. I admire their tenacity, their perky persistence in the seasons allotted them—brief lives, mostly, for the smaller birds, just a handful of years, but filled with stunning intensity.

The river has disappeared. The sky is so low, so cloud-cloaked, I can see only two hills away, the light at midday diminished as if in an overcast dawn or dusk, but it's not—it is storm light, a dim, austere subtlety. The road is gone too, of course, and, ten miles distant, the buildings of town. Gone, they are gone from sight, and I pause for a moment to hold them before my inner attention—the smokestack from the physical plant on the campus, the curve in the road where once, on Thanksgiving, I saw a few dozen turkeys crossing the river.

Yesterday's ice has encased the visible world. The short grass crunches underfoot, the rough-leafed dogwood, actually leafless since late October, is cast in a second bark of ice that smoothes and rounds each twig. Not a visitor in marl, I think, but, more nearly, marble. The tallgrass bends across the trail, its wind-ragged seed heads stilled, as if in the palest of amber. Today there's breeze enough for a wind chill near zero, but only a few minute snowflakes tick against my hood, hardly enough to register in the field of sight. Two deer on the near hillside also pause with lifted heads as I regard them; then they ripple into motion, the only muscular movement in this swath of landscape since I've stopped walking to watch. A quarter-mile back, a harrier's dark shape followed the hilltop, but it slipped from sight, and now, in the lowering clouds, even the bison across the draw have vanished. I stand in this limited, but utterly unintimate periphery of vision, the deer having crossed the trackless trail into apparent disappearance.

This is our life in the world of forms, the shapes the visible world presents to our perception, the mundane amazement of it. Today the yard holds crows, tearing the air with their calls. I wonder whether, while I was gone last fall, they stripped the dead

opossum I found weeks later beside the viburnum, its reptili-
anlike snout extending from a bedraggled snood of fur, all that
was left of it. Flickers hammer the suet; angle-shaped wrens
forage under the line of cedars. Each junco moves across the
snow like a metonym for winter days: preponderance of dark,
with a bright white underside of light. Day and night. Earth and
snow. The temperature holds still at twenty degrees, while in
the luxury of meditation, I sink but don't quite disappear into
the selflessness of observation, always structured in the realm
of comparison, language.

Of course, I spoke to the bird I'd wrapped in a hand towel and
brought indoors to recover. What was the window but the hard
separation between her world and mine, the transparent soph-
istry that wounds only those who mistake it for the open world
it resembles, who do not see solidity that hangs, vertical, within
the atrium of air. So I said a few sentences of encouragement,
in a conversational, friendly tone. And when the chickadee flew
off into its accustomed existence, I expect, though I don't really
remember, I told it goodbye.

Sometimes I think language, like breathing, functions as
both autonomic and sympathetic nervous system, deeply self-
conscious as I sit here typing in the chilly north room of my
study, but unbidden, almost unnoticed in the world of dreams.
Talking in one's sleep is only part of what I mean here. The theory that dreams are the brain's random firing of imagery, much
favored in contemporary sleep studies, does not explain the
mind's desire to order such activity, to give it form in narrative
or symbol. To find significance. And this is surely part of what
language offers us, when we sit alone in thought, unconversant
with any specific, identified other: we have the company of language, the comfort of its signifying rise and fall. In this, it gives
us, constantly, reliably, ourselves.

What was I reading? *Beowulf.* A translation, Seamus Heaney's, not the prose version I'd first studied as a teenager, enjoying the kennings and bored by the recitation of the warrior's lineage, the insistence on man-priced revenge. But lineage, identity, is vital in the poem—who is an *us*, who a *them*, and what constitutes kinship and resultant reciprocity. And when the danger of the wild world, undisciplined by the relationship of thane and lord, enters Hrothgar's Hall in the living flesh of Grendel, the smaller band of Danes are unable to man the forces needed to protect themselves. They need more distant kinsmen, the tribe of Geats, who with their superhero, Beowulf himself, come to restore order: to slay Grendel and right again the toppled benches, repair the hall, which can then hold and celebrate the fine words and gifts that will follow.

As a youth, I found a kind of campy humor in the prospect of the Danes, asleep from their mead, only one guard posted, set up for the nightly destruction and waste. Campy, too—if you resisted the serious shadow of the thing—was the image of Beowulf ripping Grendel's arm from its socket and hanging the hand with its claw as a gory trophy above the heads of the celebrant men. Passed-out frat boys, plundered while they snored. I thought of a particular house and its reputation for debauchery—the House of the Yellow Snow, the brothers called themselves. I thought of a story told and retold at preteen slumber parties: "Where's my golden arm?"

But it *was* surprising to read stories so old—an epic from another millennium, telling of an age two centuries, at least, before the poem's composition. Surprising and difficult. Despite my urge to render them as drunken Sigma Nus or Phi Gammas, it's an alien world the poem presents, with symbols and nuances as foreign as the language that is really—though evolved and unrecognizable—our own.

Or is it? This time, I reexamine the notion of Grendel and his mother as "monsters," textually confined and contained by the concept of hell, of evil, of Cain who killed his own brother. "As long as either lived," says Heaney's translation, "he was hateful to the other." And there in the original, "wæs gehwæþer oðrum lifegende lāð." For that is what, or who, Grendel seems to be—the ultimate outsider, the dangerous other. oðra, oðrum. What strikes me now is the concept of *otherness*, played out across the northern landscape of fens and bogs and moors and crags. Grendel and his mother reflect the lives of the Geats and the Danes, the struggle and combat, and even the exacting revenge, when his unnamed mother comes to the hall to kill Hrothgar's valued thane Aeschere, as if demanding a man-price of blood—certainly not gold—for the loss of Grendel. These are not the nonhuman lives, familiar as birds or imagined as dragons, which we sometimes define as the animal kingdom. They're too nearly like us, even within the strange skin of their difference. As Tolkien himself pointed out, Grendel "is most frequently called simply a foe: feond, lað, sceaða, feorhgeniðla, laðgeteona, all words applicable to enemies of any kind." Even mann-cynn, humankind. That's part of the horror of their near cannibalism, their feasting on the flesh of the fallen men.

Hand, arm, shoulder—and claw. This is the token of victory that Beowulf hangs in the hall, torn from the body of his foe. The claw seems animal. David Quammen, writing about bears in Europe, thinks suddenly, pointedly, of Grendel—but arm, hand—well, I think *hand* unmistakably suggests opposable thumb. This is the body that walks erect, even as it runs away, mortally wounded, toward the lake or the mere, under far marshy hills.

On the tallgrass prairie, in winter, I try to imagine the steppes of another era, the Pleistocene world when, in the last glacial maximum, grasslands wrapped Europe's periglacial landscape, from the Atlantic coast of modern France to the deep interior of Eurasia. A million years ago, during the Kansas glacial period, if there had been anyone to stand on this particular hillside, she would have been able to see the ice sheet that extended from the north. How, I wonder, does a steppe fundamentally differ from a prairie? Both are grasslands, both mostly treeless. From the dictionary, I infer that a steppe implies greater vastness, distance on what one might pun a *mammoth* scale. And more prone to shortgrass than tall. Here the oaks along the creek, the cedars shagged with snow on the unburned watershed, the sanded curve of the river where, in winter, bald eagles perch in the high branches of cottonwoods—these are features of the present era, this contemporary constellation of lives half a dozen miles from the interstate. Then, too, geologists point out that there really are no contemporary analogs for the biomes of the last ice age. We can compare temperatures, find that parts of Europe (and the Great Plains of America) existed in the same shivering grip that now holds the arctic realm. But at lower latitudes, more winter sunlight would have struck the earth, insolation as it's called, especially given the complicated wobble of axis that the earth has undergone. At the Last Glacial Maximum, in the Upper Paleolithic, the summer sun rose even higher in the skies than it does today. In such a glut of sunlight, despite the winter's cold, the earth might have uttered a surprising vocabulary of plants, as well as beasts.

I'm living alone. It is winter. For hours I might walk in silence, in the cedar and sycamore woods by the creek, where, if you follow the ridge, you come out behind the zoo and stand bizarrely behind two layers of chain link, gazing at tigers and Siberian cranes, caged on the Kansas hillside. Midweek, midwinter, the zoo has few visitors; there's no one around. When my friend Gina calls, though, and together we venture farther afield into the season's first snowfall, a few weeks before Christmas, it's a matter of chance coupled with wind chill that we meet no one else on the trail. We do, however, find footsteps, two tracks that follow the low path, avoiding the high exposure of the ridge and that seem to trace a conversational pace from the creek crossing to the old homestead site that marks a spring in the hillside. We don't see the people, but we don't much wonder about who they might be either.

But for most of human prehistory we were not alone. Paleontologists have discarded the linear concept of the Descent of Man, the timeline image that depicted a neat, orderly sequence of one hominid form replaced by another, each walking across millennia to reach the evolutionary summit, *Homo sapiens sapiens*. No, they say, evolution works like an unruly bush, a flourish of branches self-pruning and rebranching, dropping dead twigs to the accumulating dust and humus, the compost heap of deep time. We were not alone—throughout the millions of years of hominid history, there were often others, like but unlike us, along the periphery of our own unfoldings. And in Europe, during millennia of climate fluctuations that, when drawn on a graph, spike and plunge like stalactites or icicles, the anatomically modern people we call Cro-Magnon shared the Old World with another kind of person, *Homo sapiens neanderthalensis*. For perhaps ten thousand years their cultures shared the same landscape. Is it possible that such memory could persist, far beyond the life span of any single language, beyond any people's specific traditions or their stories of origin? Behavioral ecologists point out that certain fears—spiders, snakes—that still dwell in the modern mind might be relicts of a much earlier, prehuman existence. Tropical primates, they say, have far more to fear from these threats than people do, and vervet monkeys show deep, instinctive terror, with particular distress calls that "mean" only one thing—SNAKE!

In the first days of the new year, descriptions of the Boxing Day tsunamis that ripped people from shores throughout the Indian Ocean continue to fill the newscasts. On the radio, voices try to convey the disbelief, the destruction, the despair. The worst natural disaster in history, it's called. By tens of thousands the death toll mounts. Our newspaper prints two photographs of Banda Aceh, one before the waves hit, and one after. Half the land, it appears, is gone, the earth apparently scoured out by the power of water, replaced with the sea. What, I wonder, if the world it had struck was preliterate? How long would the tales of the world-warping waves, the floods of destruction, be told and retold? If the survivors stayed put, the land itself would remind them, but for how many generations, before the natural history slipped from its remembered place in human history? If the people moved on, would they take their story with them, lifting it free from the ground of specific landscapes and transplanting it, casting its mythic power into their lives in whatever new places they came to call home?

At the Pleistocene's end, the melting icecaps raised the seas, and shorelines lifted a few hundred feet above their former level. Geologists say that, for a period, global temperatures even exceeded those of today, and the deepening seas, in times of storm, would have suddenly flooded far inland. Some speculate that the prominent role of floods throughout the world's mythologies may be an echo, a ripple mark, of those pre-

Holocene floods, the last blast of change from the age of ice. A "transgression," it's called, in the language of glacial study, when the rising seas advance beyond their former shores.

Now that the tsunami's floods have receded and villagers try to put lives back together, the people won't eat fish from the local catch, not now, since they're sure the animals have been feeding on corpses. Their missing family, maybe. Who could bear it?

The linguist Charles N. Li calls language a "terrestrial imperative," an adaptation forced on the hominid mind by the dangerous descent from trees to the savannah. As they stood erect, our ancient hominid ancestors acquired a narrower pelvis, even as the adult brain grew, and so, over time, the infants they bore became tinier, less developed—more helpless as they entered the world. They couldn't even grasp their mothers securely to be swung up into a night nest safe above the ground. So, in this view, language rose up from the earth on which the australopithecines walked. It was a way for them to symbolically clasp one another in kinship, developing larger, more cohesive social groups to protect themselves from life's myriad threats. I find myself adopting the distancing language of scholarship, as I write—"cohesive social groups"—for, after all, it's difficult to imagine this story as personal history. In those days, our ancestors weren't yet farmers, not even hunters—they were, mostly, scavengers, cleverly vying with vultures and hyenas for other animals' kills.

Is that how it came to us, the near-miracle of language? Was it two million years ago, when, the bones tell us, the brains of our distant ancestors suddenly began growing increasingly larger? Was it 800,000 years ago, when the migrations out of Africa first took *Homo heidelbergensis* into the territories of Asia and Europe? Was it far more recent, only when *Homo sapiens*, perhaps some 120,000 years ago, once again began the many-generationed journey from east-central Africa, along the ocean's margins, from one continent to another, to another? Is language—or at least its incipiently symbolic forerunner, protolanguage—an evolutionary development from the Pliocene? Or did it come to us from the changes that ice brought to the world, the challenges of the Pleistocene landscape?

In the earlier view, language appeared as slowly as tool use, from crude, functional beginnings. It began as a simple conceptual lexicon, limited morphemes that preceded the structure and mechanical possibility of grammar or syntax. Earliest speech, says Li, was a "vehicle for human communication" but "not an instrument of thought." Its symbolism might be more iconic than abstract, the expressions tied more to the present than the past or the future. In this, it sounds to me unlike language as I understand it, as I experience it, writing here in the lamplight of an early winter evening, trying hard to wield this fine tool, this beloved and sensual instrument of thought. "A vehicle for human communication" sounds like a "new, improved" range of animal calls—danger, food, sex, us, other—though some linguists insist that animal calls have "functions," not "meanings." (And sometimes researchers have a very hard time determining whether the oldest stones they find have really been "worked," or whether they are happy accidents of natural breakage.)

There's something missing here: the role of affect in our speech. What's called episodic memory is what's at play in propositions—clauses, basically, such as "Ice covers the yard." Episodic-declarative memory, the recognition and processing, ultimately, of spatial relation and motion itself, takes place in the brain's limbic system, in the hippocampus. That's the place of emotion, where we feel, and in feeling, know that we are. Language, then, is the mind's articulation of limbic response, the emotional wave—neuronal, chemical—in response to the varying shocks of the world. "Tool" seems too bloodless, too unimpassioned, to pass for the intensity—joy or sorrow—that is speech in the mouth, in the hand. Language itself is the life of the mind.

It's also, says Owen Barfield, the inner insistence on the human place within the natural world. It's the power of symbolization, the perceptive generosity, I think, of the human spirit to chime the inner with the outer realm, to find conceptual and experiential harmony of self and surroundings. "The mind of man," says Barfield, "is not . . . 'a lazy onlooker' on an external world but itself a structural component of the world it contemplates." This linguistic "participation of the knower in the known," he points out, is not the way of discursive communication, a book-ended shelving of metaphoric thought between the hard confines of literal utterance. No, he says, this "historical fallacy of born literalness" belies the very history of words themselves. Language is not a reductive procedure, sluicing and sloshing away sediment until the heavy gold nugget of successful group dynamics lies alone in the pan. It is the alchemy of the artistic impulse, the bright glister and gleam of figurative thought.

"How did they do it? Where did such courage come from?" My father and I talk on the phone, wondering at the adventurous strength that set people out, into the wholly unknown. He's thinking of the Polynesian peopling of the Pacific, the boat trips across the impossible waters that stretched out of sight. In his teens, in the navy, he traveled the ocean, above and below, in the cold, cramped secrecy of submarines.

"They had to be young," I imagine. These weren't multigenerational migrations, most likely, the old people gazing out at the water to what lay beyond, or working hard to keep up—they were youthful men and women at the exhilarating peak of their athletic lives, for whom the sensory delight of travel and challenge is a joy. The image I have is high summer: my brother, full pack on his back, gazes into a future that's shaped like a high mountain meadow, a near-tundra proliferation of alpine flowers waiting until we descend. Even though I'm older than he, and have no intimations of immortality, this is what I see.

"Yes," my father agrees. "And, in their self-belief, invincible."

But later I imagine it differently. Not the flush of exploration, the bold choice to strike out for new worlds. Response to climate change most likely isn't a reasoned decision—let's pack up and head upriver, and see if there's more game and grass beyond those peaks. (Our own so-called debate about contemporary climate change suggests that stasis would be the likely "choice.") So migration might not be a deliberation, a preference, but a rushed and desperate escape. The panicked scramble away from the mud slides, the fires, the ravaged beaches. No, we won't stay and try to rebuild; the wreckage is too great, too terrible to contend with. Catastrophism, to adopt the geologist's term, where the sudden spasm of change marks both land and surviving inhabitant.

But these either/or speculations are reductive. By now, it's an entire world we're talking about, and tens upon tens of thousands of years.

It's three degrees this morning. I've been counting. Ten days without full sunlight; the ice and subsequent snow have fused into a slick, hard sheen across the ground. The frozen suet in the feeder draws woodpeckers and wrens; the sunflower seed brings finches and cardinals. A hermit thrush lives in the neighborhood, but he stays across the parking lot's frozen waste and hasn't shown up in my yard yet this season, though I've kept hopeful watch.

As the sun rises without the temperature following suit, I pull on layers, both synthetic and woolen, and head out into winter. The roadways are clear, but the short grass near the cemetery pokes through a tough crust that doesn't seem to even register my weight. I pass through a quick, hillside sequence of woods—cedar, then oak, then, after the last slide toward the riparian bottomland, cottonwood and sycamore. In some sunny spots the snow is so hard I don't even leave tracks, and the moment I stop moving the cold leans heavily against my skin. At one point, the creek's opaque edges give way to a transparent surface I want to test, but don't dare. As if behind nothing, a sycamore leaf sails, submerged, in clear view. Hoar frost has dusted, like a few fallen blossoms, the frozen skin of the stream. Above riffles, where in better weather I often see a kingfisher, the ice hasn't quite sealed the creek. Feathery, fractilic, a shatter-faced edge of ice fronts the current. From upstream I can hear the sudden, surprising sounds of ice: the dry-sounding crack of breakage, the weird whanging sound, like rapidly shaken sheet metal, that I sometimes heard as a child, skating on the reservoir in southeastern Ohio. I stand very still, trying to see evidence from the surface of what must be the tectonic action of the ice.

Then, from the far bank, quick, lifting wing beats bring a small bird into view. It flies up from the last dangling, dead leaves of a tree-fall from last summer; it lands in the bush just below where I stand motionless, watching. A flick of the russet tail, a ruffle of feathers, fluffed out to hold heat. The hermit thrush moves to a higher branch, watches me with its dark, ringless eye, then flits to the next, nearest branch, and regards me voicelessly. I have nothing to give it, no granola, no raisins, not even words, and after a few moments the thrush returns to the fallen tree—hackberry, I think—across the ice.

Once, I remember, in summer, I knelt on a ridge top in Appalachia, high above an eroded streambed in that southern, unglaciated edge of the forested world, while a hermit thrush opened its throat into song. My family waited, elated and hushed, as long as the bird offered us pure, clear notes, the "solitary singer from the swamp," there, on the ridge, gazing at each of us in our mute turn, until, at whatever signal we couldn't discern, the bird stopped and flew off, leaving us, for long, inexpressible moments, still silent.

That was a powerful encounter, filled, as I see it, with layers of meaning. All of us artists, writers and a painter, most of the people I loved most in the world, held by the unbidden and unlooked-for visitation from a bird who seemed bent on sharing his song, and, as we liked to think, found us worthy. Of course, we framed the event with allusion, as I just did in the paragraph above, but in some ways I think that encounter and perhaps this other, in winter, are lived examples of "symbols without meaning"—that is, numinous moments that bring the outer to the inner realm, unstructured by will. In dreams, I sometimes experience birds as versions of my own psyche, the inner suddenly made outer, regarding me from a position of disquieting remove. That's not a bad approximation, really, of those fleeting contacts in the waking life. The world, I think, must have various psyches and should, in its own chosen moments, embody the concept of self-regard.

None of this helps in thinking of the ocean wreckage. I drive to the reservoir, stand beside the chilled, still plane of the lake's impounded waters, and test the thickness of the ice. It's quiet, a mosaic of light and dark, rippled and smooth, with a white border marked with prints where a dog or a coyote trotted along the slushy margin, before the serious cold. Great blue herons, several of them, flap away from the island where, in early summer, they sometimes fill the biggest trees with their gregarious nests. Yesterday I read that flamingos nesting on India's southern shore flew inland, away from the exposure of the coast, before the waves ripped through. In Sri Lanka, at Yala National Park, it seems the animals mostly escaped; from elephant to leopard, snake to monkey, the creatures saved themselves by seeking higher ground. A few villagers left, too, when the earth shook and the ocean, at first, drew back from the beaches: they had ancient stories, these people, of waves that devour the living, and so they fled inland and survived.

But other people—fishermen, tourists, children—did not have these stories. Indeed, they had no clue, and some of them raced seaward, to the suddenly open stretch of sand, collecting fish stranded when the waters drew back, as if inhaling, before the waves bore down in what we'd call a fury, a rage, or simply power that may seem indescribable, strength pulsing from the earth's crust-ruptures, death-bedecked, and washing its rush of ill tidings into the human fringe along its intemperate, impermanent strand.

Walden, Woods

I endeavored to keep a bright fire both within my house and within my breast.

Henry David Thoreau

Let's face it. I am having a love affair with my wood stove.

When I first started living alone again, for the first time in fifteen years, I thought the stove might become rather like a pet, keeping me company on long empty evenings. His name is Walden, and he fits exactly in the large limestone hearth of the fireplace that, so far as I can tell, was never functional in this house. Oh, there were fixtures from a fake log gas insert, but I mean a real fire, one that is messy and leaves ash and smoke curling around in little aromatic, insistent moments of being. Walden would crackle and maybe purr, and I'd sit on my pale couch and cry, or try not to cry, and sometimes fiddle with the television to see whether I couldn't somehow properly adjust the picture tint.

The TV was over twenty years old, inherited from my mother when she died, and the color was fading right out of it, turning a perfectly good color set to black and white. I spent days trying to fix a pair of shoes, hip urban-looking things made in Italy but with unaccountably cheap buckles, both of which snapped as if they were plastic, and I tried cutting little stiff lengths from a coat hanger and painstakingly bending them into shape with pliers and a vice grip. One worked really well, but the other mangled the shoe leather when I tried to slide it into place. Probably the thing needed to be filed smooth (I actually do own a rat-tail file, also called a mill bastard), but I didn't think of that until it was too late.

Are you seeing a pattern here? Does this sound familiar? So many things get busted or worn out in a day's time, or a week's, or a lifetime, and no matter how hard you try to repair them, to *take good care*, as we say, the forces of entropy and disintegration usually win out. You have to keep trying, of course, but the failure rate is very high. If you let yourself think about this, it's terribly depressing.

But, now, Walden—he's another matter entirely. A good wood stove—and he is quite well made, from a reputable line (no history of infirmity in that family!)—will last a good, long lifetime. And my chimney clearly draws remarkably well. In fact, the first time I hired a chimney sweep, he remarked on it, saying there really wasn't enough creosote buildup to warrant cleaning, though he charged $40 for the inspection all the same. Where I live, the power outages generally take place in spring and summer—thunderstorms are our most violent weather, accompanied at times by cyclones, twisters, tornadoes, whatever you want to call those sinewy, sudden, and destructive vortices that drop from the sky and wreak havoc, wrecking homes and landscapes in their paths. I don't believe the power has gone out in winter since I got the stove, but if it does, of course, I'm ready. Heat, light, the house centered on the hearth's great spine of limestone reaching floor to ceiling, with the bright, glowing heart of fire I will feed and keep.

Some weekend afternoons, in winter, I put bread dough near the stove to rise. Occasionally, I've set a metal bowl of butter on the cast-iron lid to melt. This is, I think, more interesting and yet more *familiar*, in the word's archaic meanings—domesticated, intimate—than sticking the stuff into glass or plastic and microwaving it to softness. I don't have the common iron kettle set on top to humidify the house, but then I don't think my house gets unduly dry in winter. Not unduly. After all, the insurance company has carefully excluded fungus, mold, or mildew from my homeowner's coverage, so I see no reason to tempt the Fates of Damage.

The fireplace hearth, a single slab of plain cement, measures seven and a half feet long and one and a half feet wide. All summer, in that clean, sunny room with a bank of floor-to-ceiling windows, it holds plants, keeping them off the refinished wood floors. In winter, it holds the small wood box—an antique crate from the Kansas City Bolt Company, sturdy enough that I could dance on it if I wanted—with all the necessary fireplace tools clustered around: great flameproof leather gloves with which you can reach right into the fire and move the wood around; the poker and the flat, ash-gathering shovel; an old pot with a lid to carry the cold ashes to the compost pile out back; the graceful screen, curved like a miniature umpire's vest, that fits neatly in the front when the two windowed doors are open like wings, so the fire joins you—safely—in the room, and talks and breathes and shifts its changing weight. Of course, the stove is slightly less efficient that way, but the atmosphere is wonderful. A small drawer beneath the firebox catches ashes and slides out—after every single fire, since it is not capacious—to be emptied. Walden is a marvel of simple, firm, dependable technology. Beneath the hinged cast-iron lid, where one loads the wood, his compact body is clad in off-white enamel finish, a lovely skin tone blending with the limestone of the fireplace itself.

The Bolt Company wood box also serves as an accurate guide for size: if a piece of wood won't fit inside, it won't, no matter how you twist and angle it, go through Walden's open lid. Eighteen inches is the limit. This is shorter than most firewood suppliers cut, so I must most emphatically specify the length or, as I did one year when my neighbor took down a dead tree, cut it myself.

And I love to split wood. I love the full, athletic experience of the swing. I love the smell of fresh-split hardwood, each tree species holding its own, identifiable scent inside. Osage orange, or as it's known more locally, "hedge," is tangy, rank like a wet animal. Oak is clean and deep. Hackberry smells a little bit like sassafras, a tree my father often cut for fuel in our woods, in Ohio. Elm smells pretty clean, too, if you can ever get it to actually split. I love the weight of pieces in my arms, the ringing clunk each makes as I load up to carry them inside. I love the feeling of accomplishment, of work well done, when the rack on my screened porch is filled, the ax is sharpened and put back in the garage and all the bark and chips, along with branches from the yard, are gathered in my kindling bin.

I named the stove Walden because—quite seriously—I wanted to gaze into his limpid flames and say, "Oh, Walden, is it you?" Then, in my unexpected solitude, I found how companionable he is, in a mute, substantial way. Some nights in winter I will fall asleep on the long couch, my glasses still on so I can watch the firelight move behind the miniature gothic arch of the doors in front. Other times I'll bring my sleeping bag and pillow and bed right down on the floor before him, stretching out limbs cramped by work or cares of the day. I'll stretch like a beagle, like a cat, and fall into my strange, insistent dream life in the fire's changing light.

The man I'm dating feels quite fond of Walden. He treats him like my younger brother, or perhaps a nephew. "Shall I feed Walden?" Dave asks. "Do you want me to bring in more wood before dark?" One day, when I was splitting elm (ridiculous woman!), and got my wedges both impossibly embedded in the grain, he came over to help me whang them out with the maul. When he trimmed a large, broken limb from an oak tree in his yard, he set it aside to wait for me to cut it up and take it home, to Walden. And when we noticed that a branch extending above my garage was dead, he loaned me his bow saw and his intrepid teenaged daughter, and he spotted the two of us while we climbed up my antique wooden ladder (too heavy to hoist and place alone), two chicks with tools taking turns with the job. So now that felled limb is also waiting. I will have to borrow a chainsaw, or finally break down and buy my own.

Last week, visiting in the East, Dave and I went to Concord, and walked around Walden Pond in a pouring rain. It was chilly and dismal, but in that I think it was perfect, for there were few visitors besides the group we came with, and mist obscured the landscape just beyond the leafy margin of the lake. Walden Pond is undergoing restoration. The path is lined with fences, while the shore recovers from years of erosion. A friend tells me that, in the 1960s, when the place became a kind of Woodstock Swimming Hole, the urine content of the Pond was higher than any other body of water in the state. Sadly, that has the ring of truth. But we walked the Pond Path happily, at least at first, before the chafe of wet socks and weight of sodden denim set in. But even then, I was happy, buoyed by the delight of actually being there.

We gazed at the damp opening of Wyman Meadow, peered frequently through trees or from each tiny beach, to see the solitary loon, just where Henry David says he should be, cruising the still water with his heavy-necked profile, until, silently, he'd sometimes dive. Once, he lifted from the water, flew due west, toward the rail line, but by the next time we stopped to look he'd realighted, back within our sight. We passed two groups of locals fishing, with their empty canvas lawn chairs pooling water while instead they stood, wet and chatting, at the water's edge. We stepped inside the stone-marked contour of the famous cabin's site, took pictures standing by the hearth, a small spot indicated with a rain-slick slab of rock.

Each time we reached another cove we checked our soggy, decomposing map: Ice Fort Cove, Long Cove, Little Cove, Deep Cove. We scrambled up the railroad grade, just finished when Thoreau went to the woods, now a commuter line for greater Boston, marked the MBTA Fitchburg Line. Across the pond, Route 126 is named, for a short distance, Walden Street. The urban thus thoroughly—yes, pun intended—contains this little sylvan respite in the Massachusetts landscape, where the maritime cape has given way to granite, hills, freshwater lakes, and, in the mid-nineteenth century, the farms and woodlots of the day. Indeed, the woods where Thoreau went to write and think (he was then working not on *Walden* but on *A Week on the Concord and Merrimack Rivers*) were second- or third-growth trees owned by Emerson for the harvest of firewood. Today, after a decade-long preservation effort, one hundred acres have been protected. That sounds like shockingly little, a child-sized park (think of Pooh Bear and the Hundred Acre Wood), but after all, this is the East, where some states are the size of counties in the West, and the smaller, dark-green folds of hills and trees have a fine closeness to them, a spatial intimacy. The distance we covered in our walk, our rain-soaked saunter, was only a couple of miles, but the place, and the afternoon itself, seemed *large*, as Whitman would have said, and as young people say today, with no idea whom they quote.

Although the bathhouse (marked "seasonal" on the damp wad of map) looked closed, I slipped inside and changed into the bathing suit I'd brought in hopes the weather might turn fair enough to swim. It didn't, but I decided to go in. Already wet from the waist down, but warmed by Gore-Tex on my upper body so the air, at fifty-eight degrees, didn't seem downright forbidding, I ran across the sandy beach, splashing in the shallow water until, thigh-high, I had to stop and stand, and dive. I came up gasping, swam a few token strokes, laughed at the rain, the loon, the slate-gray lake, Dave taking pictures in the wake of all my mirth. Oh, yes, the day was large.

As I write this, I am far from home. I'm still staying in the deciduous East, in a great mansion-turned-artists'-colony, where my only responsibilities are writing, reading, thinking, and occasionally doing my own laundry. (My fingernails have never grown this long and neat.) It's been a late spring here, cold and wet, and some of the artists (composers, mostly) who have little studios off in the woods report often that they've "had" to build a fire in their wood stoves to warm things up. I'm envious. Each day I jog through the century-old forest of the former estate, surveying how crews have been thinning the forest. Evidently it has been decided that these woods are far too thick, unmanaged, and new muddy tracks have been gashed along the hilltops, with great carcasses of evergreen, mostly, lying alongside these new rutted tracks, and occasional stacks of newly cut wood left here and there like little installation illustrations of Robert Frost. Huge stumps stand about in the dappled sunlight, or the mist, depending on the weather. (Mostly these days, they stand in rain, but then I'm not around to witness them. While the rain falls, I stay at my desk, or in my reading chair, way up under the eaves in my little two-room suite with slanted ceilings, obviously servants' quarters from an earlier era.) I'd love to lay a fire in one of those small workspaces, off in the tiny cabins in the woods. I think in winter it must be marvelous here, the grounds all dressed in snow, the nineteenth-century casement windows shut against the New England cold, and fires burning in the smaller dwellings. The mansion will be closed, then, I suppose because it would be too hard to really heat. Now, firelight never brightens the authentic Tiffany glass inlay adorning the great hall's fireplace.

It's a mosaic of a phoenix, wings spread and lifted from the orange-glass flames beneath. It faces to its right (the onlooker's left), with a red tongue protruding from its open bill, a bright red eye like a western grebe, and a vivid green spot atop the upper mandible, not unlike the shield above the bill on a king eider. From wingtip to wingtip, the bird measures sixty-seven inches, though if the wings were fully extended, outstretched as if the bird were soaring high above the flames, the mythic wingspan would be greater, since in this stylized pose, the wings are bent and curved, much like an anhinga drying in the sun. The primary feathers are long and graceful; from the head, four plumes nine inches long are starred with golden orbs of glass. From the head's crest to the base of the flames that obscure the presumptive tail, the rising bird measures twenty-eight inches. Those flames are gorgeous, almost exactly the color of the rugs before it on the parquet floor—and, of course, the color of firelight from clean, well-seasoned wood, reflecting off of glass, or brass, or maybe even real gold. One afternoon, in the quiet, dim room, I take my giant flashlight (regular resident of the car, which I keep beneath the seat along with a small fire extinguisher for road emergencies) and shine it along the rich image, but the beam seems feeble in the cavernous chamber. So I flick off the light, measure the body, and go back to my desk beneath the gabled eaves.

Here I sit among my gatherings from the woods: a few wildflowers in a jar (red columbine and what appear to be wild geranium); a hawk feather (I studied the bird book, and it looks just like the belly of the broad-winged hawk, one of my father's favorite birds); and this small chunk of rock, dull white quartz lined and pocked with mineral incursions, what look, to me, like tiny incrustations of lime. One side—the prettier side, which I consider the top—is corrugated like the surface of a molar from a grazing animal, long since vanished.

Dave gave it to me after we had left Concord on a crowded, humid bus with the others on our field trip and after hot, steamy showers had restored our bodies to self-regulating heat, the offending denim and soaked jackets hung up to dry along with my wet bathing suit. Now it rests on the painted wooden surface of my desk. It is the size of a nickel. It is coin of the realm. It's almost exactly the dimension of the little glass mosaic pieces of the phoenix on the hearth downstairs.

It is a tiny piece of Walden's large, abiding shore.

Cañonicity

Today abstraction is no longer that of the map . . . or the concept. . . .The territory no longer precedes the map, nor does it survive it . . . today it is the territory whose shreds slowly rot across the extent of the map.

Jean Baudrillard

Nothing is less real than realism. Details are confusing. It is only by selection, by elimination, by emphasis, that we get at the real meaning of things.

Georgia O'Keeffe

I. Quartermaster Sandstone

In the landscape of the plains, there are so many reasons for concluding that the lateral line is the world's predominant fact as well as its ubiquitous abstraction. There is always that point of horizontal disappearance, beyond which all things drop from sight: the sun, the wheeling stars, whatever landmark, or small waving figure, you move away from in your travels. In the eroding cutbank of a prairie stream, you see the soil's "horizon lines," the visible layers of buried realms. "O horizon," say the scientists, marking the floor where, in organic profusion, the brief-lived plants fall back to the rich afterlife of leaf litter and eventual decay. The other layers descend, one after another, each named in a way illuminating and signifying to those whose work it is to know the workings of the ground: "A horizon," where worms churn minerals and humus into topsoil; "E horizon," for *eluviation*, where minerals leach out, leaving a silica line of white, as if someone had drawn a broad band of chalk across the visible cross-section that we call the soil column; and on through other lettered layers, arrayed like a vertical eye chart in the optometrist's office—to "R" or "D" horizons—bedrock.

The terminology is more nuanced for the upper layers, those closest to where we scratch out our existence. Bedrock itself is another matter, and one can catch brief glimpses of its history in the sudden gouges of road cuts or the slow erosion of canyons through plains country. Standing in a Texas or New Mexico canyon, perhaps not even in ear- or eyeshot of the snaky stream that's whittled and rubbed these features into being— mesa, hoodoo, canyon wall—you can scan upward from the point beneath your feet, up, upward, gazing at the world's former surfaces. Third week of March, having passed another bar in the personal timeline I call my own life—my forty-fourth birthday—I sat wrapped in my sleeping bag, watching dawn illuminate the opposite wall of Palo Duro Canyon. I was perched on the Permian, outside a stone cabin nestled into bright-red Quartermaster sand- and mudstone, a messy, erosional formation that has slipped and flowed in the past few days' heavy rain and hail, darkening the waters of what the Comanche called Kecheahquehono, the Prairie Dog Town Fork of the Red River. Above the pale line of unleafed cottonwoods along the stream and the reddish stems of salt cedar that crowd the banks, the canyon's cliffs lift into the morning's equinoctial light. Still wet, the red rock can't quite be said to gleam, but it does seem deeply dark and rich, a different hue altogether from the paler, dusty dullness into which it will fade by midday, when the rains are over and the drying wind asserts its pastel hand. I'm listening to blue-headed turkeys that look like weird German Expressionist paintings; they are gobbling on the hilltop, and two great-horned owls are faintly calling from down among the cottonwoods, while the sun continues arcing higher, calling out the smaller birds to peck and twitter among mesquite and juniper. It really rained like hell last night, leaving little ponds and puddles on the tiny cabin's stone floor, and I think the birds must be very glad to see the sun's quickening light.

Still seated, wrapped in down and ripstop nylon, I'm taking in all I can see. From here, I can best gaze upstream, up toward the canyon's most famous landmarks, the yellow-and-lavender sweep of Dockum Group sandstones and shales called Spanish Skirts, and the famous Lighthouse, a pillar of stone we'll hike to later in the day. The Lighthouse stands beside another tower, Castle Rock, and a great cleft of air—wind, most often—separates them, inviting the hiker to clamber up and gaze both north and south across the juniper-dotted landscape. But invisible to me, at least, is the first of two major geologic unconformities, vast gaps in the sedimentary record. I can see where one age leaves off—the brick-red Permian, from the age of shallow, landlocked seas—and another begins: the late Triassic's Tecovas Formation, laid down in times of swamp and stream. But even up close, after the bright morning scramble and hike, there's no sign of cataclysm, no hint of catastrophe. I can't *see* an absence. Only my notebook tells me that some forty million years, at least, are missing from the visual record of the rock, time enough for hundreds, even thousands of feet of sediments to be laid down, hardened, and, ages later, eroded away. Another such unconformity occurs between the upper layer of the Dockum Group—the Trujillo Formation sandstones—and the caprock of the canyon, the Ogallala sandstone of the buffy upper rim. There's no trace, say the geologists, of two entire eras, the Jurassic and the Cretaceous, nor of most of the Tertiary. Nearly 170 million years of geologic history are utterly missing from the upper levels of the canyon.

Still, the scientists study and conjecture. They search for the "source material" of the existing stone, and believe that those colorful Spanish Skirts were laid down by streams that flowed precisely opposite to today's rivers—they were gently flowing northwesterly, into long-since-vanished shallow basins. Those waters laid down palettes of recombined sediment—much of the silt was local, eroded from those bright red Permian beds. But hints of more distant sources are also there, in the Tecovas stone: pebbles of quartz and heavy minerals may have come from an area of geologic deformation and subduction—a late Paleozoic tectonic belt extending from Mississippi and Arkansas southwestward through Texas and into Mexico. In the Trujillo Formation, one layer up, geologists study the brush strokes of the ancient rivers—paleocurrent structures, they say, reveal the direction and intensity of flow of those depositional streams.

One afternoon, a few hours after wind-driven spring snow hurried and skittered atop the rim, I walk briskly downstream, heading nearly due east where the river flows past the artificial boundary of my blurry-featured map. It's waterproof but ill suited for the back-country hiker. Picnic areas and the names of developed trails in a five-mile stretch of map are highlighted in neat boxes, but the contour lines of every cliff or mesa bleed together in a muddy curve, a brown abstraction of height or depth. I move fast because I want to get off the map, away from the narrative clamor of the Goodnight Cabin, a reconstructed dugout similar to one the Texas cattleman Charles Goodnight built when he first ran all the bison out of the canyon to make way for his cows; away from the amphitheater with its wheel-away backdrop of false-front western buildings and waiting parking lot; away from the Visitor Center and Trading Post, the Cottonwood Picnic Area with its swing sets and chainsawed trees ("they were afraid a tree might fall and kill a kid," a local tells me later). I'm nearly trotting, moving downstream.

I pause when I see bobcat tracks in the fresh mud. I speed up when I rise into tallgrass, some of it half a foot taller than I can reach. In the day's last light, I climb a small hill and look downstream, the narrow river a sinewy line that curves in varying degrees of southeasterliness. I look in the cottonwoods, pale and bare limbed, for a glimpse of an owl. And I think of Georgia O'Keeffe, writing to Alfred Stieglitz in New York in 1916, still two years before she'd move to the city to join him. It was September, and she wrote, "The plains—the wonderful great big sky—makes me want to breathe so deep that I'll break." She mused, "It seems so funny that a week ago it was the mountains I thought the most wonderful—and today it's the plains—I guess it's the feeling of bigness in both that just carries me away." That particular day, she wasn't describing the canyon that she often came to, but the caprock plains above. I muse over her pointed comment, as I sit with my back to the developed park: "I feel it's a pity to disfigure such a wonderful country with people of any kind."

II. The Dockum Group: Tecovas Shales

She came west to teach. The Normal School in Canyon, Texas, was about a decade old and needed a "Director of the Art Department." In reality, O'Keeffe *was* the art department: the yearbooks for the time she taught there reveal precisely one teacher of art—herself—among a total college faculty of twenty-six. (English, I note, does somewhat better, with three teachers; they all seem to gaze right back at me from the cameo oval of their captured likenesses.) But it was also the time in her life when she was "becoming O'Keeffe," discovering, as she herself much later wrote, "what to say . . . with my materials." Though she'd always been an enthusiastic outdoors person, a dedicated hiker and camper, she was instantly taken with the starkness, the windy, light-flooded landscape of the Texas Panhandle Plains and the surprising canyon that opens up the escarpment of what the Spanish explorers called the Llano Estacado, the "Staked Plains." (Just why they called it that has become a matter of conjecture for historians like Dan Flores—did it refer to all those yucca plants, little "Spanish Bayonets" that plagued the passer-through? Did they become disoriented in the country's vast horizontality and drive survey stakes into the patchy grassland to mark their way? The name's origins, whatever they may be, are now obscure.) In any case, O'Keeffe soon had a personal stake in this landscape, too. In addition to the preponderance of sky, which she evoked in her watercolor "Evening Star" series and a few sunrise pieces ("Light Coming on the Plains"), she climbed down into the 850-foot depths of Palo Duro Canyon and reveled in the color—the reds and yellows, especially. It's a different world from the blue hills and low mountains she had been painting, back in Virginia. She clearly had to be out in it, as often as possible.

There are a couple of early watercolors of O'Keeffe's that I particularly enjoy for their hint and whiff of the life lived out of doors. "Tent Door at Night," one is called, and the catalogers and scholars have appropriated the name for its companion piece as well. The use of form is the same in both: a triangular patch of blue is framed by the drooping (half-lifted? half-closed?) curtains of the tent walls, and by a lumpy lower line suggestive of rumpled bedding inside. Off center, the support pole bisects the blue plane of the night outside and gives the composition a perched, impermanent sense; with morning, surely, the entire perception will be struck and packed away. What differs among them is the use of color and tone. It seems O'Keeffe was exploring what would happen to a world of forms if the only variable were color. (I don't know why I use the subjunctive here. Daily, the world itself presents us this phenomenon: morning light on the rock formation; high, white glare on the inlet strand; purpling evening on the distant line of hills.)

In one of these early paintings, there's greater variation of palette, and the triangular patch of sky is mottled blue and white. In the other, the tent's a cleaner combination of gray or black and blue, and the sky's a pure, undifferentiated blue wash. The point of view is low, the way one *does* sit in a tent, gazing outward. Low to the ground, readying for sleep, or later, waking to dawn, one is temporarily tucked down from the upright verticality of the spine, the posture of the perambulatory life beneath the sky. Both these pieces may have been studies for an oil she completed at about the same time, in her final weeks in Virginia before moving west to Texas, or just after, while the eastern landscape still resonated in her imagination. The oil, a handsome piece, I think, presents the softened angles of the tent in dull red, orange, and green, trimmed with black.

The tent pole disappears into the textured blue-dark wedge of the world outside, the clarity of air that's waiting, full of possibility. I like to think of her sitting there, watching the world change beneath her gaze.

Art criticism focuses on the authenticity of feeling in O'Keeffe's abstract work. The term *abstract expressionism* is a marvelously handy portmanteau for what's of aesthetic value in such pieces. Here's William Innes Homer describing the ethos of Alfred Stieglitz's Studio 291, the gallery (and the man) that first brought O'Keeffe's work before the public: "The work of art had to be a frank expression of the feelings of the individual who produced it, without regard for conventional rules or the styles of any other artists." Arthur Wesley Dow's theories of art (which O'Keeffe first met through her teacher at the University of Virginia, Alon Bement), called for "filling space in a beautiful way"—while using, says art historian Marjorie Balge-Crozier, "the facts of nature to express an idea or emotion" and eschewing detailed realism. All the technique is in service to feeling, "to create works that are emotional equivalences for her experiences." John Canady declared, in 1964, that "abstraction has made the identification of form with expression nearly complete." Sharyn Udall takes it even further, writing in 2004: "The core self is born within the creative event, as the story is told or the picture painted." As I consider these comments, I'm struck by how the intention of the artist seems still to be held front and nearly center, rather like that tent pole in O'Keeffe's pieces, the vertical "I" that rises up between the viewer and the sky beyond. The emphasis is not on the viewer, not on the shared "making of meaning" that we might, in our postmodernity, tell ourselves that each event of observation will entail. Instead, it's on the artist, the singular maker, and the "frank expression" of feeling.

And O'Keeffe herself discussed her work this way: "The unexplainable thing in nature makes me feel the world is big far beyond my understanding—to understand maybe by trying to put it into form. To find the feeling of infinity on the horizon line or just over the next hill." But Marsden Hartley, whose landscape paintings I also love, phrased it rather differently: "I have made the complete return to nature," he wrote, "and nature is, as we all know, presumably an intellectual idea. I am satisfied that painting also is like nature, an intellectual idea, and that the laws of nature as presented to the mind through the eye—and the eye is the painter's first and last vehicle—are the means of transport to the real mode of thought; the only legitimate source of aesthetic experience for the intelligent painter." The sublime is—can you see the pun coming?—a very big tent, transubstantiational even, and can exist as both feeling and intellectual idea, simultaneously.

And that's a pretty good way to describe my own reaction, standing in the gallery, inches from the paper or canvas of those early landscapes. It's a transubstantiation of thought into feeling and back again; it's the irrational but fully intelligible certainty that the self—my self—is somehow a crucible for this manifestation of the world's ongoing multiplicity. I love the way these Latinate nouns pile up, like bands of color, blocks of form, as I, too, aim for "frank expression." As O'Keeffe wrote to her friend, Anita Pollitzer, a few weeks after arriving in the little college town of Canyon, Texas: "I think all the world has turned into what I'm seeing."

Dan Flores identifies Palo Duro Canyon as "the place of her original Western infatuation." When O'Keeffe discovered

Abiquiu, New Mexico, and the various landforms that commanded her color-flushed imagination, it was the same landscape, the same geologic and visual world, only "drawn on the larger scale of the farther west." Flores points out that the first images of the Southwest presented to eastern audiences came from Palo Duro. So did some of the first dismissals of these studies-in-verisimilitude as being unreal, unbelievable. In 1876, Ernest H. Ruffner made six watercolors of the canyon, during his attempt with Charles A. J. McCauley to retrace the earlier, 1852 explorations of the Red River's headwaters. These paintings' "hues elicited laughter and disbelief when he showed them in eastern Kansas," Flores writes; no one back East had ever seen such vibrant colors on such striking landforms. The images were never published, lost, he laments, from the history of visual encounters with the remarkable Southwest.

As the day clears and the wind drives every cloud beyond the confines of the visible world—the canyon's rim of Ogallala caprock—I can hardly believe how clear and crisp the air becomes. Although the trail's still blocked with muddy pools, and Sunday Wash is sticky at each trail crossing, mucky and soft from last night's deluge, the air presents its signature clarity, the near-sere brightness of the West. The Lighthouse Trail rounds the relative height of Capitol Peak (a shape I think may be reproduced in O'Keeffe's "Special No. 22," a vividly colored oil-on-board from 1916 or 1917). The morning is devoid of other hikers, so our tracks are the first to skirt or skid the muddy spots; coyotes have been here, already, but no one else. We slow for a while along the wash and look to see what's been eroded out in the recent fast water. Clovis points? we wonder—we're only a morning's drive away from the New Mexico namesake of that Paleo-Indian hunting culture. And Pleistocene bones and tusks still sometimes tumble from the friable stream banks in the Llano Estacado, bones O'Keeffe might have enjoyed, too, had she found any—though when she visited the canyon, it was still two decades before she'd begin placing bleached cow skulls and pelvises against the brilliant sky and colored landscape, farther west. But we find only interestingly shaped pebbles and stones and a conglomerate of sand-crusted clay the size of a grapefruit, which explodes dully and surprisingly when I drop it to the stony streambed. The neat form is gone then, shattered.

And at the trail's end, when I climb into the high, level gap between stone pedestals that make the Lighthouse, I realize that the flat, late-morning light has reduced things again to an unnuanced state: rock, sky, and this jacketed figure, me, standing in the rushing wind that by afternoon will drive snow across the plains to tumble over the canyon's edge. Once, in January, O'Keeffe wrote to her friend Anita Pollitzer that she "went to the Canyon in a tearing norther—snow flying and bitter cold—it was terrible—but great."

III. The Dockum Group: Trujillo Sandstone

A few of O'Keeffe's most striking pieces from the Palo Duro period in Texas are oils. One is "Red Landscape," an oil-on-board piece that shows the richly red sandstone as keenly steep, almost as if rolling in deep waves. The sky is pale, holding what seems to me to be sunrise, a more angular presentation of color and shape, with white and apricot and pale pink, and palest pale blue. Others O'Keeffe titled "Specials," a name I like to think she gave to pieces she was especially pleased with. Some of her Specials are pure abstraction, such as an earlier composition she said was a rendition of a headache. But some are expressionist landscapes, like "No. 22 Special," a rounded hill or near-mesa where the hot- and dry-looking red and orange of the land meets an area of greeny-yellow sky, an aureole above the hilltop, beneath the darker blue. I think it looks remarkably like the form and shape of Capitol Peak, though the day I walked beneath that brick-red hill, the sky was widely, brightly blue, the sun having already left its crepuscular cusp with the near horizon. Other "Specials" continue to present the world of the canyon as geometrically curved: plunging J's of framing cliff walls or mesas, with rounded, rising-dough hills in the center field of vision and small rounded forms that fill and cluster along the canyon floor, like red abstractions of shrubs or other, perhaps moving, figures.

One of these paintings is itself now lost. Or rather: stolen. "No. 21 Special," the goldenest, most rounded of these studies, with a line of puffy yellow clouds in the sky echoing the line of red spheres on the ground below, was stolen in 2003 from the Fine Arts Museum in Santa Fe, along with "Red Canna" (which, fortunately, was recovered), which O'Keeffe painted in 1919. It was, as they say, an "inside job"—a security guard was convicted in the theft.

I've looked at sketches for these pieces—time darkened, square patches of paper which, scholar Barbara Lynes tells me, O'Keeffe made from a long, narrow strip, "similar to what goes into a cash register. She folded the long sheet accordion-like and tore it into smaller pieces along the folds." Not, then, a real sketchbook, like you'd take in your pocket or your pack into the field. Not like the sketchbooks she sometimes actually used (one of which I examine in the O'Keeffe Research Center, opening the fragile cover and turning the pages, until a sudden splash of pastel color is before me: a tiny watercolor landscape, but one that predates her time in Texas by about a decade). The sketches try out different arrangements of lines and forms, all bearing strong resemblance to the finished Specials—but with some interesting differences. The sketches show a world with horizontal, flat-and-angular lines—that is, mesas—set against the curving and plunging shapes of swoop and wave. Between the experimental pencil outline and the declarative oil, she changed her mind about the composition and left out the reminders of the horizontality beyond the canyon walls, the (missing) mesas' insistence on the pervasive plains.

Lynes has pointed out other examples of this kind of altera- tion of the lay of the land in O'Keeffe's work. She's interested in a later period for the artist, the great New Mexico landscapes that arguably made O'Keeffe the most famous American painter of the twentieth century. She says these pieces are part of a de- liberate move on O'Keeffe's part toward more representational images, which she undertook in the 1920s. To put a stop to the eagerly Freudian discussions of her work, O'Keeffe "redefined herself primarily as a painter of recognizable forms." And yet, Lynes argues convincingly, "these works are the opposite of verisimilitude" and instead reveal "her lifelong commitment to abstraction." O'Keeffe makes changes in the relative sizes of the forms she reproduces—hills, cliffs, mesas—and changes their textures into "flattened planes of muted color." My fa- vorite of the examples is the painting "My Red Hills (1938)," in which O'Keeffe actually combines two different perspectives of the landscape she reproduces. Lynes visited the hill itself, not far from the artist's home in Abiquiu, New Mexico, and found that a part of the painting records what one sees from a spe- cific location, where the painter presumably sat and sketched. But behind that first line of hills, O'Keeffe includes "two re- ceding ridges of hills . . . [that] occur in the landscape but can only be seen by climbing to the top of a nearby hill and looking down at this cluster of red hills from an entirely different perspective." That is, I think, the painting records the landscape as it is known to that vigorous walker, whose daily routine for years included long walks after breakfast, before the serious, stationary work of the day's painting. The piece becomes an interesting variation on the idea of landscape—it's not just what the world looks like to the artist's eye but what she knows almost as habitat—a world lived in, wandered through, a texture known by grace of movement.

Once, O'Keeffe is said to have shown one of her Palo Duro paintings to another resident of the town of Canyon, Texas, explaining that the piece showed how she *felt* about the landscape. Well, the woman replied, if that's how you felt about the canyon, you must have had a stomach ache. Now I look at "My Red Hills" and think, she must have felt that adrenaline flush of crossing wide country, knowing the land with the lift and fall of the foot, the movement of one's own shadow under the sun's high, precessional perspective, the slip and roll of loose ground tumbling downhill beneath as one steps and stumbles higher up.

As I write, I'm drawing on those not-so-distant source materials, laying depositional sentences, the horizontal lines of sedimentary thought, across the blank plane. Oh, I think, Oh, Horizon.

IV. Unconformity

A decade ago, I stood in the fresh-smelling galleries of the newly opened campus art museum, gazing at a group of watercolors, the "Canyon Suite," from those early years in Texas. I loved the show—I'd never seen the other known watercolors from that period, housed here and there in various museums and collections across the country. A relative newcomer to the plains myself (the rolling mesa hills of the tallgrass prairie in eastern Kansas), I was energetically trying to get the sense of the place, to learn the names of plants, the layers of limestone with their sharp nodes of flint, the exhilarating vista of the wide, bright sky. One spring morning, I rose before dawn to shiver in a blind and watch male prairie chickens dance their mating dance, rolling their bizarre, round-sounding calls across the level lek, trying to lure in the females. I wrote poems about my growing aesthetics of the horizontal. And here were paintings from O'Keeffe's own reachings toward place, renditions of the southern prairie and its canyon places, what she called sudden "slits" in the plains. Here they were, in the brand new Beach Museum; they'd come as a visiting exhibit shortly after serving as the inaugural show at the new Kemper Museum in Kansas City. Wealthy philanthropist Crosby Kemper had purchased them in 1993 from a Santa Fe art dealer named Gerald Peters, and although he'd been solicited by the National Gallery to donate the full set—in fact, the pieces had actually been stored in the gallery's vaults while Peters was looking for a buyer—Kemper had decided to bring them to his museum, as a kind of cornerstone for the permanent collection. That year, the director of the National Gallery sent a letter to Kemper, saying, "I am writing to confirm our eagerness to add them to this national collection, where they would be an immensely important asset . . . the watercolors could be an astonishing addition to our holdings . . . [and] would offer an unrivaled opportunity to study the origins of O'Keeffe's art." But Kemper brought these national treasures home; now here they were, hanging inches before me.

And there was a charming story about their discovery. In 1918, O'Keeffe had become very ill, stricken during the great influenza outbreak brought back from Europe, first to Fort Riley, Kansas—a few minutes' drive from my new home—during World War I. She took a leave of absence from the college and recovered in the home of a friend near San Antonio, a woman who was also recuperating from illness—in her case, tuberculosis. But O'Keeffe didn't return to teaching; she'd grown frustrated with the constricting politics of the campus and the town of Canyon's gung-ho, anti-German feeling. In June, she decided to move to New York and take up painting full time, with the romantic and financial support of Alfred Stieglitz, whom she'd later marry.

It seemed she had left these pieces behind. There was a student, Ted Reid, with whom she'd developed a friendship close enough that some of the college faculty ladies had rebuked him, telling him he must never visit her in her boardinghouse room and must stop wandering across the landscape with O'Keeffe, unchaperoned. She gave the paintings to Reid, the story goes, perhaps before her stay in San Antonio, but at any rate before she headed to New York. Decades passed. Other art teachers came and went in Canyon, Texas. One of them, arriving in 1949, was Emilio Caballero, himself an abstract landscape painter and, by many accounts, a great enthusiast of O'Keeffe's work. He, too, had studied at Columbia University's Teachers College in New York before coming to West Texas A&M. One town resident told a reporter, "he had this obsession with O'Keeffe," even considering himself to have "some kind of an astral relationship" with the famous painter. He was a popular, much-beloved teacher on the campus. He went on to become head of the West Texas State art department in 1955, a position he held for twenty years before being forced out of the office. When Caballero was being squeezed from the chairmanship, Reid evidently stopped by the office to offer friendly company. "Ted Reid came by to commiserate with me," Caballero explained. "As he got up to leave, he asked if he could leave his package with me," promising to pick it up later.

But Reid never did.

Instead, it was stored in Caballero's garage, along with many boxes of materials he'd moved out of his campus office—evidently he was something of a packrat—and was forgotten until Caballero and his wife moved to a new house and came across the package as they sorted through what would move with them and what would be tossed. Without opening the package, Caballero said, he gave it to his daughter-in-law, Terry Lee Caballero. In the kind of small-world twists of fate that sometimes coil so tightly in small towns, she happened to be the granddaughter of Ted Reid, who had died four years earlier, in 1983. (O'Keeffe herself had died in 1986.)

Caballero had already had some luck in sorting through old art department trash. In the 1950s, his wife Mary had helped clean out an art classroom on the campus when the department was preparing to move to a new building. Great piles of paper, old sketches and paintings, and other materials were to be thrown away, but, as Mary later recalled, "I selected a small group of paintings that appealed to me." Among them were five works that the Caballeros sold during the 1970s to art dealers as early O'Keeffes, each for a couple of thousand dollars or so. One of these, reportedly, has been authenticated in the catalogue raisonné, but none of the others.

"We did it as a lark," Terry Lee Caballero told *Washington Post* reporter Jo Ann Lewis. "We just found these watercolors in a box in my father-in-law's garage when we were helping him move. And we were astonished because they looked so much like O'Keeffe. We never said they were by O'Keeffe." She insists they called in the experts, people who could determine fact from speculation. Nonetheless, she did eventually sign a bill of sale declaring: "Seller believes the Works on Paper are genuine and authentic art works created by Georgia O'Keeffe"—the seller received about a million dollars for this "lark." Ultimately the group sold to Kemper for about $5 million. Doris Bry, one-time assistant and agent for O'Keeffe, has said: "One of the sad things in O'Keeffe history is that people see O'Keeffe and they see dollar bills. They don't see works of art."

Some of the pieces in the Canyon Suite I liked far more than others. Most were on paper that had darkened badly and looked rather as though they'd been bruised, like fruit, by rough handling. Some seemed, to my amateur's eye, far less carefully made, with sloppy lines that bled (bruised, I think again) into one another. But some were captivating. The subtle, hushed colors of one titled "Dusk in the Canyon" actually looked very good against the brown of the aged paper, and the soft pink shapes of the hills seemed nearly animate, like some large mammals seated on the ground. (I think now, as I write, of the words of art critic Paul Rosenfeld, from 1924: "There are canvases of O'Keeffe's that make one to feel life in the dim regions where human, animal, and plant are one, indistinguishable.") Of course, I bought the catalog, a poorly bound thing that now sprawls loose pages across my floor. Another favorite was "Canyon Landscape," which, when I stare at it, shows the rhythmic sense of those side canyons crisscrossing through the red rock of the canyon, folding one behind the other, until they reach the horizontal wash of sky.

But within a few years there was a sudden flood of controversy. The long-awaited catalogue raisonné was published, a definitive two-volume set sponsored by the National Gallery and conducted by Barbara Buhler Lynes, an O'Keeffe scholar and now curator of the O'Keeffe Museum in Santa Fe. Together with Judith Walsh, the senior paper conservator at the National Gallery, Lynes had determined that the Canyon Suite collection could not have been the work of O'Keeffe, as it had been represented. Kemper's first reaction was stunned outrage; he even suggested to the *Wall Street Journal* that the decision was a kind of revenge since he'd not honored the National Gallery's request to give them the paintings. I think his reaction is understandable, for he had little to go on. He'd simply received a formal letter in October 1999, stating "research caused numerous works on paper to be omitted from the catalogue raisonné, including those that have been referred to as 'The Canyon Suite.'"

The research wasn't specified then, but over the subsequent weeks and months press reports summarized the evidence established by Judith Walsh and Barbara Lynes; and Mark Stevenson, a paper conservator hired by Kemper himself, later concurred. At issue was the paper. Despite the asserted provenance of the group—painted during 1916–1918—the scholars found that "some of the papers weren't available until the 1960s. Others were from the 30s," as one reporter phrased the information repeated in story after story. The specifics have not been presented definitively in scholarly publications, but the short of it is that several of the pieces were on paper that was manufactured well after the mid-teens, the very time that the paintings were claimed to have been painted.

This is the sticking point, the rock-hard fact that has discredited the little bundle of watercolors. Since some of them cannot be what they were said to be, the whole group is now suspect. But there are other aspects of the narrative that are questionable, too. Michael R. Grauer, art curator at the Panhandle Plains Historical Museum in Canyon, says it doesn't make sense to him that O'Keeffe would have left such a large group of paintings in the hands of a friend. "Artists trade stuff all the time," he mused in conversation with me. "But not a whole portfolio." Mark Stevenson, the paper restoration specialist hired by Kemper, agrees. He told reporters: "Here was a woman who didn't like to sell her paintings, much less give them away, supposedly giving 28 works to someone who was leaving her [Reid planned to enlist in the army, against O'Keeffe's advice]. I don't think so." And why exactly did Reid then carry a package of the artwork to Caballero's office and ask him to keep it temporarily? J. W. Reid, Ted's son, told a reporter flatly, "I don't believe it," explaining that the men were acquaintances, not close friends. (According to one account, Caballero took a flying class taught by Ted Reid while he was a student at West Texas in the 1940s.) Further, says the son, Reid joined the president of West Texas A&M in requesting that O'Keeffe donate a picture to the school. The men traveled together to the artist's home in New Mexico to make their case. "I'm sure if my dad had any of those paintings then he would have given one to the college," he told reporters Steve Paul and Mike McGraw from the Kansas City Star.

It turned out there had been a question about one of the pieces early on. Peters sent the whole group—then twenty-nine paintings—to Keiko Keyes, a paper conservator. Because some of the suite had suffered damage, mending was necessary, at the very least. Keyes found that one of the twenty-nine pieces had a watermark indicating it had been manufactured decades later than the supposed period of composition. Peters contacted the

Caballeros, who reportedly suggested that since Reid stayed in touch with O'Keeffe long after her departure from Canyon, she could have given the piece to him at a later time. But Peters removed the painting and offered the remaining twenty-eight pieces for sale as the suite. He also thought that one looked "stylistically" different from the rest and so shouldn't be included. With the outliers gone, the suite was presented, along with its purported narrative.

In trying to map the shape of this story, to puzzle over its side canyons and sudden dead ends, I keep coming back to the matter of paper. I'm relying heavily on press accounts, notes from various museum "vertical file" clippings, and downloaded stories from newspaper databases. As I leaf through these stories and see the same quotations appear and reappear, I'm struck by a glimmer of irony, like alabaster in sandstone. Judith Walsh discussed in some detail the single time she found O'Keeffe to have used newsprint: it's for the three-work series "Light Coming on the Plains," a 1917 group of watercolors that have been authenticated as the artist's legitimate work. She analyzed the technique, the effects of the paper on the composition, and her words again imply the artist's intentions as well as the way color and texture suggest a brevity of breathlessness in the opening moments of a witnessed daybreak. "The suffusing light of dawn that dispels the deep blue of night," Walsh writes, "was achieved by using ox-gall or another dispersal agent to the wet watercolor, causing one color to separate from the other. The slightly fuzzy cartridge paper that O'Keeffe routinely used during this period did not have a slick enough surface to allow the paint to move as needed to achieve this effect."

It's an interesting group of paintings, great arcs of progressively paler blue hinting at the sun's first appearance over the flat line of the prairie horizon, but time has not been kind to the color here. The paper, as old newsprint always does, has darkened badly and gives a dirty look to each one, as if each sunrise fell upon a world of dust and drought. Both the subject matter and the contrapoise of arc and line reappear in some of the Canyon Suite series; but none of these latter repeats so perfectly the variation on line and shape from the authenticated series.

Which, I wonder, are the papers from the 1930s, when dust storms really did ravage the Texas Panhandle? Which are from the right time period but are simply the wrong kind of paper—too cheap for O'Keeffe's tastes? How many constitute each group, and what about the others? How can I separate the issues—forensics, as Grauer terms it, from aesthetics? Several people, including Gerald Peters and Michael Grauer, hold out the possibility that perhaps a few of these watercolors actually were by O'Keeffe's hand. Perhaps one or two (but not the "whole portfolio") were given to Ted Reid. After all, he had a car and had sometimes driven O'Keeffe to Palo Duro Canyon, where she did such interesting work. Perhaps some were found in that classroom, along with the others Mary Caballero had saved from destruction. But, said Peters, in a phrase repeated in various news stories, "it appears as though someone added something to the pot."

Dan Keegan was director of the Kemper Museum when the controversy broke. He seems to have chosen his words carefully in an interview with the *Washington Post*. "Fake is a difficult word," he mused, "because we don't know how these works came to be, and we don't know the intent. My definition of 'fake' is that someone creates a work of art to look like the work of another artist. And do we have that in this case? I don't know. Because the way these works came to be is not clear to us. . . . And the facts presented to us prove that these could not be the work of Georgia O'Keeffe." Mark Stevenson determined, in a reporter's words, that "the 'suite' was really the work of several hands during several decades."

"Just look at them, and compare them with accepted watercolors in the *Catalogue Raisonné*," said Ruth Fine. And Doris Bry, who worked as O'Keeffe's assistant and agent in New York for many years—until she was forced out of the artist's financial affairs when O'Keeffe developed a keen relationship with Juan Hamilton in the mid-1970s—was even blunter. "One of the things that irritated me is that they were so bad," she told a reporter in 2000. Grete Meilman, an art expert for Sotheby's who reportedly rejected the suite in the 1980s, said, "This was the period when she painted some of her most beautiful pieces, and these don't fit that description. Her sense of confidence doesn't seem to be there."

So there are several currents of persuasion here, which individually and together erode the credibility of the "Suite" as a group produced at a particular time, but also leave questions hanging, dislodged and unresolved. First, forensics, or technical evidence, which exposes the irregularities in paper. This discredits the group because of the anachronism of paper manufactured after the paintings were supposed to have been created. Second, the connoisseurship, which declares that the pieces don't look authentic because of poor execution and matters of style—the synecdoche of the "hand" does not reach back to connect convincingly with the implied artist we believe we *know* from her legitimate work. Third, skepticism about the romantic story itself; even without the technical evidence, one finds much to wonder about in the tale of the paintings' emergence and sale. (Indeed, one wonders—I wonder—whether such a provenance would have been found plausible in the first place, had the painter been one of her male contemporaries, and not Miss O'Keeffe, the then-unmarried woman painter whose work was quickly defined as "a woman on paper" and read in light of her sex and all her contemporaries' gender expectations. Maybe so; but I rather doubt it.) Finally, O'Keeffe's own memoirs. In 1976, she wrote: "When I knew that I was going to stay in New York, I sent for things I had left in Texas. They came in a barrel, and among them were all my old drawings and paintings. I put them in with the waste paper trash to throw away and that night when Stieglitz and I came home after dark, the paintings and drawings were blowing all over the street. We left them there and went in."

Together, the evidence seems overwhelming. It certainly convinced Kemper, who decided to take Peters up on an earlier guarantee to refund the purchase price. It convinced Peters, although in later interviews he held out the possibility that one or more might be authentic, even if he'd never try to sell them again. But I'd like greater connection among these lines of thought. I'd like to know which images are on the telltale paper and whether those are images I and other viewers consider as showing a poor hand? If so, that might leave another intriguing confluence: what if the prettiest paintings—Barbara Bloemink, former director of the Kemper Museum, says "some of them are very beautiful"—the ones that seem most successful as abstractions of the landscape, the most affective to the viewer—what if those were on paper that *could be* legitimate? Not the usual paper, mind you—Walsh and Lynes insist that she used high-quality cartridge paper almost exclusively. But she is known, for at least those three aforementioned paintings, to have strayed from that preference. *What if?* The scholars haven't published the details of this information, and they decline to talk about it. "Wish I could help you, but I can't. Maybe at some point I'll be able to, but not now," Lynes e-mailed me.

But Steve Paul of the *Kansas City Star* kindly sends me some of his notes from extensive research the paper conducted for a whole series of articles, some of which analyze the degree of difficulty in recognizing the various pieces as fakes. Drawing on interviews with Stevenson, who attended a meeting with Kemper, Lynes, and Walsh, the reporters arrange those source materials. They write that "Dusk in the Canyon," (one of my favorites) is "easily dismissed," with "muted colors and haphazard brushwork"; yet they also quote Peters as saying the painting "seems just right." Its technical betrayal is that it's on a paperboard material "apparently never used by O'Keeffe."

The clinchers didn't travel to my town though. These are the ones on paper that simply didn't exist during O'Keeffe's Canyon, Texas stay: "Autumn on the Plains" was painted "on a handmade paper that's been described as coming from the second half of the twentieth century," according to Paul. The other, "Train Coming In," is evidently very similar to a legitimate piece, "with a haunting, deliberate quality," but was painted on the paper made in the 1930s. When my interlibrary loan request comes in and I have the Kemper exhibit catalog in hand, I flip to the unfamiliar images. Here they are: "Autumn on the Plains" looks like an eastern landscape, full of the deciduous range of color. It's painted on a clean, textured handmade paper utterly unlike the others. I don't much like it. "Train Coming In" similarly looks clean, unweathered by time. Dominated by white and blue-purple, it's a cool abstraction, quite unlike her other, legitimate train image from the period.

But the one that makes me hold my breath isn't even part of the one-time Kemper's suite. "Abstraction, Dark" is identified as "property of Gerald and Kathleen Peters" (though I learn later from Lynes that it was donated to the Kemper after the catalog had been published). It is quite stunning. The paper is slightly yellowed, and there's a background of tawny near gold, but the image itself is framed in black. Three separate forms lift, like stone hoodoos, from the horizontal foreground. The central shape is phallic, a dark-tipped thrust of gray and palest pink; it's flanked by smaller, shouldered forms in shades of red just barely touched with black. I look at it for several long moments, and then I realize: the profile in the center is the Lighthouse. There in the watercolor I see the very curve of the tower's caprock tip against the sky. The composition is much stylized, of course, carefully composed in a way you could never see no matter where you stood in Palo Duro Canyon. But the individual elements are there: the outline of the tower, the color of the stone, and a sympathetic humanization of the enduring landscape features. It's a wonderful piece, sensual and rich, whoever the artist. And the paper? Steve Paul's notes tell me it's not from the wrong time period—just the wrong material. It's "groundwood," a cheap stock that the scholars have determined O'Keeffe never used in her legitimated work.

For weeks I've been dealing with geology's analog of unconformity, the fascinating gap of missing material, missing information. I feel now that I'm left against some box canyon wall, uncertain where to turn, gazing at a blank dead end of unidentifiable stone. I've studied the legitimate landscape paintings and those that have been discredited. I've walked and slept and awakened in Palo Duro Canyon, to see the palpable fact of the land play out its ever-changing light and weather. And, shaking my head at the cheesy development of the park, the simulated backdrops for the myth of the Conquering Cowboy, I've thought of Jean Baudrillard, the French theorist and philosopher who wrote devastatingly about the death and disappearance of sincerity from American material culture.

"To dissimulate is to pretend not to have what one has," he wrote. Dissimulation is fakery and "therefore leaves the principle of reality intact; the difference is always clear, it is simply masked." With fakes, we still know what the real is, out there, but what he calls simulation is another matter. "To simulate is to feign what one doesn't have." Once simulation—the creation of imagery utterly devoid of reference to something "real"—has affected the way a culture looks at things, he claims, there's no turning back. In a cascade effect, imagery loses its connective, indicative power, tumbling uncontrollably down that precipitous slope. "Such would be the successive phases of the image," Baudrillard explains: "it is the reflection of a profound reality; it masks and denatures a profound reality; it masks the *absence* of a profound reality; it has no relation to any reality whatsoever: it is its own pure simulacrum."

By this definition, the discredited O'Keeffes are dissimulations, pretending not to be what researchers found them to be—pieces by various hands made in various decades. But what if you regard them simply as landscape paintings "by Anon" and remove the question of authorship? Someone painted them—perhaps their reflective quality was not to *produce a copy of O'Keeffe* but to paint an expressive response to the landscape, albeit under the influence of O'Keeffe's vision, the way students will often adopt the style and interest of important teachers and models. What if you lay the question of their copying atop, not the "reality" of O'Keeffe's own career and work, but the objective reality behind her landscape-allusive abstract art? What role does the literal territory play here, the "real" world behind art, behind dissimulated art?

For there's another strange layer to the story. After reading of the controversy in the newspapers, a man from Santa Fe announced that some are by his hand. Jacobo "Jackie" Suazo lived with O'Keeffe as an adolescent. His older brother worked as a gardener for the painter, and the younger boy became a kind of foster son to O'Keeffe, he says, living in her Abiquiu home from the late 1940s until he left for the Marine Corps in 1953. He says he often painted with her, and she encouraged him in his own efforts. (Other men report that they "helped" O'Keeffe paint during her later years, when her eyesight was failing her.) After seeing a photograph of one of the disputed pieces in a Santa Fe paper, Suazo drove to Kansas City and contacted the Kemper Museum director, who agreed to show him the pieces.

"I realized I did three of them and some Mother O'Keeffe did. Some I didn't recognize," he told Gretchen Reynolds of the *New York Times*. The *Kansas City Star* reported his meeting with Museum Director Keegan and the paintings themselves: "I touched them and I started crying," he said. Suazo owns an old drawing pad that the O'Keeffe Foundation in Santa Fe returned to him from the artist's estate and suggests that the paper may be similar to that of the disputed Canyon Suite series. Not long after his trip to Kansas City, he contacted an attorney and filed with the U.S. Copyright Office, claiming sole authorship of three of the pieces and joint authorship of others. In 2001, the Copyright Office approved this claim. Suazo's attorney carefully specified what this means for the images. "His claims don't relate to ownership of the actual works, but only to the reproduction rights." He's evidently trying to publish a memoir, what he calls "outstanding and important history about the association and collaboration between Mother O'Keeffe and I," but he's had no luck finding a publisher. I wonder what role the copyrighted paintings would play. If any of them really are his work, they have no connection to Palo Duro Canyon whatsoever. All the titles affixed to the pieces would become absurd, referencing their history as dissimulation. But that, too, is a big, uncertain "if."

In the postmodern age, Baudrillard complains, "Something has disappeared: the sovereign difference between the one [territory] and the other [the map], that constituted the charm of abstraction." We've lost our conviction in the relationship between signifier and signified, between reality and mimesis. But I think it's possible here to hold on to a different precession of the image: the landscape scene and the landscapes rendered need not be taken as evidence that the land itself has lost its power to ground us. As writer Dan Flores has pointed out, the landscape of Palo Duro Canyon is part and parcel of that which O'Keeffe later chose for her home and constant subject. The canyon at the eastern edge of the Llano Estacado is separated from the New Mexican landforms and rivers around Abiquiu by the artificial boundaries of geography, not geology—the political lines are abstracted from history and inscribed on our allusive renditions of the place itself. The land stretches, beneath its tawny skin of grass and furze of juniper, beneath the pointed leaves of yucca and the sprawling bristle of cactus, along the ancient structure of escarpments (Canadian, Mescalero, Caprock), to the foothills of western mountains. There, where the High Plains meet the upthrust of the Sangre de Christo range, in that beautiful point of connectivity, Georgia O'Keeffe spent decades walking and painting, and keeping many of her own thoughts to herself.

It's a puzzle and a glory, to try to see and understand the making of an artist's vision. Somehow, somewhere along the way, in the arc from childhood (precocious or unremarkable, whichever may be the case) to full maturity, the artist arrives at the inner place of perceptive originality. Despite the early training and success and the praise for her apprentice work from William Merritt Chase, O'Keeffe's juvenilia is often unremarkable. I've held a sketchbook from 1905–1906, when she was eighteen or nineteen; the sketches there are mostly figures, a few clichéd landscapes the size of my palm. Penciled inside the cover is an unattributed, hackneyed verse, probably significant to the young person who was leaving her family to study, to work, to find her way in the world:

Good-by is the word that carries to rest
Its weight on the heart of the lightest breast;
And awakens the soul to the thought of gloom,
The word of all words I would entomb.

How far she'd leave these conventional expressions—the woman in a hat, the rural scenes, the sentimental rhyme of "rest" and "breast." Marsden Hartley would write of her work, in 1921: "She looks as if she had ridden the millions of miles of her every known imaginary horizon, and has left all her horses lying dead in their tracks."

V. Ogallala Caprock

In poetry, says contemporary poet Charles Wright, "Landscape [is a] discredited subject" and the journal or daybook, keeping track of those *facts of nature* and their play upon the mind and emotions throughout the zodiacal wheel's precession of days and seasons, is a "discredited form." Still, Wright keeps on with his work, an ongoing meditation on the place of the self in the world, the role of seeing, the landscape as a phenomenological power to the eye and mind. And I tell you again, it was the last week of March 2006 when I was in Palo Duro Canyon. The cottonwoods hadn't yet blurred themselves into a pale wash of color beneath one's gaze, softened by tender growth and their pursuit of chlorophyll's seasonal engine. The wet, red mud froze on my boots. In the quartermaster sand- and siltstone, horizontal bands of alabaster glistened and shone like ice, like quartz, and when sections of the rock sloughed off along the stream, the pieces gleamed like teeth broken from some giant prehistoric jaw, though no such creatures would have patrolled the Permian seas that really laid down that stone. I tell you what it looked like, a handsome anachronism. I'm drawing on sincerity—*I was there*—and artifice: turns of phrase, figurative language, the power of metaphor to pull that great sleight of hand or outright transformation, to make you see *as if*.

In the 1940s, from her home in New Mexico, O'Keeffe wrote to her friend the abstract landscape painter, Arthur Dove: "I wish you could see what I see outside the window. The earth pink and yellow cliffs to the north—the full pale moon about to go down in an early morning lavender sky behind a very long beautiful tree-covered mesa to the west"—and she goes on, continuing to describe, to scribe, the world before her eyes. "I wish you could see it."

In the Mind's Eye

> [I]t's no happenstance that artistic forms often seem to
> mimic those in nature—"seem to mimic" because they are, in
> fact, simply different manifestations of those same forms.
> William L. Fox

I. Form Constants

Close your eyes. Press your fingers gently against the inner edge
of each eyeball, then move the pressure toward your temples.
You're seeing things, aren't you? Probably a gold grid work,
shimmering and glimmering, or a field of scintillating dots.
If you rub your eyes, you may see stars. If you alternate pressure and its release, keeping your eyes shut all the while, you
may see all kinds of geometric forms or squiggly lines, including what may look like the pattern of your own blood vessels in
the eyeball or the eyelid. As if you are seeing yourself from inside yourself.

These are entoptic images, meaning, via Greek, "within vision" or "within the eye." They are a self-generated, minute universe of forms, abstractions, free of intentional figuration. You
aren't trying to make yourself see a particular shape, are you?
They're the ultimate ephemera, more fleeting even than the
flesh that gives them brief, brilliant life. Phosphene, researchers also say, meaning phos, light coupled with phainein, to show.

But who is the audience for this light show? Only yourself. For each of us, only one's self. I remember, in childhood, in that dull smear of boredom that only the young enjoy, engaging in just this kind of self-stimulation, filling time by painting myself a golden world, which then metamorphosed into black and red. Outside the first bedroom window I remember, at 1621 Ninth Street in Boulder, Colorado, I could look out and see the Flatiron Mountains. Later, in Ohio, my window at 46 Grosvenor opened onto the slant of the porch roof, with a view of a great sycamore tree across the street where an elderly couple lived in what I thought—then—was a very distinguished-looking house. I must have spent hours gazing out these windows, then shifting perspective to stare at the screens on the windows, the dead insects and dust clustered in the corners. But other times, I recall, I'd lie on my bed, or on the floor, and stare at dust motes in shafts of sunlight. I'd rub my eyes and see dust motes there, too, and then the panoply of inner fireworks, as I identified them, that responded to the movement of my palms against my eyelids.

You probably did, too, now that I mention it. For "form constants" is a related term, through which scholars emphasize their conviction that, as results of the optic nervous system, these images are cross-cultural universals, the biological heritage of any human being alive now or in the preceding millennia that were peopled by this particular form of hominid, *Homo sapiens*. Form constants need no specific stimuli, no blow to the head, your wind knocked out as you lie gasping, blinking, beside your bike, your horse, the rock face you tried to climb. No hallucinogens. Only your own breathing, blood-coursing body, accessing what seems to be some aspect of the inner architecture of your neural system's synaptic life.

Archaeologists identify a number of these entoptic forms and say they are the referents behind much of the oldest rock art throughout the American West. Grids, zigzags, spirals, groups of dots, meandering lines, starbursts, crosses, honey-combs of contiguous closed forms . . . these shapes, some say, could be ritually induced and enhanced—through trance, in vision quests or shamanic spiritual journeys—and then traced or, perhaps, in something a little like *recollection in tranquility*, retraced in paint or pecked art on the dark, hard varnish coating desert rocks.

I spread out maps. I buy a new compass. I make lists of places to visit, within a long day's drive, and study written descriptions of what I'll find and how to get there. Or I fill all my water bottles, pack provisions, check the tent to be sure the stakes are there, all ten of them and an extra one, just in case. I cancel plans when desert rain pounds the dry Mojave, leaving some roads slick as a potter's wheel, others washed out altogether. When that happens, I go with the flow, change course, head somewhere else. As winter opens into desert spring, I'm on the trail of rock art left for thousands of years in the desert South-west, some images faint and faded as the varnish slowly returns to darken again the incised stone, some disappearing as the surface erodes, like figures, names, and dates in old New England graveyards, some chipped and blistered where twentieth-century vandals have blasted them with shotguns, or paint, or carved their own infamous initials across the surface of surviving art. The desert in late winter feels less inhospitable, less inhuman, than it has in the brief, midsummer visits I've made in years past—though then I traveled only in the Chihuahuan, and now, for a few weeks, I'm even farther west, living in the Mojave.

Yes, it seems less inhuman, even though the back roads, parks, and parking lots are nearly empty, far less clotted with tourists. The landscape itself seems to be resting before the grim glare of summer heat and the demands of dry tenacity. And after a weekend of rain, the world must be deeply, with a biologic metaphysicality, refreshed.

II. Grapevine Canyon

The barrel cacti that seem scattered like boulders across the hillside are rosy fingered, red petaled, but each rufus point is sharp, stiff, spiny. Beauty comes hard, here, and so the little stream that tumbles down the hillside, below Avikwa'ame, Spirit Mountain in the Yuman language of the Great Basin dwellers, is a tiny microcosm of amelioration. Rushes grow in two or three spots where, appropriately, the rushing water slows. Beyond the visual barrier of tumbled boulders and balanced rocks, in a small round dip in the landscape, a cottonwood stands rooted in the sweep of sand, surprising and lovely against the surrounding Mojave. It's the only real tree I'll see all afternoon, amidst the wide panorama of stone, black brush and brittlebush, Joshua tree and almost-blooming cholla. At first I think it may be dead (there have been five years of drought in this difficult countryside), but as I step closer I see hard fat buds on all its pale fingers.

The petroglyphs begin much lower down, right where the stream first reaches the wide plain—or plane, I think suddenly—of the wash. The boulders at this gateway to a wetter world are marked and marked again with the artistic matter of abstract aesthetics: the grids and boxes, diamond chains, the lines and dots that seem like punctuation to the mute counsel of stone and the welcome music of moving water. Some scholars see this place as a mythopoetic stage, a cosmogenic site of a Mojave creation tale, involving characters like Frog, a daughter of the oldest spirit, Matavilya, and Frog's brother, Mastamho, who created the Colorado River, the ocean, the mountain itself, from which each aperture of headwater opens to the world of air. Desert marigold and desert dandelion are already in flower in the sun-bathed microclimate where worlds meet—basin and range, sand and bloom. In recent centuries, I've read, Paiute and Shoshone people frequented this site, considering it Mastamho's Home and conducting shamanic rituals. Initiates evidently retraced existing images, leaving the lines thick and deep. A few panels are so closely and overlappingly inscribed they seem a textured residue of artistic activity, where individual shapes are almost indecipherable among the blur of light and dark.

In bright, dry sunlight, I sit and eat my lunch and scan the rockface with binoculars. In shadow, I find a perfect rectangle, marked in just a few alternating solid and open squares. A closeup of a checkerboard, perhaps a foot in width and two in height. Or a tiny section of a nine-patch quilt. But this is no initiates' workbook, fudged by subsequent reworking. Although in shadow, it's obviously old, the pecked lines darkened with returning varnish. What I like best, however, is its placement on the stone itself. Directly below the image, a rectangular block of rock the size and shape of the inscribed form has fallen away, so that the artwork offers a replacement shape, an artificial completion to the missing stone.

That's not an explanation for the work; it's not an interpretation of some ancient symbol. I don't know what a checkerboard might "mean," or whether, centuries or millennia ago, someone sat, in shade or sunlight, recording symbols from narrative or spontaneous, unstoried shapes from within the neural workings of the mind. At rest in the desert, I'm only noticing the lay of things, the patterns, with their polyvalent variations, of the human in the larger realms.

III. Varnish

"Vernissage," a lovely collection of Romance-language syllables, contains in its etymology the interchangeability of *v* and *b*, deriving, if you follow the word-path back, from Berenik, a North African city of great antiquity, where, the dictionary tells us, "natural resins were first used as varnish." Vernissage has two meanings in the contemporary lexicon: a pre-view or private showing of an art exhibit before it opens to the public, and a reception in celebration of a show's opening. Both the private and the public; both the glimpse and the gathering. I learn this word the same day my friend Janie writes that she's having a show of her recent work in New York; landscapes and abstract pieces, she says. She prefers to paint the latter, and from what I've seen I agree that they are her best work, but it's the landscapes that actually *sell*. "Those pesky landscapes," she calls them.

The pale sandstone cliffs of Utah, the basalt boulders of Southern California, the red sandstone monoliths of Nevada— throughout the desert Southwest, the world itself has painted, patinated, patiently colored some of the old stone surfaces with the dark, hardened veneer of what is called desert varnish. The process is minute, the result of tiny bacteria shaped like spheres, rods, or pears that colonize the rocks and make their living on the bright, dry edge between air and stone. This austere ecotone is theirs alone. *Metallogenium* or *Pedomicrobium*, kinds of "appendaged bacteria," send out their microscopic filaments across the surface where even lichens fail to thrive. They eat rock and air and precipitate oxides, micron by micron. Manganese for black, iron for red. *That's for remembrance.* And for thoughts.

How old such stains may be is still open to debate and will be, I'm sure, the object of much study, but it seems some ten thousand years are likely needed for a slick, hard rind to grow. Under the scanning electron microscope, one can see and even photograph the pattern of this deposition: dry, dusty times leave a smooth appearance, called *lamellate* for its layered look. Wetter times of greater vegetation growth result, with a delightful if coincidental symbolism, in depositions that are called *botryoidal* and look like miniature berry bunches, juniper, say, in a micromorphology that seems, I think, like a kind of eye-rhyme too small to be seen unaided in the field.

Amazingly, researchers have sketched out a sedimentary sequence, a band of colors a little like an Agnes Martin painting, regularly alternating dark and light, brown and orange. It's utterly functional, however. It becomes a chronometric ruler, with darker bands corresponding to wetter periods in the planet's history, like the sudden cooling spell called the Younger Dryas that falls along the temporal boundary between the Pleistocene and Holocene epochs, or, if you glance farther down, to earlier geologic happenings called Heinrich Events, when great chunks of Laurentide ice collapsed into the Atlantic, changing the ocean currents' patterns and leading to a wetter, cooler climate in the northern hemisphere from shore to shore.

When these darker pigments, shadows of the earth's circumferential processes, creep back into the miniature canyons of an incised line, they change the visual tenor of the image before us. Old petroglyphs hold these shadows, like the changed perspective of a desert evening after the sun has dropped behind the nearest ridge. At a glance, you can tell whether a collection of images are of the same age, or whether any single panel has been composed over centuries, its imagery both dark and light. Researchers can further focus the chronometric gaze: with tiny scrapings, samplings, they can date the repatinated varnish and so approximate the time of composition. My favorite of the methods described is a kind of miniature fossil study, in which the growing varnish traps and seals over flecks and bits of organic matter—pollen, say, or a bit of ash that soon is encased in the slow recoloring of stone, like minute insects caught in hardening amber. Through carbon-14 dating, this residue of far-distant life can be dated, at least as far back as some forty thousand years. Another process involves not the study of carbon's decomposition but what's called cation-ratio dating. Here the fractional relations of constituent elements leach, or shift, resulting over long periods of time—far longer than the upward limit of carbon-14 dating—in a calibration against which samples of the desert varnish can be measured. You can picture the researchers hiking over rough and forbidding terrain to glean these tiny traces of matter, then making their way back to distant labs where, far from the art's position in the world, they try to tie it to some far-off point in time.

In the Coso Mountains, in southeastern California, the rock art has an ancient lineage. Some images are recent additions: they depict men with both long penises and bows and arrows, suggesting some hypermasculine, tough-guy cult of the past fifteen hundred years. Paiute people may have pecked some of these images as recently as the nineteenth century, when their shamans still headed out to the usually dry canyons to record their visions, dreaming of the power to make rains come. It's said that to kill a sheep means, metaphorically, to bring the rain.

But others, the scientists have shown us, are truly ancient. At the head of Little Petroglyph Canyon, still marked on some maps with the older name, Renegade Canyon, and in the early twentieth century occasionally called Sand Canyon, are images dated to the Pleistocene. Sixteen thousand, five hundred years ago. I type the number as words and letters, not numerals, to watch it stretch across the horizontal line of thought. These could be pre-Clovis people, immigrants from across the much-imagined "land bridge" during the age of glaciers. What did they carve, or more precisely, what is left to us from them? A stippled rockface, pocked and puckered with cupules, so-called pit-and-groove engravings that seem wholly revarnished with the color of time. A few geometric forms, these "entoptics," tracings from the mind's eye. And, perhaps, the body of the great sheep, whose outline is carved deep, deep, into the water- and time-scoured canyon bed. It has either withstood long ages of floods or has been painstakingly recarved, regenerating its curved belly even as the stone that holds it is abraded away. One spot near the canyon's head hints at the work of researchers, as well as the ancient artists. A closely spaced lattice of vertical lines, colored over with dark varnish, stretches across the stone's slight curve. Much of this petroglyph has been overgrown with bright orange lichen, but a neatly shaped square is free of growth—scraped carefully and painstakingly, I think, the fungus and algae deposited in some clean jar or tube for transport back to the technological complexity of the laboratory. The remaining image, sheared of its fluffy coat of slow growth, looks almost like a square field, plowed but unplanted, as seen from an airplane making its descent.

We drive to Ridgecrest, California, on the first Friday in March, after a particularly wet February, and throughout our journey the wetness continues. In the distance, rain rakes the desert, hanging in slanted, diagonal shafts, looking exactly like the common rock art form that's sometimes described as a "comb" or "rake," or like the unfurled wing of the thunderbird or a horned, fringe-coated rain dancer. As we top a small rise, the road is suddenly awash with slush—hail has fallen, moments before, and in the storm light all the hills shine silver between the dark, wet sagebrush.

That evening, lightning laces together the edges of the sky, and once, in the restaurant where we eat burgers and steaks, the lights go out briefly, and everyone gasps. But the morning of the scheduled tour dawns promisingly, with cool, clearing skies. A small party of seven, attended with friendliness and vigilance by two guides, we caravan onto the China Lake Naval Air Weapons Station and drive windingly through fields (forests?—they're so tall!) of Joshua trees. At Wild Horse Mesa, we round a bend and come face to face with the namesake horses, manes in the wind, heads attentive in the morning light. All around are mountains: the Cosos, the Panamints, and to the west, the shockingly high and snow-bright Sierra Nevadas. We are in the world of basin and range, nearly ringed with rugged peaks.

It's cold. And still rather windy, in the raw March morning. Throughout the canyon, pools of water fill the sculpted tanks and basins carved by countless other wet, and wetter, times, forcing us to climb around and over, and even in one case, wade right through them. One of the guides is elated and surprised. "I've never seen water in this canyon," she says. Most often, now, this is a land of drought, not flood. The name of the range, "Coso," derives from a Paiute word for fire, and the dark volcanic basalt that litters the landscape does look charred and burned, as is, in fact an entire hillside where the Joshua trees have been blackened and brought down.

After weeks of anticipation, we're here. For over a mile, the images line the walls: sheep, some with cloven hooves, some with balls instead of feet, and some footless, with simple, stiff, stick legs. Many seem to depict the act of sheep-motion: leaping, flying, great horns curved across their backs. Some have been pierced with spears or arrows. One, a faint image on a pale cliff, is nearly eight feet across; the light must catch it right or it will disappear beneath your gaze. A row of stick figures, arms and legs and thin-lined heads, some of which fork into hints of horns, parades statically across the stone, headed as if uphill and around the corner of the rock. "Journey," I think the image says. "Line dance," think others. In any case, here the rock reflects the human form in motion, in the nearly elemental stasis of stone; the shape of the group takes precedence over the depiction of any individual body. Minimalism, this is, with the human form reduced to the level of the line.

Elsewhere, we exclaim over the patterned bodies of humanoid figures—shaman or spirit beings, some archaeologists insist. One has a spiral for a face, suggesting the power of the whirlwind, the animated body of air that transects two realms, at least, with its vertical reach. Atlatls. Spear or arrow points. But also the geometric, abstract designs that defy a narrative interpretation. They are the shapes of themselves, of intentionality, of, perhaps, pure hypnotic presence, the act of the mind's attention to nothing beyond itself.

IV. Amphitheater

By now the cottonwood has small, pale green leaves. A pair of phainopeplas, perky in their blue-black feather crests, sweetly feed one another mistletoe berries, and the namesake grapevines are now just starting to leaf out. I'm back for another visit to Grapevine Canyon, and the intervening weeks of wet weather have left the streambed fuller. The water now meanders noticeably farther toward the east before disappearing in the abrasive, pale quartz delta of the wash. I wanted Dave to see this place, and he strolls in the late-day light, photographing the profusion of flowers, the birds in their courtship rituals. Bee balm, curved-bill thrasher. The desert life flits and blossoms in the sandy fan of what we call the canyon's mouth.

At the lowest rung of the escalier of tumbling water, where the channel abruptly opens from its squeezed passage between boulders into the plane of the wash, I stop for a moment and listen with excitement to two waterfalls. The first is behind me, the curve and tumble of the stream I've crossed and climbed atop to reach the upper canyon. The other is directly before me, an even louder rushing, an almost-roaring of water beneath the surface of the hill. For a moment, puzzled, I look for the outlet of this subterranean current and wonder at its voiced suggestion of an even wetter world beneath my feet. But, taking two steps back, I find the sound abruptly stops. One step forward; it's there again, though not so loud. One step, then another. But there is no opening among the rocks, no rivulet where the underground waterfall joins the surface waters.

I'm standing in a room-sized echo chamber, where the face of stone before me, covered with petroglyphs, must catch and amplify the sound of the swollen stream. One step, then another. I keep repositioning myself within the auditory convergence of two worlds and notice, slowly, another sound, a *swish* and *slip*, downstream a few yards. Turning to watch, I see the three-inch height of sand that is the northern border of the current slump into the water, as the current slowly whiptails itself across the flat potential of the wash. Tomorrow morning, when we return, the current will have meandered south again, and the ephemeral echo will have ended, no matter where we stand.

But now, suddenly, voices. A group of people arrives, four women and a man wearing white tennis shoes. He leaps atop the nearest of the boulders freckled with petroglyphs and begins giving a lecture, pointing to the images. He speaks in English, with the lilt of an Indian accent, and one of the women calls out a question—"Is that the picture of the canyon?"

"Yes," he calls in response. "It shows the journey through the canyon that the people took." They're pointing to a horizontal petroglyph that stretches like a gap-toothed jaw, a single line suggesting positive and negative space: the flat-topped presence of a row of mesas and the echoing flat-bottomed canyons alongside. I draw closer.

"Do you mind if I listen?" I ask.

"No," he responds, and pauses. "You're in for a treat."

And as the daylight dims, the sun dipping behind the upper reaches of the canyon, he identifies the spiral shape as the point of emergence, where the people came up from the world below into this one. On one boulder he shows the back of the great dragon, or Gila monster, on which they traveled. He points out the vertical ladder, a span of horizontal steps, which they used to climb atop the beast's back. Even without images to point to, he tells the story I've read about Mahatma's creation of the Colorado River, and he gestures widely to the east, where, hundreds of feet below where we stand, the river is even now cutting its way down, flowing south. Then he jumps down from the rock where he's been standing, crosses the stream, and climbs atop another. The women follow much more slowly; unlike him, none of them wears athletic shoes, and I feel suddenly self-conscious in my hiking boots and the ease with which I cross the stream behind him.

Looking down and away, I notice a glyph I hadn't paid attention to before: a stick figure, head, arms, torso, one arm—its left, if I assume it's facing me—raised with all five fingers spread wide. Beside it, images of atlatls, the shapes of human footprints. But instead of legs, the figure rests atop the rake, the comb, the shape some researchers call an entoptic, but which I cannot help but see as pelting rain. This person wears a skirt of rain, or walks, as rainclouds do across the basins of the West, on legs of a cloudburst. Here, in the echo chamber of the canyon's mouth, a figure waits who, when moving, walks with the rain.

Soon the man says, "And that's all I know," and I'm sure that is my cue to go. I thank them all for including me and walk back down the wash, looking for Dave, who has also been listening, he tells me, as he pursued the birds in the wash. The Indians remain awhile by the glyphs, and then as dusk gathers they return to join us in the parking lot where Dave is loading up his equipment. The man comes over with an open zip-lock bag and gives us each a pinch of dried sage, telling us we should make an offering to the rocks and thank them for the stories. We do, and I thank him again, as well.

"There's more to tell," he says, "but we can't say it once the sun has set. We just ran out of time."

V. Sleeping in the Panamints

Again, I drove a long way to get here. The car holds minimal gear—the tent, the stove, four days' worth of food. Though I plan to be here only three, I think it's best to be always over-prepared. Maps, of course. I fill the gas tank just before entering the park and drive past Badwater, the salt-drenched lake shadow in the lowest chapped, cupped palm of Death Valley, where this week the waters are choppy, muddy from the whisking wind, and they stretch for miles along the north-south axis of the park. Yesterday, I hear, someone launched a kayak in the shallows, a playful gesture in this record-year pool of residual rainwater. And just outside the park, along a stretch of dirt road, with a speed limit posted at twenty miles per hour, I waded thigh high into waters refilling the bowl of Silver Lake, marked "dry" on the map but neither dry nor silver on the day I briefly thought of swimming farther out to see how deep it got.

On a Saturday afternoon in February, I claim the last tent site in Wildrose Campground, perched at just over forty-one hundred feet in the Panamint range. The campground has well water, cold and sweet tasting, far better than I would have expected in such a geologically surly-seeming place; a few metal picnic tables; and a single latrine. Wildrose Canyon stretches roughly east-west, and as I fix dinner on the camp stove that first night, I can watch the sun setting precisely in the V-shaped notch where the canyon empties into Panamint Valley to the west.

The map's spread out on the table, weighted at each corner with a stone. Death Valley itself, formed by two tectonic faults, one on either side of the Panamint range, looks to me like an unhealed wound, and I compare the raw raggedness I saw, driving here, of what seems truly to be a *crust* of earth against the contour lines of this pleasing facsimile, shaded light green to denote wilderness, that lays out points of interest, geologic features, and the peaks I hope to climb. A young woman ventures over from another part of the campground. The rest of her party—a group of college students volunteering labor in the park—have gone elsewhere to take showers, but she sits out at the picnic table for awhile, reading, then comes over to chat.

"Do you always camp alone?" she asks with a whetted interest.

"Well, no," I begin, but don't quite know what to tell her. She's too young to know anything of divorce, of disappointment, of the *need* to go alone. But in the face of my uncertain reticence, she continues talking, a wellspring of enthusiasm. She tells me of a place she camped alone, once, in Washington state where she grew up. It turns out I know the place. Her face in the lowering sun is self-illuminated as she tells me of her solitary adventure, how marvelous it was; her muscles fairly ripple with the adventure of it. And I still don't have to say anything; it's enough to smile back at her exuberance, to ask the occasional question, to look out together at the approaching sunset. And then, before her companions return, she heads back to her picnic table, gazing up and out.

The next day the maps fail me. In the morning as I climb Wildrose Mountain, the trail disappears. There are patches of snow, of course, but the trail isn't buried when I lose it; it simply has ceased to exist on the southern slope, washed over, perhaps erased, by rain or melting snow. What's odd is the feeling that I know exactly where I am in the landscape, though it's utterly unfamiliar terrain. I can actually *feel* the position of the trailhead below. I can see precisely where, far above, the saddle gently curves upwards toward the west, to the summit. So, with compass in one hand and hiking stick in the other, I strike out, twenty degrees west of due north, in a steep ascent through pinyon and juniper, prickly pear, stone, and occasional pile of shaded snow.

I reach the saddle slightly before noon and find the trail again, just where I thought it should be. This time I head west below the upper rim, staying in the southern slope of sun, since just over the ridge the snow's still deep, sharp in its ice crust and glitter. Only two sets of footprints already mark the snow; below, the ranger told me that yesterday was the first day this season that anyone had reached the top because of lingering drifts. So I have footsteps to follow, a kind of mute companionship as I hike alone. At the top at high noon, I can circle, slowly, and regard the world's circumferential reach.

To the south, I see Telescope Peak, at over eleven thousand feet, the highest mountain in the park. Beyond it, perhaps twenty or thirty miles away, lie the myriad images of Little Petroglyph Canyon—some five thousand forms cluster in that tiny crack in the vast, dry world. To the east, Death Valley itself lies mostly hollow and dull, scooped out to 282 feet below sea level. Today, Badwater basin holds a shallow lake of water within the dried paste of salt flats and the sere severity of dirt and rock. I scan it with binoculars, looking down on what must be another realm. Above, Telescope Peak is the boreal world, still forested and snow packed, while below, Death Valley seems prostrate with its sand dunes and salt flats, the desert in its lowest extremity. A few white plumes lift from the surface—dry geysers, they seem, or perfect spirals of smoke rising from some ghost of a vanished fire. Whirlwinds, they appear to pace the basin's length with a legless gait, headed toward some unglimpsed, unknown—at least to me—and un-languaged purpose. Bizarre, I think, to imagine the valley in Pleistocene times, when Lake Manly filled the basin—116 miles long, 600 feet deep. But, lightheaded and exuberant in the chilly mountain wind, that's what I do: gaze down at the wide, dry basins and imagine the world in the age of glaciers, and just after: wet, wave-laved, cloaked with a furze of plant life where the desert now seems sere and bare. To the west, Lake Panamint once filled another long valley; to the north, Owens Lake (today mostly a name's anachronism since it's nearly drained by the aqueducts that rush toward Los Angeles) joined this chain of ice age waters. It was a western landscape, where the basins cradled people on the shores of great lakes beneath the mountain ranges. And much later, perhaps four thousand years ago, in the cooler, rainier times geologists call Pluvials, the lakes refilled again.

Alone, I stand almost ninety-five hundred feet above Badwater, that nearest ancient lakebed, and shiver in the high bright air. I put on my jacket and drain a water bottle. I hear a whish, a swish of sound and look up to see another whirlwind, a hundred feet or so away, this one a swirling cup of lifting snow. Then just as suddenly as it appeared, it's gone.

That night, at 6:00, a solitary coyote howls, and by 6:30 it's totally dark. Most of the others camped at Wildrose have cleared out, the weekend over. As the stars appear overhead, I lie outside the tent, bundled in my sleeping bag, watching and blinking, drowsy beneath the moonless, star-perforated expanse of sky. All night I doze midway between ascension and descent, while the temperature drops to just one degree above freezing. At one point I wake, remembering images from the Coso site, across the mountain from where I sleep. I see again the fringed and patterned-body figure with a spiral for a face; another shows what is surely a boat, with what seems to be a single paddler in its very center, headed somewhere. Literal, perhaps narrative, it is deeply transcendent of the single, solid human form it shows, and I lie very still, gazing outward from my point against the earth, into the moonless, late-night sky that is darkness, darkness interspersed with hints of forms.

Here the Animal

"*Le dos, l'oreille, l'oeil, le front, le museau, le coup, la poitrine, le ventre
. . .*" The voices in French, in the acoustic chamber of the cave,
trace the body without a touch. Sometimes a hand-held light
follows along for emphasis: the fine, floating red dot of a laser
pointer or the beam of a flashlight. Here the animal is a horse;
here an aurochs. A bison, and another. They sprawl across the
surface of stone, they wallow in its curves and hollows and
plunge toward the declivities that disappear in further darkness. I say the names of the caves to myself as well, to impress
upon my image-sotted memory the composition of the whole:
the place, the artwork, the voice of the guide—now a woman,
in Niaux, impossibly young and delightful when she stands in
the center of a vaulted chamber and sings aloud a high, long
note to show us the echoes; now a man whose hands keep moving before his face, and in the space between us where we're
cramped in the tiny passageway of Les Combarelles, he seems
even now to be holding and shaping something unseen; now
a woman with long, dyed hair and an accent of perfect clarity,
who at the Abri de Cap Blanc sells the tickets, directs one to the
restrooms, and conducts, each hour, tours of the carved horses
on the shelter's back wall.

"Voilà," say the guides, that indispensable and ubiquitous
French word, which, in this particular instance, suggests its
most literal translation, "look there," though in amusement

we've realized it can mean "here you are," "well, there you go," and, by way of introduction, "this is . . ." or, fatalistically, "that's just how things are." Voilà.

We do look. We look at the image; we look at the rock. We look here at the shadows, cast by the modern glare of nickel-cadmium battery or electric light (*voici l'ombre*), and there we watch the guide splash a dim tint against the wall from a shrouded bulb while he speaks of torches and tallow lamps. I've seen such a lamp in the museum display case across from the hotel and watched the video presentation *This Is How to Make a Lamp*, with the hollowed stone bowl, the wad of dry moss, the melted lumps of fat. Imagine, commands the guide, the way firelight would bring out the relief, the musculature, in the rock. "*Musculature*," he says, his mouth holding the French tension and precision, lingering on the vowels and liquids as if they are palpable shapes.

In Rouffignac, nodules of flint stand out in the limestone walls like huge, floppy fungous growths—they're stained a reddish-orange color by dissolved iron oxide, and rounded and lobed, so at first I don't connect them with the word, *silex*, which I know from the shaped flints that, spread out in displays, point to the cultural change of millennia: Solutrean, Azilian. But here in the cave wall, small rounded bumps of flint become eyes for the animals, the bodies traced around them in manganese oxide. Here a mammoth seems to have one such node of flint balanced, like a surprise or a gift, on the tip of his long, curved tusk. Another curls the trunk around two such protrusions, as if they were small objects it wanted to pick up. There, the rough texture of stone makes the beard of a bison; there, it's the mane of a horse. Another point of texture—a bump or a hole, I can't tell which in the dim light—has become in a mammoth its anal operculum, its ice-age anatomy depicted on the body of the cave with such precision that, when an actual mammoth was found in Siberian tundra, researchers could recognize both form and function—the flap of flesh could help prevent heat loss from the animal's sensitive derrière. Here, a horse head is drawn on a large node of flint, so it looks outward at the visitor, an alert and charismatic gargoyle adorning a subterranean chamber.

In what is called, like a nineteenth-century naturalist's collection, "The Bison Cabinet," deep within the main passageway of Font-de-Gaume, black bison seem to sprawl in all directions, if such muscle-bound, high-humped forms can accurately be said to sprawl. Perhaps ten of them fill a small alcove, well above our heads as we gather in twos or threes to see. The deepest concave holds the highest of these painted shapes; its rounded hump and shoulders follow the rounded hollow in the stone, while the cave wall's curve continues past its back, and seems to trace the higher profile of a mammoth looking in the opposite direction. Just below, this morphing of forms is answered in another composition, where the painted curve of the horn says bison, but the high-domed head, above the hump, suggests the profile of a woolly mammoth. "Our ancestors," the guides always say, the artists were *nos ancêtres*, claimed through the kinship of continuity. I like this; the guides emphasize not them, the distant others, but us.

In Les Combarelles, a lion gazes from the wall, its eye bright white in the guide's flashlight, where a pebble or flint from the sedimentary substrate already was focused outward. Oh, obviously an eye, around which the thick, strong face has been incised. A swelling in the stone itself has become the beast's cheek, and the ear is engraved to be leaning forward, as attentive as the eye to what lies ahead. Some thirteen thousand years ago, perhaps, a person held a light before the wall, ran a hand across the surface, and thought, in whatever language lived in his or her mind: lion. Perhaps even said the word aloud, while lying cramped and uncomfortable in the tiny passageway that ran far back—some thousand feet into the limestone cliff above the Vézère River and its tributary, la Beune. The cave was low and narrow, and the artist would have had to crawl in on hands and knees or perhaps slither forward, an awkward approximation of a snake, and most likely couldn't have turned around when the work was done. Back he'd have to slide, a few inches at a time, over the cold hard floor, head sometimes scraping the roof above. Perhaps by then the lamp had gone out, and the bruising trip was made in utter darkness.

Long before, only water filled the corridor, a subterranean stream that cut its channel though cretaceous layers. The guide shows us le sol, the level of the ground in Magdalenian times, and tells us again, in French I just manage to grasp before his train of thought flows on, how we must try to imagine the difficulty, the danger, even, as part of the artwork's mastery. We wonder about what might be called, imperfectly, the performative aspect of composition, there in the narrow dark, the privacy of the work. No audience could enter then, as we do today—the floor has since been excavated more than three feet to let us stand, single file, and face in turns the wall on either side. And we move on, toward the superposition of a horse with a mammoth—the same line serves as back for each beast, so the rock becomes two animals, or the multiplicity of animation, or the glimpsed potential of the living earth. We move on, and the guide points our attention to a basin, scoured out by centuries of water as it once swirled past this curve in the cave. The finger bone of a human was found there, he said.

Two days ago, I read an art historian's suggestion about the role of artistic expression in evolutionary development, or, as he says, the "arrival" of "the human personality," some two hundred thousand years ago. Here's what he says: "Art came before everything. It certainly came before writing. . . . It almost certainly came before speech. . . . The evolving genetic code which made humans rationalise themselves into art was the same force which produced rational speech noises, so that the two processes were intimately connected from the start." I haven't stopped thinking about the idea, though I'm still not certain what to make of it. Intimately linked, I think, yes, but art before speech? Of course, for me, speech, song, written word—these are the art I am closest to daily. When I talk to them about this claim, some of my friends who paint seem unsurprised—they point out that you don't need language to either appreciate or make visual art—indeed, clichés announce shabbily, cheaply, the superlative power of pictures over words. And yet another painter friend is leaving New York to study poetry—a bold move in an age when poetry is, as my poet-father says sadly, mostly dead in the culture. "It's an important anthropological fact," he says, and I realize he's right—people are somehow different in what they expect from themselves, from language, or, as he says, "in what the language does to them."

But written poetry is just one mode of art—art in the "body" of language. I wonder what other modes of art have disappeared, utterly mutable, from the landscape, throughout all those years of exploration and inhabitation. A genetic anthropologist I've read is sure our ancestors left Africa already artists—dancing, singing, painting. Another scholar, Ellen Dissanayake, declares that art itself is a manifestation of a larger impulse that is evolutionarily selected for—the practice of "making special"—through ritual, adornment, even heightened and unusual language use. And a rock art specialist, Paul Bahn, launching into his *Illustrated History of Prehistoric Art*, quotes Edvard Grieg in order to place the artistic impulse within the human emotional life, which is exquisite in its mutability: "Art is really the surplus longing that cannot find expression in life or in other ways." With this thought in mind, the interiority of parietal art—on the walls of the caves, the *avens*, the *grottes*, the *chambres* and *voutes*, and within the walls of the mind, the lobes of our thought and perception—seems deeply touching. Decorated caves, then, become the inward home for the outward signs of the inward state, a layering of denotation—the symbol we glimpse and that which we can only guess at, beyond the collapsed chasm of lost narrative.

There would have been stories, mythologies, surely, in which the human personality confronted others, some known to us in modern guises (bison, ibex, horse). But others we know mostly through bones, like the extinct bears who withdrew for long Pleistocene winters into the reaches of so many caves, leaving the bowl-shaped depressions where they settled in to sleep; or the mammoths we knew first through bones, then drawings, then, almost impossibly, through the frozen carcasses encased for millennia in Siberian tundra and sheathed beneath ice. So, we imagine, the painted world was keenly allusive, the animals alive to the artists in ways that extended beyond their knowledge of migration routes, calving grounds, preferred forage. I think, when I look at the beasts carved and especially painted in the great caves in southern France, that these are not the word made flesh, but something rather like it. They are the flesh made less suddenly mortal through the painted line; they are some spirit of the mammalian world caught, unlike any actual body with its antlers and pelt, and transferred to the improbable body of the earth, the cave wall's muscled surface.

In Chauvet Cave, deep in the limestone cliffs that overlook the Ardèche River, I stood before a panel of lions. It's a famous image, now reproduced with as much enthusiasm and interpretation as the so-called swimming stags of Lascaux, though it's nearly twice as old. Wildlife biologists have commented on the accuracy with which the panel depicts modern lions' hunting behavior and body language—the animals' posture, their facial expressions. Scholars of the Pleistocene say these images confirm that the species extant then lacked the great mane of today's African males, since both male and female behavior seems implied by one particular pair, both maneless—the smaller, presumably female lion rubs along the flank of her larger companion, another "realistic," premating posture. From this single collection, a viewer can conclude that Europe's ice age felines were akin to those of today's American West, the mountain lion or cougar—shorthaired and pale—but they probably lived in social groups, like the matriarchal prides of modern Africa. I've never seen a mountain lion, though they sometimes venture into Kansas, and I often wander farther west, into the territory they search, in this century, for prey. I wonder, often, what I'd do if, rounding a bend in isolate country, I encountered one. Get tall, say the experts. Look dangerous; be ready to fight back. I rather doubt, though, that I'll be tested; I don't often venture so far afield.

Lions are rare in Paleolithic art, but Chauvet Cave holds seventy-one of them, drawn in charcoal, with usually just the head and shoulders shown. In the cave's deepest chamber, a group pursues a herd of bison—a cluster of dark heads and uplifted horns. The predators stretch their faces forward, nose first, as if pulled by invisible threads of desire and scent. Some of their eyes are alarmingly wide, the whites obviously scraped into the cave surface. The head of one seems tensed below the shoulders, as if ready to strike, while the mouth is ajar in another—the moment, perhaps, of a quick, eager breath, or the hint of a low, now silent, growl.

Those lions are extinct, of course. So is the megaloceros, the giant deer of the age of ice, whose antlers spanned some twelve feet across. It's also called the Irish elk because so many—mostly males, emaciated from the stress of rutting season—stumbled into peat bogs and sank into inky tannin. Gone, too, is the woolly rhinoceros, painted in Chauvet with a dark belly band like a saddle blanket across its bulging girth. So is the mammoth, an animal whose image I've wanted so much to see here in the art of the Aurignacians and Magdalenians, the people who lived within sight and sound, at least sometimes, of these past-tense mammals, these no-longer-beings.

Charismatic megafauna is the term often used for the large animals, so often disappearing from the landscape, that draw public attention and concern. They're usually mammals, too—I've never seen, for example, the Komodo dragon—large and impressive as it is, with its poison spit and snaggle teeth—referred to this way. Did I say *disappearing* from the landscape? That's true, of course, since the large tracts of intact habitat such creatures need are increasingly fractured, converted to cropland, or otherwise altered from the earlier ecosystems in which such beasts evolved. But *megafauna* also serves as a convenient label for the Pleistocene species that did not join us in the artificial garden, the agricultural age, that is the geologic era of the Holocene. *Extinct megafauna*—the Latinate noun, clumped together in the noun-phrase style of a Germanic language—both holds and obscures a list of vanished animals: bears, sloths, mammoths and mastodons, great wolves and cats. In the Museé de la Préhistoire, in the charming valley town of Les Eyzies-de-Ta-yac, stands a reconstruction of megaloceros: the antlers, per-haps the hoofs, are originals. The hide appears to be moose. It nearly makes one gasp, to see the height and girth there, stuffed, almost in the flesh. And one thinks of Darwin, shak-ing his head over the post-Pleistocene extinctions: "It is impos-sible to reflect on the state of the American continent without astonishment. Formerly it must have swarmed with great mon-sters; now we find mere pygmies compared with the anteced-ent, allied races."

But *monsters* doesn't carry the hint of romance, of desire, of charismatic appreciation that I think the great herbivores, at least, call up from us. Too often the word refers to things "un-natural, ugly, malformed, deformed, frightening," to list a few of the adjectives that stipple, unpleasantly, the various defini-tions I find when I look it up. These creatures were, perhaps, sublime, but they were also beautiful; at least, that's how the ancient artists make us see them. And, for those of us who've never seen a grizzly, or a tiger, or a cougar in the wild, the carni-vores, without the near and present danger of their power, will also likely inspire the indrawn breath of delight as well as fear.

There is a composition in Chauvet Cave, called "The Panel of the Engraved Horse," in which a horse is certainly prominent. Traced, most likely with a finger, or in some places a stone or bone tool, into the pale clay and heavily weathered limestone, the horse is adorned with a curving line along its side. In pro-file, the mane stands out stiffly, a mere thickening of the line where, if one looks closely enough, one can see fingerprints where the artists paused in the work, pressing against the clay. At least two mammoths follow it, heading right to left: there is the high dome of each forehead, the secondary hump along the back. From the bits of clay pushed aside, one can see which direction the artist's hand moved along the wall, which lines were superimposed in sequence on the others. And one sees the wall's previous markings: bear claw marks left from the years—thousands upon thousands, surely—when the cave bears slept in their mud nests, outlasting the winter to waken in the ice age spring, to stretch, and scratch, and then emerge. Or, since so many bones also punctuate the floor, slept into the depths of their own deaths.

One archaeologist, Yanik Le Guillou, has remarked on the visual association between the work of bears and that of Aurignacian people: "It is interesting to note," he says simply, "the systematic connection of animal clawmarks and engravings, as if the former had attracted the latter." In one location, out of sight from the prepared pathway, are finely engraved lines that "could," he says, if included with claw marks on which they've been superimposed, "make the shape of a mammoth." This seems to me a fascinating variation on a common Paleolithic practice: to follow the preexistent line, crack, or bulge, and with paint or blade, to *complete* whatever is already, incipiently, present. Always already, I think.

"The forces of the environment act as formative influences only when they evoke creative responses from the organism." The microbiologist and Pulitzer Prize–winning author René Dubos wrote that sentence a generation ago. He wasn't talking about Paleolithic art; he wasn't talking about art, at all—he was exploring the nature-nurture debate, discussing genetic potential and experiential stimulus, the problem, ultimately, of heritability and free will. But it's a useful sentence, flexible though precise, and I've been mulling it over while I think about the great beasts pictured on cave walls and our modern attraction to them. It's not merely academic, intellectual. Sure, we marvel over their great age. We discuss, as Stephen Jay Gould did not long after the public announcements of Chauvet's artistic holdings, the conflict between our stereotypic view of "cave men" as primitive, hardscrabble hunters, pursuers of meat who left mostly bones and stones behind—and the aesthetic power of their creative work.

Pablo Picasso, the world-famous figure of modernist painting, commented repeatedly on the power of cave paintings, and when I look at the marvelous bison of Niaux, the confidence of their lines, the mixture of caricature and precision, I think of him. Here's what he said in 1943, in conversations with the Parisian photographer Brassaï: "Man began to make images only because he discovered them nearly formed around him, already within reach. He saw them in a bone, in the bumps of a cave, in a piece of wood. One form suggested a woman to him, another a buffalo, still another the head of a monster."

Monster, again. But sometimes it's true. There is the famous engraved "sorcerer" from the cave Les Trois Frères, which seems to dance in a nearly upright posture, though not quite. His head, shaggy, with animal ears, is turned toward the viewer, beneath a sketched pair of antlers; his thighs, buttocks, feet, and penis seem quite human, though he dangles a foxlike tail. Also in Trois Frères, a clearly upright bison also seems to dance atop human legs. In published renditions a dark spot at the groin may approximate his phallus, and an odd, bow-shaped tracing from his nostrils could suggest the shape of sound. He approaches the body of a reindeer, who turns toward him, across her shoulder, a bison's face. But the bow-song bison-man, his bison-reindeer partner, and many other figures are clustered in a dizzying cloud of lines and images—perspective is lost in a near chaos, an exuberance of forms. Life moves and swirls, right here before our eyes. And there is the "bison-man" from Chauvet, with a vaguely human arm dangling from the buffalo's shoulder, beneath its charcoal-dark face. This weird image wraps around a splendid stalactite, as if it lives in three dimensions, to pose its bushy, curly head above the image of a woman's pubis.

In Chaucer's time a monster was "a mythical creature which is part animal and part human, or combines elements of two or more animal forms." Such examples seem like perfect, ancient illustrations of the earliest meaning of the word as it appears in written English. I think again of Picasso, commenting on modernity, after the great discoveries in Lascaux and elsewhere along the Dordogne: "we have discovered nothing new in art in 17,000 years."

But perhaps we've lost things along the way. Portable art, of course, and flints and buttons and atlatls—much has been dropped into the dirt underfoot. Picasso commented on this preservational power of deposition, too: "The earth doesn't have a housekeeper to do the dusting," he said to Brassaï. "And the dust that falls on it every day remains there. Everything that's come down to us from the past has been conserved by dust." Those are losses to be refound, reclaimed. But if art recalls, and responds to, the world its makers woke to daily, walked through, dreamed of—and just beyond—sometimes it holds up metaphoric mirrors to a vanished lamp. The aurochs, progenitor of modern cattle, leaps and strains its lovely body through the invisible dust that's settled, deep within the caverns that once were lit with torch and animal fat. The aurochs persisted in Poland until 1627; for centuries, it had coexisted with cattle in the settled landscapes of Europe. So it's a bridge between two geologic eras—Pleistocene and Holocene—between, that is, the world before the farmer's garden and the *entrecôte*, grilled *á point* or *saignant*, and served upon the terrace, where we sip our wine and listen, almost unbelieving, to nightingales from the tall hedgerow. The agricultural world of the present era and the hunter-gatherer's world, the animate landscape. (I think, turning over the handsome flatware at Le Moulin Ancien, where I wait for risotto with black truffles, what a fine fact it is that a spoon is called in French a *cuillère*; hunter-gatherers are called *chasseurs-cueilleurs*.)

Magdalenian artists—and before them, Gravettian, and before them, Aurignacian—painted or carved the horse, the aurochs, as beasts of beauty and power. The work articulates desire but never, as we say today, commodity. The horses they painted well before, we think, they ever caught handfuls of mane and leapt astride. They painted bears, the animals who also marked the walls within the earth. They painted mammoths.

Most of the mammoths in Chauvet were drawn along the periphery—in hidden alcoves beyond the easy reach of cameras, or in chambers where researchers are hesitant to venture and disturb the floor. Jean Clottes, the head researcher for the team at work on Chauvet, tells me with some regret that he might have been able to take me to see the mysterious panel of scraped mammoths, which I've seen in photographs and puzzled over. But two other members of our five-person group would have trouble with the terrain and the tight space, he says, "and it's awkward to take just one person, and leave the rest behind." He's right, of course, and I am profoundly lucky to be here at all. I'm not complaining.

What I consider the prettiest mammoth I've seen in my travels into caves appears not far from the entrance into Chauvet.

It's small, a red-ocher outline that has been painted on a great rippled concretion of calcite, a stilled, milky cataract. When we approach, the stone glistens in the light of our headlamps. A curved protrusion in the mass has become the mammoth's back and head. But even more perfectly, the legs and trunk follow—echo, I think in the acoustic cave—the vertical shape of the stalagmitic flow. And once you've seen the animal traced in red, the entire cascade seems to take up the form and becomes a natural panel of mammoths, paused and pale within the stone.

But the calcitic deposition is still at work. As the researchers say, "the mass is still partially active," and we can see the effect: the back half of the mammoth has vanished into a veil of new calcite, which might, in time, overtake the shoulder, the head, the leg, the trunk. The painting long predated the decline and disappearance of mammoths from the European landscape, but to the contemporary viewer, for whom the animals live only through depictions and imagination, the slow obliteration seems symbolic.

It's another glorious evening along the Vézère. From the terrace at Les Glycinnes, a restaurant frequented later in the season by the rich and well-born in Europe, we can watch the nearly summer solstice sunset change the patterns of light on the far cliffs. A pine tree in the garden perfectly shades our table, and Dave wonders whether, as the sun moves, the attentive staff each evening will shift the table slightly, preserving this seemingly accidental luxury.

We've ordered beef tonight, not the ubiquitous Provençal duck. "Isn't it fine," says Dave, smiling broadly, "that our ancestors domesticated the aurochs?" He studies the wine list, then asks the waiter for a recommendation among *les vins du région*. He's enjoying *terroire*, the principle of definition among the nation's innumerable wineries. Each type is not identified by grape species, but by the region where it's grown; the body of the wine combines the grape's inherent attributes with the variables of weather, climate, soil, slope—the body of the place in which the vine is rooted. It's a marvelous principle, I think, and roll the idea around in my mouth: *la terroire de l'art*.

Today we visited l'Abri de Cap Blanc, a limestone overhang where Magdalenian people made their home: they prepared their meals, they slept in relative shelter, and, once, they buried the dead, a woman perhaps twenty years old. They left behind hearthstones much reddened by fire, bones of the reindeer they'd cooked and eaten, pendants and beads, burins and scrapers—this was no sanctuary, no ritual site, but a home. And the back wall, some forty feet of the cliff face, was a high-relief panel of sculpted, life-sized horses. That is, most are horses, but one is a composite figure, a horse facing to the right, whose back becomes, as it extends along the wall, the back of a bison, facing left. The images are damaged, of course, broken both by time and the carelessness of the workers who, in 1909, dug along this shelter looking for trophies—the points, the blades, the portable art—that their employer thought might be buried there. It took awhile before they noticed the shapes on the wall, and by then their shovels had already chipped away the legs of at least one of the horses. Later, they decided to clean the surface and scrubbed it vigorously with brushes, removing the traces of paint that still clung to the stone. And when the job was done, they left the dirt heaped about, the preservational dust of millennia, perhaps, scattered about with the wine bottles they'd emptied at some point in their work.

There's a broken ring in the wall visible along one of the animals' backs—did it serve some household purpose? the guide suggests. We look where she directs our gaze. What might a woman hang there, I wonder: tools she wanted to keep off the floor? A basket of berries the children had gathered, or herbs, drying for the months ahead? Jewelry awaiting a special occasion? Flowers, picked some mornings along the hillside? I love the idea of people living against—with, that is—the monumental presence of the sculpted stone, talking and planning and cooking and sleeping and waking, grieving and making love. Only three such friezes are known in the world, and they're all in southern France.

Here, the animals stand in profile, some with an eye still opening outward, gazing down at the small crowd of visitors who have filed into the viewing chamber. Once, the horses stood more nearly at floor level, but the exhibit maintains the actual depth to which excavations were carried out, displaying in the foreground the skeleton's curled shape—somebody's ancestor, maybe, laid in the earth, la terre, so close to where a family kept on with the business of living, with the litter and clutter of daily refuse, the footprints trampling one another in the dust. And the light, if the sun touched the back wall of the south-facing home, or the dancing cast of firelight glazed the stone—the light must surely, sometimes, have lifted into relief the shadows of animals moving across the landscape, coming to stand so close to the people who watched them, loved them even, across varying distances.

La Descente

There are many ways, probably, to enter another world. One such, according to traditions "since time immemorial" in the American Southwest, is to rise up, to emerge from a world beneath this one into the sunlit gasp of new possibility. You can see this belief inscribed in Pueblo tales of emergence, in the *sipapus* that punctuate each ritual *kiva* with a connecting symbolic navel of stone or clay, and in the ladders that span the gap between the private world of the home and the public space of plaza and rooftop vista everywhere in the desert's solarium dome of sky and air. So it makes sense, I think, that another way is to descend. In a metaphoric, if not historical logic, it makes sense, too, that the descent as I've experienced it is older by far, taking place in another continent, across substantial seas and the abstract apportionments of time zones.

I got there in the usual way for our age: cramped for hours in the bizarre, expensive discomfort of a transatlantic flight, my seatbelt always fastened and a tiny television offering up comedy, movies, and cartoons by way of distraction, interrupted by disappointing snacks and miniature sips of "complimentary" beverages. Then herded into lines and holding areas, penned up and verified until I felt, under waves of sleep-deprived tension, the deep reptilian brain demanding that I fight the security agent directing me to take off my shoes and submit to a patdown before proceeding, for the second time, to what is called, as if in parodying Orwellian newspeak, "Customs." Global travel and a viral fear of terrorism are now, I suppose, evidence that we're in another world—"everything is different, now," as people say, shrugging, about our institutional incivility—but that's not the kind of other world I wish to think about today. Instead, I'm trying to will myself back in memory to landscapes in southern France, with the still-white heights of the Hautes-Pyréneés just out of sight, beyond the nearer slant of green hills, or the abrupt plunge of limestone cliffs giving way to cultivated vineyards and small, riparian woodlots along the river's edge. Landscape, and vista. Memory, and possibility.

I. Labastide

We step-slid our way down, past saplings and bracken, past a single, stationary snail, below a spray of white blossoms—elderberry, it looked like—extending from the sheer rockface above. Crows scolded us as intruders, although we never even saw their nest, high in some tree, much less marauded their eggs or preciously ugly babies. At the bottom of the slope, we suited up for a brief journey into the underworld: sweaters or jackets, coveralls or rain pants, boots. Various headlamps. Last-minute battery checks. Our guide, an archaeologist named Yanik Le Guillou, who has responsibility for the conservation of all Paleolithic caves in the region, unlocked two heavy iron gates. And, once we'd all stepped in, depositing our packs and other shoes in the shadow of the cave wall, inside the iron bars, he locked the gates behind us. We were in; the slanted forest—and whoever might have wished to follow us from it—were out.

The cave is called Labastide, after the nearby village. It's an interesting coincidence, this place name. Though *bastide* can refer to a fortress, a stronghold, these hamlet-bastides are economic bastions from the fourteenth century, when the rising power of the merchant class began to threaten that of the nobles. The latter established market towns—commanded and paid for their construction, I suppose—to be convenient and to keep the wealth nearby, accessible, but tucked under the shadow of the noble's chateau and that of his ostensible largesse and wisdom.

It's a damp, increasingly dark, and slippery route we follow into *la grotte de Labastide*. First, we bear right, skirting a dark hole jagged along the visible edge with fallen rock. We stoop, and duck, and pass single file along what serves as trail here— a firm, slick clay surface heading farther into the hillside. My headlamp is much weaker than the halogen bulbs the professionals wear, and I'm glad to follow along, resorting to all fours when the way seems especially steep or slick. But Labastide is a relatively spacious cave—not so echoingly long as Rouffignac, where one can take an electric train along some seven miles of cavern to view mammoths on the walls and ceilings; nor so wide and vaulted as Bédeilhac, where, during World War II, an air munitions factory was installed underground to be safe from the Axis bombers and where, in 1972, a local pilot managed to land a small plane as part of a much-trumpeted publicity stunt. Behind its iron gates, Labastide remains undeveloped, the uneven floor hinting at the careful route the Magdalenians themselves would have taken to enter the space.

Since the 1940s, Robert Simmonet has been studying whatever remains of the people who entered this cave to leave traces of their works and days behind. At times they lived here, cooking meals and leaving refuse of bone. That's unusual among decorated caves of the Paleolithic; more often the living spaces were open-air sites, or day-lit shelters and alcoves. The great, painted caves were something else entirely—places for meditation or ritual, locations in which to seek and make ways to sense the ineffable, the spiritual depths that reside somewhere within our skin. The people left flints behind, too, blades and flakes that can be traced to a network of supply sites, an ancient map of Magdalenian travel across the geologic constant of outcrop and quarry. Simmonet found several handsome stone blades tucked into crevices—placed for safekeeping, perhaps, in an inviting niche? Or—could this be possible?—stolen from their owner, hidden away by the long-anonymous thief until taken again and placed in drawers, well labeled, in the researcher's study? Or, far more likely, deposited like offerings at some unseen—by us, at least—shrine? One researcher, David Lewis-Williams, remarks on what he calls the *interactions* evidently valued by Paleolithic people: painters "transforming" the shape of the rock or depositing blades or bones into crevices—filling the absence with some human-placed presence.

Perhaps fifteen thousand years ago, the people who moved across the landscape in sight of the Pyrénéés spent some portion of their lives in this dark hold. They engraved the walls and stationary boulders that stand like solid islands in the directionless dark, as well as little flat pieces of stone called "plaquettes," a large pile of which, having been examined painstakingly by Monsieur Simmonet, rests near our path. But the engravings mostly elude my untutored eye, no matter how obliquely I shine my battery-powered light and turn my head, and try to change again my point of view. When we gather in twos or threes—the students, the professionals, the guests— to consult the charts that tell us something *should* be here (a bison with symbols on its side, a horse turned to face toward the distant entrance, an ibex balanced beneath its tall curved ant-lers), I strain forward. Absurdly, I squint in the dim shadows. I sit back on my heels.

"Let's see, what do we have here?" asks Kathy, the most talented seer in my group. I see rough rock: colorless, dull. Only when she traces the line of some super-subtle shoulder or rump do I nod my head in recognition.

"I swear," says Kristen, a tall young woman whose thesis will discuss newly discovered earthen mounds in Louisiana, some unrecognized culture in the New World, "I think sometimes people were just sitting around after dinner, hardly paying attention . . ."

For the moment, I have to agree. "Emery boards," I say. "What they really wanted was emery boards," and we laugh briefly, crouched before the vague scratchings. But yes, fleetingly, I could glimpse the suggestion, the incomplete hint of an implied form. And isn't that the way with abstraction? Isn't that, really, its essence—the glimpse, the flash along synapse, the brief *yes* in the mind?

We slip and clamber to a high ledge, or a cliff within the cave; a precipitous plunge surrounds what feels like a peninsula where, in the dark, we crowd as carefully as we can to see where Sebastien, another young archaeologist who recently completed a doctoral thesis on flints in the region, says there is a bison figure. This may be, I think, the Defecating Bison I've read mention of, but I hesitate to ask. At any rate, I can't see any outline clearly enough to decide whether it's humorous or grotesque, or even mammalian. I keep thinking of the slippery edge, and it occurs to me that it could be considered bitterly ironic if the ledge became a kind of bison jump, a kill site where the twenty-first-century hunters-of-images fell to their deaths.

From this high point, however, you can just barely see the light of the entrance. Simonnet has marked the precise location with a metal pole, and we take turns positioning ourselves to catch that distant, sunlit glimpse. One by one, we see it: *yes.*

Farther along, I follow Kristen after she emerges from a tight, hidden alcove where her professor, Meg Conkey, waits with light in hand to show us the best of the trip's engravings. One at a time, we climb to the opening, at chest or neck height, and enter a tunnel formed by two adjacent boulders. Turn left, Meg directs, and straddle a crevice in the stone. I do, and there on the rockface is the face of an ibex, its eye alert in the beam of Meg's lamp, its horns curving back toward the dark as it gazes outward, as if it heard us coming and, in surprise, has lifted its head to look.

One afternoon, thousands of miles from the caves and karsts of southern France, I slog through a couple of French articles that Simmonet published on Labastide in particular and the Paleolithic landscape of the region more generally. In dramatic language he describes how the land of the Aquitaine basin would have seemed to Magdalenian people. The Pyréneés would have provided a constant, unmistakable line of landmarks, each peak's profile like a reverse notch in a mental map the traveler would not have to carry with him since he moved across its veritable, self-identifying body. You couldn't become disoriented; you always knew precisely where you were.

"Such long-distance landmarks," he says, ". . . necessarily give a sense of mastery of place; they permit one to anticipate access to distant territories, and they signal the existence of such places, even if the lands themselves are unknown. The effect is one of security, in presenting real limits while exciting curiosity about what lies beyond." I love this writing, even as I realign his thoughts into English. Simmonet is describing, through landscape, the way nomadic people could always be at home in the world, even while engaged in a journey of several days. And he imagines the beauty of that world in "favorable weather"—"clear skies and, ideally, bright light. Sometimes the picture is completed with a winter brilliance of snowy peaks." The daily variance of weather, he says, played out against the backdrop of seasonal predictability is how "one perceives climate in real life." So by the end of a sentence he's transported himself, and us if we'll follow, to the flank of the glaciers, the land beneath that climactic and climatic winter brilliance.

"The barrier of the Pyrénées," Simmonet says, "is a horizon that does not recede to the south, whereas west-east travel shows limits receding endlessly into the sight of other limits." However, he insists, "it is quite remarkable that, from certain points, the Aquitaine region can in large part be seen at once. The eyes of the traveler can't help but notice the mountain range that, wherever one might be, encloses the southern horizon beneath the sun," while, as he demonstrates with line drawings of the mountains' profiles and the distant shores of two seas, "It is remarkable that at the end of this progression, while not having lost sight of the Atlantic world, one also has in the visual field the heights that belong to Mediterranean regions." He muses, rhetorically: "How to express this undeniable contact between two worlds that today are so contrasting?" And for himself, I think, there is a longing to express some point of contact between the subterranean and surface worlds, as if his own experiences, his life's work, are a kind of axial chamber or a ventilated passageway, between them. How to express the feeling I sense in the French syntax? I sit at my table, never quite lost in the thought. I get up and pace the house, before I sit back down to the task.

As a young man, doing his earliest research in the cave, Simmonet worked shifts of fifteen hours or more below ground and, he says, would sometimes spend thirty-six hours without sleeping. This led to slight hallucinations, and he speculated on the possibility that the original artists, similarly focused, similarly ensconced in their subterranean work, might have had similar experiences. Here again is my translation: "In weak light, the image of forms persisted alone, after draining of their color; we could then see the lines evoking the exterior world of the countryside in the sinuous streaks of white calcite which filled the vault of the chamber."

Just past the niche with the pretty ibex, the rest of the group moves on. Some hundreds of yards farther are still more images—a goose or a duck, among others, and a composition called the Bison Frieze. One must wade through a river of mud, a veritable inundation, in order to reach them. Now I understand the wisdom of the tall rubber boots the others carried across the pasture and pulled on at the cave's mouth. Our hiking boots won't do well in the mud the lamps illuminate—shin high, sometimes, Yanik assures us, in his impeccable English, knee high. So Dave and I are left behind, while the shouts and chatter of the others echo until they pass out of range, and the cave is silent.

But we aren't alone. We're sitting on a fallen rock, conveniently benchlike, before the cave's one great painting: high on a boulder, nearly life sized, painted in black and red above our heads, there is a horse. A Pleistocene horse, a Magdalenian horse, a painted rendition of the short-maned, thick-necked wild horse of the European steppes. Black manganese dioxide lines its bristly mane; red ocher, sometimes shaded and mixed with black, fills in the stocky body. This is surely the Przewalski horse, the last wild species of *equus*, a survivor from the days that preceded domestication. Within the painted head, the eye has been incised to give it three-dimensional relief; faint, white rays of a star surround a convex pupil, and we shine our light repeatedly to catch the faded pattern. The ear, too, has been carved to give dimension, but the remaining shape of the body comes from the rock itself. A crack defines the rump and the slight inward curve of the rear leg, while the tail is a flying bustle of long lines of color, ocher and black. We shake our lights, to catch the motion frozen in the darkened form. We trace the bulging contours of its legs and belly, where the rock itself seems muscled underneath the painted pelt. We can hardly believe that we are here, unsupervised, unguided, trusted to simply stay put in the center of our own desire and appreciation of the form before us.

And, more than once, in the chilly hour we have with the singular image and the silence, we switch off the lights and sit very still together, not speaking in the wordless dark, before an invisible horse that still, we know, remains, and, for a magical time, as long as the others are gone, we're worlds away from everything else on earth.

II. Along the Ardèche

I'd been reading, of course. And examining the photographs, the amazing images in great oversized books, some of which folded out into panels a yard long. I'd learned new vocabulary, words I certainly didn't remember from my college classes over twenty years before—par exemple, *fouiller*, to excavate; *falaise*, cliff; *gisements*, layers or beds—and I'd practiced placing adjectives after nouns in French phrases that might, I thought, be useful, as well as approximately polite. I'd written careful, though no doubt error-studded letters of inquiry, made reservations. I'd been dreaming of animals, dreaming of caves. I'd sat in a small, back-row seat in a French language class held in a room where in other years I sometimes teach, and worried over my homework, the difficult grammar, and when called upon I answered in my best approximation of the tone and tongue, and repeated aloud the inevitable corrections offered by the patient professor. I'd written more, even more careful, letters, using, in supplication, the subjunctive mode—*pourriez-vous, s'il vous plait?* And—gasp—I'd somehow been granted permission to enter one of the greatest, most significant Paleolithic cave art sites in the world. La Grotte Chauvet, where the oldest art has been most assuredly, most conclusively, through the replicability of repeated testing, dated to over thirty thousand years before the present. How had this happened to me? How marvelous!

We met in an unpaved restaurant parking lot, shook hands and made introductions, and then there were forms to sign. I would not wear jewelry into the cave, I wouldn't eat, or drink, or spit—*crachat!*—in the world below. I would take no photographs, wear no backpack; I'd dress in the coveralls and shoes provided; I would hold no one but myself responsible for any injury, et cetera, et cetera. I asked a few questions, I turned the several pages, and of course I signed the forms. Thereby I became part of a select group: only five people at a time can enter the cave to work, in the company of watchful guides. Jean Clottes would lead us. He's worked with the images of Chauvet almost since the cave's discovery in 1994, and he directs the research efforts there. Two others, Paule Rodrigues and Charles

Challveau, attended to all the technical aspects of the trip. The other viewers were African rock art specialists: Alec Campbell and his wife, Judy; and David Coulson and his wife, Deborah. And me.

As we made the sloping climb to the cliff, Deborah picked wildflowers—an offering she wished to leave at the entrance—and told me of her work as a landscape designer. The scholars chatted, old acquaintances. I asked several questions of Paule and Charles, who, *par exemple*, told me the name of the oak trees that line the cliff (*chêne-verts*, live oaks). They'd taken interesting paths to arrive in their positions as guides to the oldest parietal art in the world: one had studied art history, the other civil engineering. Gently they both admonished Deborah when they noticed her bouquet: these woods along the Ardèche are a natural reserve, and one mustn't disturb the plant life. "You cannot take them back with you," Charles said.

But when we arrive at the entrance, and she quietly places her flowers against an outcropping of rock, no one scolds. Instead, there's a flurry of preparatory activity. Charles and Paule unlock the gate to a small alcove, adjacent to the cave itself, where there's a little office with tables, various monitoring equipment, a telephone. And, surprisingly, a coffee maker. While the rest of us are urged to make use of the woods, since there will be no restroom breaks during the visit, coffee is brewed, chocolate is set out, and soon we are having these light refreshments, as if to fortify us with the world-traveled drug of caffeine before our journey into darkness. We drink from tiny paper cups; they're whisked away into a waste can that someone will have to empty by packing it all out, back down the hill. After this polite ritual, we suit up. We get special clothes for the occasion: everyone is provided with coveralls, ingeniously designed with a complex of zippers; we're also encircled with climbers' belts, to be able to clip in with carabiners for the descent, some thirty feet to the first chamber. At the entrance proper, Charles unlocks a heavy metal door, and we file inside. In the cramped antechamber, which seems to function as a sort of air lock, we take off our own shoes—boots, sandals, sneakers—and rummage among a large collection of matching rubber shoes until we find some in our own size. We wear hard hats with excellent lamps. We're ready for our transformation underground.

The images in Chauvet Cave have changed many views of the nature of Paleolithic art. First, they confound the notion that earlier images must have been crude, approximate, with the real flourishing of technique and mastery belonging to the Magdalenian period, roughly 18,000 to 11,500 years before the present. These paintings belong to an earlier culture, or "complex": the Aurignacian, an era in which, at its earliest dates, two species of humans lived in Western Europe, and especially in the Dordogne Valley and isolated pockets in Spain. In what researchers sometimes call simply the Transition, roughly 45,000 to 35,000 years before the present, Homo sapiens sapiens entered a landscape already home to Homo neanderthalensis, and the newcomers' arrival seems to have spurred a sudden flurry of cultural change among the indigenous Neanderthals, referred to as the Châtelperrion period. These latter began to wear jewelry, and their tools changed form slightly, more closely resembling those of the Aurignacians. They may have begun to adorn themselves with ocher paint. But they didn't—so far as we know—join their new neighbors in the practice of cave painting. Only the persons who, generations upon generations later, become "us" throughout the diaspora of empire and emigration, were the artists who decorated the earth as well as themselves, and who left rich tableaus of engraved and painted bestiaries where sometimes, astonishingly, the art survived for millennia.

At Chauvet, the painters would not have lived beside their Neanderthal cousins; the artwork dates just a few thousand years too late for that. But the images preserve aspects of another world, all the same. A surprising number of woolly rhinos—rare elsewhere in Paleolithic art—are depicted throughout the cave, holding the great curves of their impressive horns, clear trumpet flourishes of power and strength. There are mammoths—many of them—placed in positions that seem to trace the cave's periphery, as if they reside ever in the distance, spatial or temporal, real or metaphorical. There may even be pictures of insects: strange, alien images that turn no eyes outward to regard the visitor, unlike the mammals that animate the walls. Our little group stops before one such panel, and we exclaim.

All along the way, we mark our passage aurally, with *oohhh* and *look!* (all the guests today are English speakers) and, stopping to gaze around, or up or down, I sometimes feel a flash of dizziness, and brace my knees against the possibility of tumbling off the metal walkway that's been laid down to protect the nearly pristine floor on which we move, single file, from room to room. If the French guides notice this kind of teetering, they rein us in with words, as well: "*Attention,*" or, in the Briticism, "Mind, now. Mind your head." Paule points out quietly, as I follow him, a spot where cave bears once rubbed a stalagmite into a fine, ivorylike polish. Jean directs our gaze deeper into the Bear Chamber, where a cave bear skull was set atop a square rock, the canines pointed downward, two once-living stalactites of enamel on this apparent altar. Or is it just where the children amused themselves, picking up bones and rocks, while the adults were at work? Both possibilities seem easy to imagine.

At some point in time, other visitors to the cave marked their way with torch wipes, rubbing the burning surface to knock off ash and renew the flame—and, perhaps, if the way was unknown to them, to leave signs of the route back up and out. This seems to be what happened about twenty-six or twenty-seven thousand years ago. A torch wipe appears, for instance, on a film of calcite that has, like a cataract, varnished and dulled part of a painted panel in the central Hillaire Chamber. None of the artwork has been dated to the same time as that carefully dated carbon, so it seems very likely a visitor, or party of visitors—like us, perhaps—came through the caverns, torchlight flickering, some three to five thousand years after the artists first illuminated the walls. As we make our way inward, stepping carefully, though never—*never*—slowly enough to take it all in, I notice these shadows of ancient fire, these sooty smudges that mark somebody else's passage through. Someone stopped, paused, *there*. And, like me, the Someone gazed at the Panel of Horses, their muscular necks, the way each head tilts at a different angle, like a line of living animals, bobbing and tossing their heads in the wind. I love the wide eye and surprised, half-open mouth of one, the smallest; another is blinking, eye shut, the nose lifted as if sensing some interesting smell.

Pleistocene culture was stunningly conservative: for the most part, technology, imagery, lifeways all persisted with only gradual change for *thousands* of years. Even so, whoever stepped into the chambers and looked, with surprise and delight, or perhaps with fear, at the painted figures leaning from the walls, from the darkness, from the inner depths of earth and stone, must have marveled at the scene. How extraordinary, how apparitional! *Who could have done this?* Perhaps the caverns had stood empty, the people who used them having moved on. Or, as we say euphemistically, passed on, killed, perhaps, by a bad winter of sickness, an earthquake, some world-shaking event that disrupted their inhabitation of the handsome limestone valley with its cold, fast river and the caves above. Perhaps a hundred generations, or more, before someone found the still-open chamber and ventured in to see.

But whoever it was, the Someone I'm imagining came from the same world, the same glacial landscape, as the one depicted on the inner walls. For us, it is quite Other. We pause before an owl, carved in clean, sure lines on a low-hanging stone, so that it seems to be perched upon nothing, upon the ancient, unchanged air of the cave. We stare at a panel of rhinos—rhinos! In Europe! A notion so absurd it was figured in a play by Ionesco!—the outlines of their horns retraced and repeated in a pattern that could indicate, some scholars think, motion, or perhaps the sense of a herd, bristling their dangerous points. I think suddenly of the work of Charles Burchfield, a mid-twentieth-century painter who used somewhat similar repetitions of angles, the outlines of objects, to indicate sound. The visual world rendered like an impletion, an infilling, of the aural realms it holds. And I suppose we all think about the extinctions, the disappearance of the living animals from the landscape, as we gaze at the images that rise up, out of the dark, as we draw near.

Sometime, many thousands of years ago, the cave was closed by a collapse of the cliff. The entrance was lost in a great self-scabbing scar of rock and rubble. Long after the dust had dissipated, plants had grown up, and people—whoever they might have been, then, living along the beautiful Ardèche—had forgotten all about the tumble and roar, as well as what was sealed behind the barrier of stone and soil—long, long afterward, the cave continued to hold its painted relics of the Pleistocene. That's one reason the images are so fresh, so undamaged: they've been preserved with very limited air exchange, little variation in temperature as the world warmed and chilled, and warmed again, outside. And, of course, for millennia there were no visitors to carve their names over the painted animals, or hold aloft their sooty torches, or spit (!), or cook, or shelter livestock, or in any other way intrude on the geologic self-sanctuarial space of the cave.

I hold a map in my pocket, though I can't see well enough to study it as we make our way from room to room. It's the work of Yanik Le Guillou, a neatly drawn chart of the chambers, looking, in outline, a little like an island from southeast Asia, carefully labeled with the names that have been given to each location, each panel of compositions. One chamber in particular, the Megaloceros Gallery (named for the image of a giant Pleistocene deer, long extinct), appears on the page like a yellow peninsula extending north by northeast (though, underground, who can tell direction?). There's a torch wipe marking the entrance to what, in the actuality of the cave, is a tunnel, a downward-sloping passage that will take us to the End Chamber. Someone marked the way, once, there; here, we shuffle single file and share a flashlight, passing it up and down the line, with which to examine more closely some of the carvings just inches away. Charles and Paule are exquisitely attentive here; one must not touch the walls, mustn't put out a hand to steady oneself, or to pause, leaning against the stone, to look. Attention, attention.

We won't be able to stay long in the End Chamber. The oxygen level, at this low, remote cove within the cave, is also low, and our guides will monitor our time here precisely, hurrying us out when we've overstayed out limit. Because of the lower oxygen ratio, the Aurignacian artists couldn't prepare their pigments on site, even though every image in the room is done in charcoal, and they'd have needed quite a bit of burned wood. Instead, they used the Megaloceros Gallery like a kind of preparatory antechamber, and as we slowly descend the slope I see several small piles of burned wood—tiny artisan's hearths.

I breathe in—*I can smell it!!* At first, I can't believe it's really the scent of char from 30,000-year-old fires, but we haven't been here long enough for light-headedness to set in and play tricks on me. I inhale again, and again. Later, Yanik assures me that, yes, it wasn't my imagination—I would, indeed, have been able to smell those old, ghosted bones of long-dead fires. Yes.

I haven't touched the walls. I haven't slipped, or stumbled, or spat, or in any way violated the surfaces of rock and clay that hold the ancient artwork. But, in the End Chamber, as I gaze at the black or gray-black images along the walls—the mammoth with the rounded feet, like balls; the panels of lions; the rhinos, the bison heads, lined up along an angle of the stone like gargoyle flourishes on a building's corner—through all this, I keep breathing in the air that's touched by hints of soot. Rarified air, ancient air, air at the lowest, furthest extreme of the cave's unfolding privacy. It's me who is changed, changing; hidden, invisible, our bodies are taking in these transubstantial tokens, images, aromas, volatiles that enter us, in through the lungs and the blood, here in the dark world. Our group examines, exclaiming, the strange "sorcerer" figure on a stalactite—what seems to be a woolly, curly-headed bison, dangling an impossibly tiny leg from the left shoulder. The lower, tapering shape of the stalactite presents what is obviously a woman's vulva, with her thighs, as well, which become in the composition tiny, vestigial-looking legs. The combination of bison and woman calls to mind the theory of André Leroi-Gourhan, who in the mid-twentieth century speculated that Pleistocene symbolism was built upon binary thinking: like the world of French nouns, a great system of masculinity and femininity, the bison representing the feminine principle, the horse representing the masculine. I wonder about the nomenclature for this figure. It's been referred to as the "bison-man," though, if there's any merit to Leroi-Gourhan's system, and judging from the beast's obvious association with the female figure, whatever transformational, shamanic, or simply metaphoric power the image presents should be considered feminine.

Interestingly, the stalactite hangs a few yards away from a portal, a niche in the cave wall with a scalloped top, which holds a charcoal drawing of a horse. From the metal walkway, if you pause at a certain spot (and, as directed, we all do), the animal seems to be emerging from the edge of the cave, into a "chamber"—the niche—distanced by perspective. A few more steps, and the entire figure is in view, framed handsomely, celebrationally, by the recess in the stone. It's a horse like those I've seen reproduced from Lascaux or Altamira: a huge, bulging chest and belly, nearly bursting with visual vitality. There they are, the horse, the bison. The cave, the stalactite. The yin and the yang of the prehistoric world, as some scholars suggest. "Imagine," says Jean Clottes, "if a shaman sat there, how the rock would frame him. He'd be facing the sorcerer, the horse at his back." It's a tremendous mental picture, and it makes the animals on the wall—those lions, those rhinos—seem all the more dangerous, powerful, when I envision a priest, or a sha-man, surrounded with such animate power.

But, far too soon, it's time to go back. It's a little disorienting to turn around on the metal mesh walkway and head slightly uphill, through the Megaloceros Gallery, our slanted passage back to the larger chambers. As we leave that lowest chamber, I turn again to see the torch wipe, which seems to me, after the impressive images, a nearly personal sign, almost like a hand raised in greeting or farewell. And so despite the amazing age of the galleries and the animate images of a lost age, the hints of symbolic meaning that continue to elude us, despite all these hints and recognitions, we are departing, to our own rich and unfinished lives.

On the way out, Jean gestures toward the northwest reaches of the cave, an area called the Chamber of the Crosshatching. We peer into the distance, while Charles shines a powerful flashlight beyond the reach of our own headlamps. The area is inaccessible to us, but the research team has found footprints there—most likely those of a child, a preadolescent about four and a half feet tall, most likely a boy, based on the shape of his feet. He seems to have come alone into the cave and walked about with his torch, deliberately marking his way with soot—some of the very torch wipes I have been noticing, and which have been carefully dated by the researchers. The cave of the floor was a little different whenever he made his visit; the trail of prints seems to deliberately avoid some low spots, as if they were filled with water, though no such pools exist today. It's touching, to imagine him moving alone through the great, dec-orated space, taking care that he won't get lost, and pausing re-peatedly before the same images that have had us alternately gasping and silent. Perhaps he was alone all day, engaged in the kind of inwardly meditative play that is quickly disappearing from modern versions of childhood, regimented into team sports, or lessons, or time with virtual opponents from video games. Perhaps he was singing to himself, or telling himself a story, when he came across the entrance to the great cave.

In fact, some researchers have speculated that the very flourishing of art and culture that we see in the Upper Paleolithic, what some call the Representational Revolution, is itself the result of childhood play. That is, of a longer childhood, in which both solitary pretend play and what has been called "complex social pretend play"—imaginary games with friends—are allowed to flourish. In this view, the artistic upwelling of millennia ago does not emerge from any cult of technology, that is, "practical problem-solving," to use Gregory Currie's terms. Instead, it is the cultural unfolding, the maturation of imagination, in a world where children had been able to engage in more extended, more complex, and ultimately more creative play. Peter Carruthers suggests that pretend games, the animating sparks of childhood, allow the mind training in "relevant and interesting" ideas, possibilities, alternatives. I like that characterization—though I'd place "interesting" first; "relevant," of course, to the postmodern mind, is itself a largely subjective and creative view. The nonrational, what can become the spiritual, has a "relevance" that is above all "interesting," pleasing and intriguing and challenging and amazing to the innermost imaginings, the partially lit perceptions that will also animate metaphor, symbol, aesthetic desire.

Even more intriguing, Lewis-Williams speculates that artwork became a cultural force of exclusion, elitism, a way to differentiate the us of Homo sapiens—the people who are not only clever or smart, but spiritual, imaginative—from the Others, the Neanderthals, the Infidels of another era. According to Lewis-Williams, the neurological structure of the anatomically modern human brain allows us all experiences of altered consciousness—the hallucinations, the visions—which we perceive as spirituality and which we standardize through the protocols and rituals of the world's various religions. Neanderthals, he suggests, with their different evolutionary neural development, could have lacked this form of in-sight, a lack that is suggested by the paucity of their creative art. If he's right, this is the dark side of the aesthetic revolution that decorated the Pleistocene landscape, and it's the earliest hint of the hurtful purposes—religious wars, pogroms, exterminations of witches or heretics—to which spirituality has been put. I think briefly of the Albigensians, hunted and killed by the hundreds in some of the same landscapes where the prehistoric hunter-gatherers adorned les grottes orneés—in which, at times, the persecuted of Europe's Middle Ages took refuge to escape the slaughter.

The boy who walked into Chauvet may have imagined himself in any of an interesting array of identities, as he moved from room to room, talking out loud perhaps to himself or to some imagined companion. But it's also possible he wasn't quite alone. Very close to his own tracks are those of a canid—a wolf or a large dog—that may have accompanied him. The researchers can't yet be sure. They haven't found a place where the prints are superimposed, one upon the other, a pattern that would show that they walked together, that afternoon, perhaps it was, or early evening, some twenty-six thousand years ago. It's possible the trails are unrelated, recording visits that occurred days or years or centuries apart. But it's also possible—imagine it!—that the tracks are intermingled traces of a joint visit. Intriguingly, studies of the canid prints show they're not quite wolflike—the length of the middle toes seems more in keeping with the proportions we know today in dogs. But the earliest domestication of the dog we've known before now dates to only fourteen thousand years ago. If all these conjunctions hold up: that the torch marks that have been definitely dated were made by that Paleolithic child; that the two traveled together, beast and boy; and that the beast had, in the language of Rudyard Kipling, become First Friend, no longer the Wild Dog of the Wet Woods . . .

Well. It's an astonishing If.

Imagine it: under the images of the untamed gaze of ancient animals, there in the Pleistocene reaches, deep underground, are hints of our own age, incipient, glimpsed in the barefoot trail over mud and clay, in the black and ocher tints on the walls. The way in—deep, beautiful and, don't forget, also terrible—and then back again.

In Situ

> There is really no such thing as Art. There are only artists.
>
> Ernst Gombrich

> "Art" is a handy monosyllable, and, provided we are aware
> of the dangers of its Western connotations, we can use it
> with caution.
>
> David Lewis-Williams

At the reception, a man in a clean-pressed shirt and a clean-shaven scowl makes a beeline for me.

"But of course, what you're talking about isn't really *art*," says the man's face in front of me. "That's a modern invention, after all."

I have no drink in my hand to swirl thoughtfully or dismissively, though what I'd really like, after reading aloud for half an hour, is a long gulp of very cold water or a lovely white wine in a handsome glass. But the table with refreshments is on the other side of the room, and for the moment it's a world away. I'm not quite sure what particular chip is on this guy's shoulder, but whatever it is, it's an itchy presence for him, and he clearly wants me to knock it off and see what happens next. So I consider the possibility.

"Well," I say evenly, "if you really wanted to talk to somebody long-dead about whatever rock art meant for him, you probably couldn't be speaking English in the first place."

He doesn't move toward this feint, not one bit. He's still worrying the anachronism of the *concept* like a piece of raggedy sock, hoping I'll tug back. Art, he insists, belongs to the modern age, and I'm not sure whether he's about to talk about commodity, or community, or the rise of the individual, or *différence*, or what. But I refuse to let go of the issue of language.

I deliberately relax the muscles under my eyebrows. "But words aren't static, though, are they?," I say. "Why *wouldn't* you want to talk about, well, what *we* see as aesthetic utterance using the best label we have for it, even if it's not part of the historical tradition you know as 'art'?"

No, of course, I don't say that, not there on my feet, watching the imaginary lines of our boxing ring and thinking of verbal footwork. But at least, I say something like it, though not as smoothly as the sentence will seem later, in memory's replay, with sports commentator Frank Deford's radio-quality voice urging me forward as I dance and weave. I still don't understand this pulse of aggression that animates the tilt of my conversant's head. He seems to think I'm some kind of imperialist, subsuming distinction under the bullying smear of a noun. I think he's picking a fight for no good reason, and as I notice how pinched his nose seems, pinched with dissatisfaction, suddenly I don't care whether he wants to artfully turn his back on the paintings and engravings I've been reaching toward for months, reaching through reading and travel and long, short-winded gazes after steep hikes to arrive.

And I suddenly think of the play by Yasmina Reza, *Art*, in which the purchase by one of the three characters of an abstract painting launches a series of bitter disagreements among them, pitting first one, then another against his friends. It all takes place indoors, of course, within the world of urban "apart-ments," and I look over for a moment at the brightly colored canvas on the wall nearby, then back to the very picture, as we say, of indignation that stands before me. And then I think, this guy means by "art," "art for art's sake" or its even earlier French incarnation, "art pour l'art," and I decide to call him, since he hasn't even introduced himself, Walter Pater.

But then the little confrontation masquerading as polite discourse is over, and Walter Pater heads away, and someone hands me a glass of water, which I do gulp, and someone else asks about a mutual friend who has been ill, and I wish for a moment I'd worn something more summery, less formal, on this warm evening of early May, and then a friend I've known, off and on, for over twenty years steps forward to exchange the ritualized but sincere greeting of a hug. What would Walter Pater do, I wondered, if we weren't here, if he'd suddenly been whisked eight hundred miles west, set down in a landscape of near-desert-under-snow, and led along a trail to stand before the painted figures, facing southwest, in what I can only call a "composition," a fine-grained sandstone cliff with weird, beautiful figures in black, or white, or oxblood-colored paint. What—what in the world—would he do?

"Beware, traveler. You are approaching the land of the horned gods . . ."

That's how Edward Abbey interprets the painted forms that address the landscape from the undressed stone of cliff and rock shelter. A riskier traveler than I, he saw a good deal more of such images. In one solo outing, he dropped down an eroded stream channel, some dozen feet into a pool of water, continuing on and down until it became clear he'd have to do the nearly impossible—retrace his steps back up, with neither rope nor companion (nor, even, I gather, much water or food beyond raisins). He managed it, he says, by balancing atop his walking stick and nearly wishing himself into vertical motion, creeping by dint of desire and desperation back up the channeled rock, heading upstream against gravity, current, and the odds. His view of rock art is likely colored by the nature of his own presence in the place, and the tenor of his traveling. The paintings are stern, "demonic," he says. Their implied authors, the ancient artists, inscribed territorial and cultural conflict, calling upon imagery to pose as warning sentries. It seems like a reasonable interpretation, really, although my own time spent in rock art country has been quite unmartial, largely unfraught by either tension or conflict. Abbey had a more pugilist persona than I, despite my little flyweight fantasy at this essay's outset, so it would make sense that he'd see Threat Postures in the desert paint. Demonic? Maybe. Transformational, surely, I think. The figures seem, to me, to posit the wonder of being, the metaphorical or spiritual complexity of being-in-a-world-of-being. The wonder of the body in the flex and extension of perception, even perception of the self as other, suddenly here. That's part of the power I find in their apparitional presence on cliff face or boulder. The image, whatever its import, is fused with location.

The road over Boulder Mountain climbs through impressive stands of aspen and pine, and the season's snow has been plowed into high, crusted banks on either side, like walls of impossibly friable limestone. My friend Gina is buoyed with enthusiasm and has used up her carefully hoarded frequent-flier miles to get here, to join me for a week of my immersion in the carved and painted landscape of the American Southwest. She has a new camera, a new daypack. I have a brand new sea-foam-colored jacket, my old coat having been stolen from a friend's parked car in Las Vegas, an indignity (okay, tension and conflict) that I've almost shaken off by now, with the excitement of the trip.

The asphalt is freshly white and slippery, and for a while Gina and I seem to be the only ones abroad, our tire tracks the first across the pass, at over nine thousand feet. Then we drop down again, into the intriguingly named particulars of Grand Staircase-Escalante National Monument. We pass Box-Death Hollow Wilderness area, travel along a stony, slanted ledge called the New Home Bench, along Dry Hollow. To the east, out of sight in the corrugated landscape, are Steep Creek, Longneck Mesa, Egg Canyon . . . and beyond that, far out of sight, lies the bizarre geologic phenomenon that is Waterpocket Fold, in the San Rafael Swell. Near where Calf Creek joins the Escalante River, we park in a tiny campground lot, only the second car there, and continue heading nearly due north. The day is clear, if a little cold, and though we have no map my guidebook describes the trail, the ruins of a few Anasazi storage bins, and the locations—more or less—of the rock art sites we've come to see. Today, we're in pursuit of imagery believed to have been left by the Fremont culture, some twelve hundred to seven hundred years ago.

We take turns scanning the canyon walls in what seem likely spots—by now, I've spent a few weeks looking for rock art, and I'm developing a bit of a mental search image for what kinds of places seemed attractive to the ancient makers. The guidebook has been helpful, here, and, in my best tour-guide voice, I read aloud: "Many examples of Fremont rock art are located very high on cliff walls in nearly inaccessible locations. The fact that the artists took considerable risks to create this rock art in these settings, and the care taken in making these images, seemingly attest to the ceremonial importance of some Fremont rock art sites."

And look, before we've warmed enough in the walk to take off our fleece hats, I think I see a splotch of color, far above the trail. We turn and follow a dry, eroded rivulet until we're high enough to really see; then we dump the packs, and hurry over loose rock and bristly plant life to the cliff's base, several hundred yards uphill. It's a steep climb, but hardly risky. Only the adrenalin of delight floods and tingles as we stand still, and catch our breath.

We stand before a painting that seems to float on the pale surface of the cliff: solid black pigment, with an incised line defining sharply the perimeter of the head; the figure is clearly life sized, though it hangs a bit above me when I stand nearby. Armless, legless, faceless, it is a body's silhouette: two wedge-shaped trapezoids—one for the head, the other for the torso—sternly inscribed in straight, unyielding lines. The composition's only curving features, two bison horns, prove that one doesn't need eyes or arms to seem tensely, tautly alert. What's most fascinating about this image, though, I think, is that despite the horned god's angular, black-and-white aspect, there is a little color: variation within severity. From the figure's shoulder, a faint red line extends a v-shape, with a thick red dot just where an elbow would define the bent angle of a more realistic arm. On the other side, off center, a long white shape, like a clean-picked fish skeleton or a stylized plant or feather, hangs vertically, across the dark body and down below the torso's lower line.

I feel I'm standing with a collage or palimpsest, a layering of color upon color, age upon age. It's a representational abstraction, surely, and, as I always do when gazing intently at a painted image, I feel it making some pull on the senses. The figure leans a little, not quite plumb and square, and I feel myself echoing the tilt, the implied possibility of movement, with my own shoulders. Then I move away, and Gina steps closer. She holds out her hand, so it looks as if the figure is balanced in her outstretched palm, and smiles, waiting for me to take the photograph.

In light that seems nearly acoustic in the quiet canyon, with only the occasional rasp of raven or the wet muttering of the current where the stream quickens its pace, we keep moving, scanning the far cliffs. Now we're looking for an image said to be three warriors who face menacingly across the succulent valley. We look across the amphitheater of open air, following the perimeter of earthbound vision, the cliffs that stand in silent answer echo to the ones our trail traces. And then we see them, *people*, clear on the other side of the canyon, on the smoothest, flattest, palest portion of the cliff, as if they're standing atop the pile of scree that sheared away to leave them, peopling the scene. And when we spot their distant forms, we plunge straight toward them, running through a head-high stand of reeds and grasses, wading the stream, and scrambling up a dusty, crumbly bank. Another faint foot trail leads to the bottom of a tall, sheer ledge, and we move around it, in some frustration, shedding jackets in the heat of our effort, until we find a way to scale and climb, using a vertical crevice like a rope, and one after the other we haul up, panting, in the sun. Ha! Only *nearly* inaccessible.

How small they looked from across the canyon, three tiny figures in the cliff's palest stone, below some two hundred feet, I'd guess, of sandstone stained in russet stripes, the residue of countless rainstorms and the periodic cascade of water from the rim above. Now that we're here, I see they're life sized— larger than I am—standing three abreast and holding hands, their broad, wedge-shaped shoulders like a fence I cannot pass. The one on the right is a perplexing figure: within and beneath the solid pigment, we can see the outline of a smaller body, also in red; its hands jut out, like crazy deformities, beneath the finished torso of the larger form. From the distance, you can't see this imperfection, but up close, it's very strange. The dangling hands are huge in proportion to the arms, and though they're blurred, as if, perhaps, by rubbing, they seem to have six or seven fingers. Had someone called out to the working artist, *That's no good—it's too short, you can't even see him from the flat spot by the stream. Start over, make them all bigger!* Or had the painter been working alone, and stopped, shaken his or her head, and thought, *No, I guess I don't like the look of those bristly hands, after all*, and then gone on to make the threesome inseparable in the invisible grasp of undifferentiated fingers? Off to the side, and lower down, another, smaller figure wears a cloak of parallel lines. He's draped in verticality: a rain cloud, maybe, or a spirit of the tall striped cliff, or some long-feathered shaman standing nearby, as if outside the panel's composition. From the distance, he's invisible, a hidden power, but here where we sit on the tilted, rock-littered ledge, he stands out sharply on the stone, changing the composition's balance.

Questions unanswered, we slide back down, recross the creek, and bushwhack into a side canyon, searching for a few, faint petroglyphs. We find them: intimate, tiny, unlike that imposing troika painted on the far more visible shelf. Like ground birds, we move about in the brush that grows against the cliff, until we reemerge, shaking off a few dead leaves. As we regain the trail, we meet another hiker, a young man walking fast enough to overtake us almost before we hear his approach.

"Did you see the pictographs?" we ask him.

"No!" he says, and opens his face with excited interest.

He missed them, then. If these were warrior figures, bracing their broad shoulders in shows of testosterone or territorial force, they didn't impress this particular trespasser. He tells us where to see an ancient granary, nestled masonry in a sheltered notch of cliff, and we describe to him the rough location of the red figures on the canyon wall. And then, anonymous but friendly, we go our separate ways.

Fremont art arises from centuries of desert subsistence living, generations of dry climate and deeper drought. The time period includes, at its close, the famous, devastating droughts that wracked the Southwest in the twelfth and thirteenth centuries, evidently acting like a perverse, dry pump to sweep the farming peoples from their earlier lifeways, emptying the great communal cities farther east and south, like those of Chaco Canyon. These centuries were the culture-shaking times in which, according to some scholars, cannibalism may have stretched another dark but bloody rain shadow across parched western earth. Acts of starvation in a drying land? Terrorism in the age of lithic technologies? Destruction of witches, those mysteriously powerful, dangerous threats to the social group? Ritual dismemberment, performed under the watch of fierce, transmogrifying gods? Researchers point to the bones found in a few specific places near the Four Corners region, not so very far, really, from where Calf Creek still carves its way a thousand feet below the region's nearest spine, the Straight Cliffs of the Escalante Rim. The bones reveal, researchers say, "the body as artifact," a record of material practice from which they hope to glimpse the afterimages, or whispers, maybe, of the acts themselves. Disarticulated skeletons: butchery for the stewpot? Or preparation for respectful burial? I wonder what the air was like here, eight hundred years ago. Was this neat canyon contested land, empty except for well-armed scouts or raiding parties who slipped past the visual fence line of the painted figures on the cliff? Or did it echo with domestic life, the clamor of voices discussing the state of the winter stores, the weeks until planting season, the laughter of women talking together?

For Gina and me, the trail ends at Calf Creek Falls, some 160 feet of year-round cataract that tumbles into a sandy pool. In the chill of the spray, in our coats and hats, we stand on the sandy crescent of beach and examine the vertically striped colors of the cliff, the occasional dangling plant rooted in some damp crevice, the mare's tail waterfall that hisses and whispers in the amplifying hollow, shivering and dimpling the surface of the pool. We gaze upward, to the lip of stone and blue embankment of sky. We talk about the patterns of verticality that mark the sedimentary rock. There is, I've read, a spur trail that, with much work, could get us to the higher level, but that's a journey for a longer day. For us, the cliff walls off the adjacent but as-if-forbidden country.

More reading around, and I'm conjuring mental companions to join in my thinking about rock art, about paintings in places. For example: Ellen Dissanayake considers the primary human *creative* impulse to precede the *aesthetic* urge. She says human beings have always striven to decorate or adorn—*making spe-*

cial, then, she says, is the basic desire. Yes, I think, this is what it's like, when I consider Horseshoe Canyon, or Head of Sinbad, or any number of cliffs and alcoves that have been embellished through carving or paint. Or is it not so much "making" it special, as "marking" the perception that it is, indeed, special? The one inveighs; the other traces. Either way, it's through the concentrated activity of the hand and eye, connecting the immaterial fire that's struck by the brain's synaptic mass with the world's substantial verity, that creativity seems, for us, to "complete" some circuit: self with circumstance.

Back home, with a keystroke, each image flashes on the computer screen. I can select each one, in an instant, as the "wallpaper" (dead metaphor) for the imagined interior space, the virtual "desktop" where I write. A finger moves; the image is replaced. Another keystroke, a finger's "click," and I move from photograph to text to read of the scientists' attempts to date the paint. I place these immaterial extensions of the experiential memory, my *phenomenomentality*, I inwardly name it—; I place text and image in my visual field, like little meditative helpers. I place them here, before me, on the laptop's bright, transportable screen.

I know this is bizarre, ironic, to contemplate the immobile and enduring figures of the decorated landscape through the portable ephemerality of a Pentium chip, but irony itself is surely ancient too, predating postmodernity's self-referencing and closed feedback loops. Especially if, for the archaic inhabitants of the San Rafael Swell, art was inseparable from the physical landscape, as David Lewis-Williams has said it was for far more contemporary hunter-gatherers. I realize that one reason I wanted so keenly, so palpably, to get there on my own two feet, to be *present* in the place itself, is because my life is so often mediated by high technology. One has to work hard, sometimes, to break out of the facsimilated mode. And yet, that's exactly what figurative language is: a facsimile through speech, a verbal likeness of being. So maybe I'm a bit pretentious in this desire to get to the source, to break on through, to get my feet wet in the facticity of experience. All the while toting around several pounds of accouterments: binoculars, notebooks, dried fruit and cereal bars, blister kits for those feet. And, oftentimes, extra dry socks in a plastic bag.

Overnight snow has topped the recent accumulations—perhaps five inches—that cover the San Rafael Swell. The whole region is a veritable textbook of geology, composed of layered depositions from the Permian, dating to almost 300 million years ago, compacted under subsequent eons of assemblage and, much later, blistered into a crusted wheal by Cretacean uplift. Once the land was a seashore, awash with the eroded grit of ancient mountains, the so-called ancestral Rockies that preceded today's sharp granitic peaks. Today, it's a semiarid, overturned bowl, corroded by weather and time into arches and chimneys and great standing headlands, with the closest peaks being the Henry Mountains to the south. It's taken us two tries to get here. On the first, we finally found our snow-besotted dirt road late in the day and decided, dusk dogging our tracks, to wait until daylight and get an early start. Now Gina and I motor across the stony landscape, shifting into four-wheel drive as soon as we leave the plowed road. We want to see the paintings shine as brightly as the aging pigment can, casting the used sunlight back to us. Today my new tires plunge into snow and mud, miles of it, and we take turns driving, sliding delightedly across the potter's-wheel surface until we reach the latest feature of erosion—road-gobbling, waist-deep gully, damply white—where we must park the car and walk the final mile or so. How tiny we seem, then, against the open vista: two female figures moving slowly beneath the wide, bright sky.

We arrive just before noon, and under junipers adrip with the warming day's melt we spread out our coats to sit on. Before us rises the clean, protected surface of the Head of Sinbad, a sandstone headland facing roughly south-southwest. We're staring at two compositions, two separate panels, balanced and composed around what seem to be shamans, all painted exquisitely in maroon-red paint. Their wide, far-watching eyes look past us, as if focused on some scene long since imagined and forgotten. We're here! We don't exist.

The figures float above us, short, stiff arms out to their sides, clutching snakes or dangling empty fingers like perfect claws. Long-bodied, their torsos define the vertical line, delicate patterns decorating the length of their impressive height. One reaches left and right toward two tall, slender shapes that could, I think, be plants; each of these has a long, stemlike center composed of a few vertical lines, topped with a caplike, curvy line like a shriveled blossom or a tiny rising snake, projecting from its top. The plants—or stylized rain showers or bizarre, striped mushrooms, or whatever they are—look quite a lot like dangling jellyfish, impossible as that image is, here above the long-dry bed of a Permian seas. But actually, these two shapes do not *preside*; they clearly *attend* the central shaman, lending the power of balance and symmetry to the scene: one is composed of even groups of lines—two short, four long, then two short again. The other presents odd numbers: one, three, one. An unmistakable snake floats stiffly above the shaman's head; a strangely postured creature (celebratory or supplicating, one can't tell which, if either) spreads wide his humanlike arms, a bushy tail dangling from his thick, animal torso.

This panel is considered the best-preserved example of Barrier Canyon–style art in existence. The paint is bright, waxy looking, seemingly unfaded by the centuries—millennia, probably—since its completion. The work is, to borrow an adjective from other contexts, quite anthropocentric, focusing mostly on human-shaped forms sometimes larger than the human scale, which seem so stylized—and sometimes metamorphosed partially into animal form—that they're usually believed to be components of shamanic belief, aesthetic power articulating ritual and channeling otherworldly strength.

The other panel, though partially damaged by water and weather, presents more of this shamanistic imagery. Here, one figure grasps a snake in its outer hand; an entourage of tiny birds encircles the feathered horns that sprout from its head. A larger bird flies above the figure's shoulder, as if heading toward its ear. A spiral petroglyph adorns the shaman's chest. To the being's right is another figure, with vacant eyes and empty hands. What seem to be two snakes wriggle through space, or across the panel's "surface," toward its head. A wash of mud from above has veiled this second shaman's face and torso, but the space between the two is stippled with small, painted forms: circles sprouting lines like cilia or fur, horseshoe shapes, red ovals with white-painted centers and straight lines, like fringe, on either end. Spirit helpers, suggest some scholars; entoptic shapes from vision trances, others elaborate further, gazing through the finely finessed paint into an animate inner world. The shamanic world-view, scholars agree, is underlain with a bedrock belief in interconnectivity. That is, upon relationship, relations. Kin. And, I think, falling back on the Old English echo, *kith*—knowledge and acquaintance. Individual shamans, writes Polly Schaafsma in one of the touchstone studies of American rock art, are "practitioners skilled in techniques of ecstasy," out-of-the-body travelers who venture into those other, mysterious realms that intersect the quotidian texture of our material lives.

In the bright, chilly quiet of midday, beneath skies devoid, just now, of real birds, we sit still, looking across the space of a few yards and many centuries, to what may be an ancient spirit world, full of motion and balance, inspiration figured in the ancient allure of bird flight, frozen in pigment in its conjunction with the shaman's head, and here depicted on the pale, fine-grained corporeity of a single, particular cliff in winter sunlight.

In summer, the hike to the Great Gallery in Horseshoe Canyon must be an endurance test of heat and sun and thirst. There's no water at the trailhead on the canyon's rim, and the traveler hikes down at least 750 feet, over bare slickrock sandstone, or sandstone littered with fine-sand dust, or sandstone marked with stone cairns, all of which would reflect and intensify the sunlight as if one were making a deliberate pilgrimage into a bread oven. But in late February, the sun is still low, relaxing in the southern portion of the sky. Ice forms overnight on puddled ruts across the rangeland, and the hiker pulls on wool and gloves before checking the pack for water bottles, patting the map in the pants-leg pocket, and leaving the car alone—no one else for miles—in the scuffed-dirt parking lot on the canyon's rim.

Horseshoe Canyon, earlier known as Barrier Canyon, contains a stunning handful of pictograph sites, including, in what's called the High Gallery or the Great Gallery farther along, examples of what archaeologists consider the "type locality" of Barrier Canyon–style art. I wonder mildly about the name change for the canyon itself, as if the very place—the trail, the surveyed acreage included as an outlier in Canyonlands National Park—would be distanced, ever so slightly, from the images who take the landscape as their namesake. Was that the intention? To cloak in different nomenclature the true location of these rare, vulnerable forms? Nah, probably not. It's likely there is a far more mundane story, involving property rights or colorful nineteenth-century Anglo history, stippled with gunshot, that I just haven't stumbled across yet.

However it's named, the canyon is a steep-walled, deeply impressive place. On the rim above, the world presents a study of the horizontal and seems to echo the wide-horizoned ocean realm it was once. But as you descend, the power of verticality rises before you, above you, in the very body of the cliffs that lift—or, depending upon how you look at them—fall and hold along their edges a furze of shadows and cottonwoods, like loose clothes dropped when the sandstone stretched itself into full height. I find myself trying to stand up straight as I descend, lifting myself from my own breastbone, as if in answer to these mute predicates involving height. Down we go, in a switchback on slickrock, down.

For hundreds of yards at a time, long stripes of color— shades of red and brown—hang like stilled ribbons waiting for some absent breeze to hustle up the canyon and lift them into the flutter and wave of dance. This dangling color suggests the drip and wash of runoff, the plunge of water, the aesthetics of the vertical fall. On the sandy floor, restored to the horizontal motion of the hike, the pilgrim pauses, gazes upward, taking in the visual vocabulary of the place—*color, line, form*, I think, drawing on some of the basics. Fundamentals, cast across bedrock. This time of year, the meandering stream holds both water and a fragile fringe of ice, the fractal engravings like feathers or ferns or impossibly subtle seepage through the transient sand. Although the patterns here are white and gray, I think of some of the watercolor landscapes my friend Laurie paints, the delicate details made by water's action on the paper.

Some twenty years ago, a park ranger named Gary Cox noticed that the paint on some of the life-sized figures that loom from the rock in the Great Gallery was flaking away, spalling from the cliff face. Using accelerator mass spectrometry and traditional radiocarbon dating, government archaeologists tried to date the image by the paint itself. They had difficulty, of course. The paint was tightly bound to a fine layer of the rock substrate, and it was impossible to separate the pigment fully from the sandstone—and whatever carbon contamination it might contain. But the tests, however imperfect, give us something quantified, an imprecise but suggestive mental benchmark for the artwork's age. They indicate a range from roughly 2000 B.C. to 300 A.D.—either way, an amazing length of time for paintings to persist out of doors. For that's the great insistent presence: this is exposed artwork, somehow sheltered enough to remain on cliffs or within shallow rock alcoves, century after century. Some scholars think that the style itself may have extended much, much longer: clay figurines found in a cave adjacent to Horseshoe Canyon have a body shape—rounded shoulders, no legs or arms, patterns engraved in the once-wet clay along the length of the torso—that is, in the illustration I've seen, remarkably similar to the anthropomorphs of the Great Gallery. They were excavated from layers dated between 5000 and 6000 B.C. Perhaps eight thousand years ago.

What do these dates mean? Could a culturally specific image, the patterned-body profile, which is often interpreted as spirits or ancestors, have lived *for up to six thousand years* in the minds of the hunter-gatherer people who roamed the San Rafael Swell? If so, it could have taken shape in various media—clay and paint, the two found in such close proximity along Horseshoe Canyon—but others, too: mutable, ephemeral, more purely organic, that is, carbon based. Utterly testable, but utterly gone. If we figure twenty years as a generation, we're talking a good three hundred generations. We're talking, as well, about something close to the average life span of an entire language family, not merely a specific tongue. This suggests that the immaterial idea, the spirit helper of the mind, would need to be as long lived as the syntaxed world, the systematized patterns of articulation, in which the stories of such figures rose up to take their place.

How long can thought itself live, itinerant, moving from one pit-house shelter—a particular cranium, home to the first-person-singular I—to another, and another, in the many-generationed emergence of us: *We?* And, both much later and simultaneously (to the storytellers dwelling two watersheds away) *Them?* Thought moves across landscapes, dragging its hard-won burdens, wheeling its handcart of close-held beliefs. If you squint a bit, and grow quiet, you can almost make out the mysterious bodies, pausing among us.

That day we met few other visitors to the canyon: just one small party. It was still early, and we were paused at the High Gallery, the first of the rock art sites along the trail. The red paint bodies hung way above the canyon floor—the artists must have scrambled to the high stone ledge above our heads. We heard voices before the others came into sight; then they rounded a clump of cottonwoods by the trail, and we exchanged quick greetings. They were Park Service personnel; the young woman turned out to be Heidi, a volunteer with whom I'd spoken by phone some days before. They'd brought Mike, an employee from the Cleveland-Lloyd Dinosaur Quarry, to show him a large dinosaur track recently discovered on the very ledge we gazed at from below. Gary, the leader, pointed the way, and we all clambered up to see the five-toed print, perhaps ten inches long, at the bottom of the Navajo sandstone layer. Gary had discovered it a few months back, and Mike had been wanting to come get a good look.

What a happy accident, I realized much later—our sudden guide was Gary Cox, the very person who found the sample used to date the canyon's images. So there we were, several yards above the canyon floor, in an unlikely conjunction, on a plateau of recorded and unrecorded footsteps. The painted figures hung, or stood, nearby. My favorite was a squat-bodied form, with two pointed legs and no apparent arms, whose spectacular torso was filled with the curved stripes of a rainbow, or—I thought suddenly of the canyon's current place name—a horseshoe. Either way, a symbol that, at least to the small group of currently assembled, was special, and figured good luck.

But it's true: in places, the painted figures have been damaged.

When we finally reach the Great Gallery and sit on a fallen cottonwood log, in the winter's almost-shade of the still-living tree, we still aren't ready for the impact. The panel of figures stretches perhaps a hundred feet in width, with some of the beings larger than life size, using my personal scale of reference: I'm five feet, four inches tall. We stand again; we sink back down. This, then, is the location-specific type: a long, tapered, slightly wedge-shaped body, shoulders more or less rounded. They look, we think, like mummies, just as all the descriptions say. But despite the "*type* locality," there's nothing generic about the images; each one is keenly detailed, exquisitely different from the rest. Some have eyes that gaze implacably outward; some are solid color, featureless in the face. Some, says Gina, look like kings, adorned with rings of white-paint dots like crowns. On some, the torsos are elaborately decorated, with lines and stripes and zigzags; others hold more images across their chests, animals or other, smaller figures.

We step forward, drawing closer. We step back. There is no one here to mediate our own experience, no guide to draw the eye here, or there, no other visitors to distract our rapt attention with their laughter or talk. We know next to nothing of the history of the artists who draped these images across the stone. Did the artwork flourish out of wet times or dry, good or bad? For how many centuries did people gather here to gaze beyond themselves, into the bodies of the rocks? Erosion has toppled boulders from one side of the composition, dropping whatever images once hung there into dust and rubble. Along the other side, the bottom edge of the panel is ragged with weathering; it's clear the rock's patina is, indeed, flaking off, and with it, the paint. The vision is falling, slowly, into ruin. Gina moves back and forth with her digital camera, recording frame by frame the forms that hang before us, in this single afternoon that, already, has begun its infinitesimal procession toward dark. We keep exclaiming to one another, trying to articulate the beauty and mystery each form embodies. Whenever we fall quiet, we can hear the whisper of slight wind in the standing stalks of last year's grass.

We talk again about the similarity we see between the vertical stripes of color that feature forth from the surrounding cliffs and the specific painted figures on the rock before us. I think, again, it's the aesthetic of the vertical, the idea of *reach*, of *height*. Here, it's not so much that form follows function, but that form follows formation, the cultural utterance recalling the phenomenology of stone. We're in the landscape, after all, of geologic wonder, with the named sequence of sandstone that can hold the mind quite still, trying to grasp deep time.

I'm glad that Gina has brought this camera and is making a record of what we've seen. I know I'll make repeated passes back through the material, months later, seeking some meaningful shape for the narrative that is our journey of encounter. In memory, we'll hold the positions of the figures, lit by the canyon's particular cast of light; we'll recall the panel as the end of a singular walk, the hike we made that very day. We'll try, as time takes us progressively further from the afternoon of our intense perception, to keep the images in their experiential context. We'll fail in some of this, details sloughing off from the complexity of our no-longer-breathless recollection, but that certainty of imperfection won't keep us from trying. Imperfect, fallible, doomed even to the smudge and wear of time; still, we approached the figures, in the landscapes where they've stayed for centuries, perhaps millennia. We were there, and came back subtly changed.

Fragments

By early afternoon, in Picket Wire Canyon in southeastern Colorado, on a mid-October day of brilliant air and sun, I am barefoot in the river. I am wearing what have been a favorite pair of trousers, soft as chamois, rolled to the knee. This will be their last outing, since I ripped out the seat earlier in the trip, scrambling up a rockface. The day feels utterly golden and blue: bright sky, warm rock, dry grass, the hours rich and long and full, and filled with happy, languid company—we are two men and two women who have hiked down to the river to see dinosaur tracks. It is almost time to turn back, to retrace our way along the dusty trail, back through the canyon's mixed-grass prairie and occasional cottonwoods, up through the scrubby pine of the canyon wall, to rejoin the drought-beiged rim of the horizontal plains. It's still another five miles; we should get started soon. But for now, we are dawdling. Dorian sits on large limestone blocks, dangling her feet in the silty current. Dave and Roger prowl the level shelf along the bank, pointing out the shapes and peculiarities of the tracks and taking photographs. I'm wading in the gentle, subtle flow, searching the bottom until I find what I'm looking for: footprints in the riverbed. I step into them, walking upstream against the feeble current. Me and Heraclitus, I think, heading back.

For a moment I'm reminded of afternoons in college, in a sun-filled classroom on the second floor of Gordy Hall, where

Professor Wieman lectured on the pre-Socratics. It was a world of metaphor, of transformation, talk of accidents and essences, doctrines of opposites and of flux, the future opening out in its surprising complexity. "Other and other waters flow down on those who step into the same rivers," wrote Heraclitus. Some say this is different from the popular paraphrase, "You can't step in the same river twice." And, of course, I can't read the original Greek, so whatever wordplay and poetry the prophet-philosopher first laid down are lost on me. It's Fragment 12 I'm talking about, which opens "*autoisi potamoisi*," and I take it by eye and on authority that the onomatopoetic whisper of the river sounds in those first words.

Here are the footprints. Trackways, they're called, clear lines of ancient footsteps heading roughly west, parallel patterns of animals who traveled together along some Mesozoic lakeshore, in the late Jurassic, some 150 million years ago. They're laid in limestone that has jointed and fractured into even blocks like great paving stones, giving the impression of a road, or some old central plaza, a *place* rather than mere *space*, where the sauropods strolled together, heading somewhere.

Dave and I spent the night camped on the rim above nearby Vogel Canyon. When we pulled in, the other vehicles were a camper, whose occupants I never saw, and a van with two "semiretired" folks who came to our picnic table almost before we had finished dinner to pay a long, chatty visit in the gathering dark. The fellow, a sculptor and aficionado of antiquities, was full of bluster and statement. At one point, he asked absurdly, "Where you live, do you have access to mammoth bones imbedded with projectile flakes?" In the dry autumn air, I grew chilly and impatient, as the last light faded and seeped away before Dave and I could stroll across the plateau and gaze down into the canyon, or maybe hike the brief descent to a spring I saw marked on the map. The day was gone; the canyon waited in the dark, unchanged by any visit from us.

At last the couple left, and we crawled into the tent to sleep under clear, cold skies, in near proximity to birds, as the place name—*vogel*, bird—would suggest: an owl in the night, early morning bluebirds as we rose in the day's first light.

At nine, we meet Roger and Dorian near the edge of the Comanche National Grasslands park in a rugged juniper-and-pinyon-ringed spot five hundred feet above the river, and descend to Picket Wire Canyon. The name is a corruption of Purgatoire, a charmingly reshaped linguistic artifact from the age of Spanish explorers, who named the stream "El Rio de las Animas Perdidas en Purgatorio," the River of the Souls Lost in Purgatory. Some explanations trace the place name to a grassfire that surrounded and consumed an exploration party, or to an expedition bound from New Mexico to Florida that disappeared into the unmapped lands of the New World. But the landscape today is anything but desperate. Our gait along the dusty trail is an unhurried saunter, and we pause often, admiring the grasses, the rocks, some persimmon-sized gourds that sprawl in drying clusters of vine. Prickly pear cactus grows in aromatic, hirsute profusion here, and we stop frequently to pluck the plump fruit, wipe away the fine bristles, as if stroking a cloth along the nap, and peel back the rind. Inside, the fruit is rich and sweet, prune-sized clusters of flesh-and-mostly-seed. They are often delicious, but labor intensive, requiring much seed spitting, and they stain our lips and fingers scarlet. Dave and Dorian discuss the seed-to-fruit ratio, and Dave says it's more like a pomegranate than a grape. "Persephone walked, spitting," I say, and we do. The seeds make a satisfying percussive sound as, like children, we spit whole mouthfuls out. Dave says he has eaten jelly made from the fruits and that it is delicious, and far more convenient.

In the bright sun, we browse and amble, looking at everything. (We notice lots of seed-filled scat, scattered in the dust.) Along a bend in the trail, several yards above a similar bend in the channel, Dave and Dorian spot a gray fox and exclaim as it disappears into the brush. But Roger and I have missed the moment, talking of poetry and teaching, and by the time we look to where our companions are pointing the animal is out of sight.

When we arrive at the river, just past noon, a sandy side path takes us down to the water, past thickets of tamarisk that mimic native willows on the bank. Immediately we find a large, three-toed allosaur track on the near side of the river, which is easily recognizable from the photographs in our guide booklet. This deep print is in fine-grained stone that feels silky to the touch. It reminds me of a turkey-foot petroglyph I once saw in New Mexico. Two less-well-formed ones are just behind the track, a record of the two steps taken before the larger, perfect print. A tiny pair of white tennis shoes, toddler sized, sits nearby, forgotten no doubt by earlier visitors. But within minutes they will remember them and come back; we'll see their owner's daddy jog back along the path and scoop them up.

The Morrison Formation, the geologic layer that contains the tracks, is deeply fossil rich, known for the bones found throughout the late nineteenth century—skeletons of the brontosaurs that would be quarried, painstakingly packed out of their distant locations, and reassembled to loom tall in museums and the public imagination. Some of its deposits are lacustrine—set down in lakes—others are fluvial, deposited by rivers. Both words, I think, are lovely, holding liquids in their Latinate construction. Though the Mesozoic Era was marked by the central sea that covered the plains states, the limestone of the Purgatoire Tracksite marks a lakeshore not a marine environment. It is believed to have been a semiarid savannah landscape, and has been compared to regions in contemporary East Africa. I like the comparison in part because we—people—at the earliest point in our species' being, lived and walked in such savannahs. Shales accompanying the limestone testify to the periodic flooding and evaporation of the ancient lake, with bits and traces of small fossils: algae, snails, seed shrimp and clam shrimp, tiny crustaceans that lived in quiet, shallow waters. Fossil ripple marks suggest it was a large lake, oxygen rich and frequently an important source of drinking water for the Jurassic animals that lived along its shores.

The largest footprints follow one another at a gentle angle from the river, several in neat parallel lines that show it was a group of beasts that walked together here. These are the footprints of sauropods: great, gregarious vegetarians whose stride stretched from 4½ to 6 feet as they swung thick legs from massive hips. The footprints themselves—ichnites, in the language of paleontology—are open basins in the rock, and I sit down beside one and put both my feet inside, as if I were about to pour warm water in to soak after the long hike. But in the drought, the river is down, the footprints are dry, and only a little powdery dust swirls beneath my toes. In one large track, prairie grass is growing, where some tough little seed must have lodged in another, wetter year of higher water. Though we stroll and linger along these most prominent prints—a half-dozen or so separate trackways—researchers have mapped more than one hundred other such individual trails, with at least thirteen hundred separate prints. We kneel to touch a smaller, three-toed track (some carnosaur, as near as I can tell from studying the guidebook) still holding unmistakable tracings from the scaly skin that pressed against the damp surface so many million years ago. Dorian and Dave take photographs, impressions I will later study, trying to match the specific shape with published pictures from what's called "the scientific literature," trying to put names and labels on the imagery we've carried home.

In the so-called Doctrine of Opposites, Heraclitus lays out the complementary constituents of the universe and hints at their relation through change. Modes of being, *cold* and *wet*, combine to form Water; *cold* and *dry* form Earth. Neither is permanent, any more than their hot-wet-dry counterparts Air and Fire. "Cold things grow warm," he says, "Warm grows cold, wet grows dry, and parched grows moist" (Fragment 126). Through these states, the cosmos oscillate, each, it would seem, by turn. There is at the heart of things, he says, a "back-turning structure [*palintropos harmonie*] like that of the bow or the lyre." This is how things fit together, how pattern and order emerge from flux, how the tensile opposition of the arms of the bow create a thing of grace and power, how the lyre, similarly strung, strummed renders, out of silence, music.

Because Heraclitus (known as "The Dark," "The Obscure") might have enjoyed these wandering associations and this wordplay, strolling along the Purgatory River and thinking of time, I cast the imagery before us in terms of the opposites. The cold, brisk air of sunrise, when Dave and I rose from our tent site on the canyon rim has given way to midday heat. Dorian and I soak our t-shirts in the river and put them back on, shiveringly cool, though quickly they rewarm between the sun and our backs. Dave follows suit, annoyed that he is wearing black, a photon-sink, as he puts it. Then we wade across the diminutive ripples of the current, and I stop briefly to change back from sandals to hiking boots, while the others move a little farther on. We pause along a stretch of rumpled stone where once the wet lakeshore was churned by sauropods, as if, like cattle, they had gathered at the edge of the impounded water, milling about and roiling the ground beneath their feet. Bioturbation is the geologic term for such disturbances, and the guidebook puns that along the Purgatoire, the earth was marked by "dino-turbation." Again, I think of Heraclitus and the echoing shape of internal rhyme. Wet things grow dry. Soft things grow hard. Motion stills. We stand and scan the limestone surface for the trampled clams and plants left as fossils in the tousled limestone. Then, with a quick swig of tepid water from the packs, we move along.

In 1911, dinosaur hunter Charles Sternberg published a slender book of poems called The Story of the Past: Or the Romance of Science. Here he recounts, in broad strokes, the narrative of his search for bones from other ages, and he presents himself as a time traveler, an amazed visitor to the Permian and Cretaceous worlds. He is, indeed, the hero of adventure, telling his tale in verse heavily metered and rhymed, a romance of the stones. From the beloved hemlock forests of his childhood in New York state he heads west on a God-inspired quest "To show to man His wondrous Work / Through all the scenes of time." In life, his travels in search of fossil skeletons took him across the plains—Kansas, Texas, Wyoming, and as far west as Oregon—but he never saw the tracks along the Purgatoire. I'm sure he would have liked to, and to "read" the text of those ancient footprints. For to Sternberg, geology held distinctly transcendental flavor: science lighted with the roseate flush of faith. "So God engraves in mouldering land / The works of his almighty hand," he wrote:

Not Moses' tablets graved by God
Seem more wondrous than the word
He left recorded in the earth,
When rocky strata had their birth.

In a long poem called "The Permian Beds of Texas," Sternberg declares: "I sail down on the Tide of Time, / My oar-beats keeping gentle rhyme." In his imagined "birch-bark boat" he "gently floats" back through millennia, describing all he sees—ancient lake and ocean, lush jungle and glade combining, unexpectedly, convention's archaic syntax with precision's scientific diction. He wrote of erosion's uncovering power:

The rains of ages have laid bare
The ancient dead once buried there,
Far, far below in limestone vault.

For Sternberg, as for some others in the late nineteenth and early twentieth centuries, tracks drew little notice. It was the bones, mostly, that they wanted, and Sternberg found some fine specimens, including the concentric skeletons of two fish, one encased within the other's belly, an ancient record of footless predator and prey.

R. T. Bird, in the employ of the American Museum of Natural History's Barnum Brown, did pay a visit to the Purgatoire in

1938. It was something of a side trip, following a summer spent in Wyoming, when he came to Pueblo, Colorado, in early November, and, joined by John Stuart MacClary, made a car trip to the track site. He was puzzled by the prints and thought they showed a brontosaur walking on its front two feet, as if partially floating in the water. He took photographs, one of which is included in his posthumous memoir, showing huge circular footprints in the jointed rock. The next day he headed farther south, and within a week he'd found a large, accessible trackway along the Paluxy River, which would hold his attention as the Purgatoire had not.

It was left to MacClary to document the footprints. He'd been interested in the site for nearly two years; in 1937 he had organized a trip with some college friends, though in his wheelchair he could not reach the prints themselves. Even so, he drew a roughly sketched map of their route down Minnie Canyon, south of the Withers Canyon route that my friends and I descended. MacClary went on to produce three small publications, which I track down in a couple of afternoons' library work. The first, from 1936, is a tiny note in *Life* magazine, a half-page spread of three photographs with a single accompanying paragraph by MacClary. One circular picture, cropped like a little spotlight falling on its subject, shows the allosaur print with a man's hat set beside it for scale. I find this source on a sunny afternoon on the fourth floor, where a nearly complete run of *Life* rests in crumbling bound volumes. This one is housed in a green preservation box, tied neatly with ribbons, since the broken spine sprawls pages that threaten to tear as I turn them. The next two must be recalled from the storage annex, and are delivered the following day. From 1938, there is a full-page description in *Scientific American*, again with three photos. One shows a plaster cast of the allosaur track and a cement replica of the track itself, which, he says, is "used as a bird-bath." (I briefly envision the cedar waxwings that come through my yard each autumn landing on the concrete lip, drinking and fluttering in a three-toed puddle of water.) MacClary describes a trackway that we didn't see in our relaxed afternoon along the river. "One three-toed trail angles to follow that of the huge four-footed creature," he writes, "obviously indicating that the carnivorous biped pursued the huge vegetarian." He goes on to interpret the gait of the two beasts: the predator had a regular, forty-eight-inch stride that "gives the impression that the killer felt confident mastery of the situation." The other trail, he says, is spaced irregularly, which "may be regarded as evidence that the herbivorous dinosaur was aware of impending conflict, which it did not relish." I can find no other description of this particular confluence of prints, and when I study a detailed map of the tracks, painstakingly surveyed in the 1980s, none of the trails seems to illustrate his account of an ancient chase.

I wonder about this discrepancy. Was MacClary simply mistaken about what he saw? Did he "read into" the limestone annals some agonistic drama, with Jurassic players, that never did take place? Or have the movement of the river and the subsequent decades of weather removed all record of the pursuit? It's true: erosion has obliterated sections of the trackways, and the very blocks on which Dorian and I sat, soaking our t-shirts on that hot October day, are only pausing their slow tumble into the current. There is an archive of destruction here at hand; it is the very width of Picket Wire Canyon, where the river has washed and wandered across its floodplain, a shallow, fluid Shiva of creation and destruction. A Forest Service publication suggests that "the majority of the main footprint bearing

bed" has been destroyed by periodic erosion, and cites a cata-
strophic flood in 1904 and another in 1965. Indeed, throughout
their management plan runs a persistent theme of loss: erosion of the tracks, degradation of the riparian habitat, deteri-
oration of prehistoric rock art along the canyon walls, "deliberate vandalism" of prehistoric and historic ruin sites. One of
the primary resolutions in that decade-old plan is to arrest the
river's erosion of the prints while maintaining its wild and scenic character.

I write to Martin Lockley, the lead researcher of the 1980s,
and he doesn't know what to make of MacClary's description
either. But real or imagined, the account lodges somewhere in
my subconscious. One night I dream of driving in a small suv
that suddenly becomes an open buggy, vulnerable like an old-
fashioned sleigh, along a winding canyon road just above a riverbank. Of course, this being an anxiety dream, I'm in the dark.
Headlights flash on the river as I make a hairpin turn, and I see
a huge crocodile rising from the water with amazing speed, and
its gaze meets mine as it begins pursuit. In a later sequence,
some ungulate, neck rising from raised shoulders like a small
giraffe from a Dali painting, crosses the road. I see, in shock,
that it has no head, but is still moving, making a stumbling escape. A lion crouches beside the road, haunches turned toward
me, but I can still see it tearing at the head it holds between its
paws.

In his third published note, a 1939 letter to *Natural History*,
MacClary reports that the three-toed tracks (represented by
two of the previously published photos) are "undoubtedly new
to science," and wonders what species could have made them.
He confides that he'd long wondered about the tracks, but had
been unable to visit them until the previous year, "because of

physical incapacity"—evidently he was an invalid, an enthusiast of paleontology who relied on reading with only rare visits to the field. He says he "had not dared hope it would ever be possible to see them." Of course, this means he probably couldn't go back again, to reexamine—reconsider—what he'd found. Back at my desk, I wonder whether it is now too late to ever see the trail of predator and prey that MacClary studied over half a century ago.

And today I wonder whether the residents along the Purgatoire River ever felt themselves living at the end of the world, in the years of the Great Depression and the Dust Bowl. Picket Wire Canyon lies at the very western edge of the Dust Bowl, along the border between Las Animas and Otero Counties. To the east and south is Baca County, one of the hardest hit places in the 1930s droughts, along with southwest Kansas and the Oklahoma Panhandle. Though the canyon hit its peak of settled inhabitants in the 1880s—about four hundred people lived and farmed there at that time—the Depression and drought later drove many from the land.

MacClary's first trip in April took place during the single worst year for dust storms, if one counts either the number of times visibility was less than a mile or the number of hours people in the region were besieged by dust in the air. Though unlike nearby Baca County, Picket Wire Canyon had not been largely plowed up for wheat production, these still must have been dark, despairing times. In the southern plains, spring during these years was marked by black blizzards, when sudden cold air masses drove down from the north and lifted the loose, dry earth in great rolling clouds, sometimes extending as high as eight thousand feet—mountains in the air above the plains. More frequently, the nearly incessant wind resulted in sand blows, where plants were buried and choked in the moving drifts. I think of the dry, sandy trails we walked along, and imagine the canyon pocked and pitted by destructive drifts.

By other standards of measurement the worst year may have been 1935. In March and April, the black blizzards descended repeatedly on the southern plains in stunning storms that could last for hours. Historian Donald Worster has detailed how fully these storms invaded the landscape of the former grasslands. By March 24 in that year, twelve consecutive days of storms had gripped the regions of southeastern Colorado and southwestern Kansas. He notes that the wind "carried away from the plains twice as much earth as men and machines had scooped out to make the Panama Canal." Then on April 14, an even greater storm swept south- and eastward from the Colorado border in what would be called Black Sunday, a terrifying visitation of particulate darkness that lasted more than four hours, killing livestock and people who were caught out of doors.

Many of the National Grasslands in the West date back to the efforts of Franklin Roosevelt's administration to remove what were called submarginal lands from agricultural production, a program whose roots lie in the 1920s, before the dust storms arrived. Between 1933 and 1943, however, the theoretical interests of social scientists received practical policy enactment through the Federal Emergency Relief Administration's program of buying up distressed land, later continued under the Resettlement Administration and the Soil Conservation Service. The 1934 Taylor Grazing Act closed the West—and there were then 80 million acres of unclaimed land—to any further homesteading.

Picket Wire Canyon, however, in the Comanche National Grassland, doesn't trace its public lands lineage to these Dust Bowl–era programs. When the Rourke family, who had ranched the area for three generations, sold their holdings—the Wineglass Ranch—in 1971, the eventual buyer was the Department of Defense. The land along the Purgatoire River became the Piñon Canyon Maneuver Site, and for twenty years the army conducted training along the riparian grassland and the caprock rims. The track site, in one army document, was referred to as one of the canyon's "uneconomic remnants," while citizens' groups called for the protection of the prehistoric prints by transferring their management from the army to the Forest Service. In 1990, Public Law 101–510, Section 2825, effected this transfer, and 16,700 acres of the larger military reserve unit were removed from the army's purview and established as the Comanche National Grassland's Picket Wire Canyonlands. A few weathered poles and phone wires still string their way across the landscape, remnants of those years in which the army conducted maneuvers in the canyon. I can hardly believe they are less than thirty years old: gray and slack and tiny in the wide, light-filled landscape, they seem far distant and diminutive, dwarfed by the stretch of open grass, the upward reach of the canyon's cliff wall, and the sere, hot sun. I think of Emily Dickinson, and how in many poems she speaks of Noon, markedly capitalized as starkly metaphysical, a philosophical or psychological state of being gripped by Realization, ravished, one could say, by Reason.

On the hike out, we feel small beneath the hot expanse of sky. I become aware of physical annoyances: a few prickly pear tines itch and chafe in my thigh, where (unthinking) I wiped a fruit against my trousers. My right foot begins to ache, the first signs—though I don't know it yet—of severe plantar fasciitis, an injury that will plague me for months afterward, and end my hopes for competing in an upcoming autumn footrace. Dave threads his bandanna beneath his cap to shield his neck, which is already sunburned. Dorian sips the warm water and complains that it is so hot it makes one want to puke; I tell her that miles away, cold water and cold beer both await us in an ice chest in the car. We pass a family pausing on their mountain bikes, and a girl of perhaps nine or ten shows us a dead tarantula she has found in the trail, looking furry and mammalian, though slightly flattened. We exclaim and thank her, and she smiles, flushed with the achievement of demonstration and instruction.

Dead cottonwood trees stand pale and smooth without their bark; a few are lined and shaded by charcoal, signs of fires from some other year. (I think briefly of the tale of the Spanish explorers, lost souls consumed by fire in the river valley.) Dry branches of cholla, weathered down to the hollow, hidden lattice of their bonelike structure, stand in desiccated clumps among the grasses. We pause along the way back to investigate old ruined home sites. There is the Lopez settlement, dating to 1871, including the remains of a Catholic "mission"—two partially standing walls from the rough-beamed church—and a graveyard with hand-carved headstones. Back behind these former buildings is a rock-shelter cave with partial masonry walls, reputed to be the Lopez family's shelter while the houses were under construction. Farther along, we explore a more recent—though also decaying—structure, with a covered cistern we peer into, hoping for snakes, and a handsome enamel-coated wood cookstove tumbled on the hillside by the house. To our surprise, we run into hunters, young men wearing blaze orange vests, with their rifles slung over their backs. Like the family, they are on bicycles, and we see them first along the river, pedaling through the high, dry grass, away from the tamarisks where they sought—unsuccessfully, evidently—mule deer. I wonder just how these wheeled predators would've handled the carcass, had they been successful. It's a very steep climb to the top, and they'd have to leave their high-tech bikes, perhaps in a little trail-side cairn, one atop another, while they struggled upward with the weight of the deer.

We drain the last of our water—all except Dorian—and slowly make the final ascent, back out of the canyon to stony rim above.

In the final days of June, the shortgrass plains are delightfully, surprisingly cool and moist. Heavy rains along the Front Range have soaked the soil and flash flooding has suddenly swelled the little streams outside the concrete-bodied cities in the foothills. Farther east and south, in its valley beneath the Dixie Bluffs, the Purgatoire is muddy and swift, but well within its banks. I'm here as a kind of postscript to our autumn visit to the Picket Wire. I want to try to find the little town of Higbee, which the map shows on Highway 109 south of La Junta, along an area of the river called Nine Mile Bottom. Higbee was established in 1866 by a settler most recently from Trinidad, one Uriel Higbee, along with Jesse Nelson and his wife, Susan (a niece of Kit Carson); William and Manuelita Richards; Samuel Smith, and a few others. Soon they joined forces to build an earthen dam along the Purgatoire, for irrigation and flood control. With iron spades and cottonwood shovels they worked from 1868 to 1870 to change the river just enough to allow them agricultural purchase along its banks and floodplain. By the 1930s, there was a "ditch caretaker's house" to oversee a more sophisticated diversion channel, paved with stone and cement, and a lock control system. L. C. (Lawrence) Ridennoure was the ditch caretaker by then, and he lived with his family in the stucco house; the building was provided as part of his salary. Born in 1895, he had served as a private first class in World War I, and with his wife, Etha Lynn (born 1904), he was now raising children—Betty Jo, Lawrence, Ben, and the baby, Ted—in the valley.

It was Betty Jo who told her high school teacher, Mr. Don Hayes, about the tracks, and shortly afterward MacClary learned of them as well. I gathered this much from reading throughout the winter, leisurely poking around, and when I learned that Betty Jo was still living, I wrote to her in her retirement home in Arizona. She replied to my questions in sentence fragments, sometimes only one-word answers, penned right onto my letter. From her I learned of the "ditch house"; she also told me that in 1941 she and MacClary "spent a long time writing about the tracks." But she said, in sometimes spidery writing, changing pens midway from blue to black, she's "not in the best of health"; she was not a loquacious correspondent. So I'm eager to see the spot, to flesh out her story from the spare, historical framework of ink-on-paper.

Right near mile-marker 39, on Highway 109, is a turnoff for Nine Mile Bottom on the Higbee Road. A dilapidated white wooden sign lists just over a dozen residents, their names and the mileage to their homes. A few of these dangle loosely from the frame, and I wonder whether the people have moved away or just don't have the time or interest to nail back their single-board planks in this lettered landmark. Not far from the turnoff is the Higbee Cemetery, with an iron entrance gate and a cistern beside it spreading out a network of hoses for watering the grave sites. Also near the entrance is a metal sign mapping the burial plots: each grave is marked, and the names of the dead are handwritten in faded marker. Though no doubt intended to be permanent, a few are too faint to read. Others are evidently unknown, simply empty locations, sideways U's on the map.

In a cool, light rain (welcome weather for late June!), I wander through the tiny graveyard, noting the large number of veterans (Civil War through Vietnam), the dead infants (most often marked with dateless concrete rectangles, names like Baby Wood or Baby Carson). Barrel cactus and sideoats grama grass punctuate plantings of iris and the occasional hardscrabble rose bush; low, leathery lilacs spread over the Carson family plot. Here, among the irises, are the Ridennoures, three of them (L. C., Etha Lynn, and their son Ted C., 1934–1992). Nearby, neat sheets of Astroturf cover the McGowns like bright green afghans, weighted around their perimeters with rounded river stones. A couple named the Martins, dead before I was born, share a single piece of petrified wood for their headstone. Several Hispanic families have little wooden fences, chipped figures of Mary, piles of stones, and faded plastic flowers to keep company with the grave site. Here are the names I recognize of founding families: Nelson, Lopez. No Higbees, though, and when I'd asked Betty Jo if there were any Higbee descendants in the valley when she was a child, she wrote, simply, "no." I suppose Uriel himself must have moved on to something else. Overhead, a golden eagle circles the valley, and the air is very quiet.

The road runs southeast, roughly parallel to the river; we're several miles downstream from the dinosaur track site. The morning continues cool, and we drive farther south amidst alfalfa fields and a small stand of irrigated corn. Blue grosbeaks and orioles move between cottonwoods and phone lines; once, in the distance, I see a small group of vultures gazing intently into the field, closely attending something dead, or perhaps nearly so. We pass an old adobe-and-stucco ruin, a building that has simply folded in upon itself and is melting back into the ground. And then, high on a rocky knoll, with the Dakota sandstone bluffs above and beyond, unmistakable, is the ditch house, with the muddy Purgatoire waters below. I grin, and squint up toward the metal roof weighted against the wind with stones along one side.

In town, I visit the Otero County Museum. I want to see whether they have any other images or information on Betty Jo, the dinosaur tracks, the decades of the Dust Bowl. In the cavernous building, there are plenty of artifacts to examine: hand-drawn fire-hose carts for fighting wildfires; a stage coach from the nineteenth century; a barbed-wire collection, a directory for the local ranches' brands. A local man named John Liken donated his arrowhead collection to the museum, along with a careful annotation of where each point was found; most were from out of state, but a few are from the area. Two dark, much-worn points were found in "the vicinity of Dixie Bluffs along the Anderson Arroyo." An amber-colored, unfinished-looking piece perhaps an inch long "was found south of La Junta"; only one small point was from "the Picketwire River, Godfrey Canyon, Higbee." The collection is neatly and artfully arranged, a geometric pattern of points and their hand-numbered labels, framed behind glass and hanging like a picture on the wall.

In an exhibit dedicated to the early schools of the area, I find a ledger listing each building, its years of use, and the land-office deed for the property. On the second page is a description that matches the old, crumpled adobe-and-stucco building along the road, roughly two miles from the highway. The Higbee School, the ledger says, was "Constructed as a former saloon and other in the 1880's years," before it assumed its later, less commercially recreational, use. "This building evacuated in October year 1962 as school building," declares the ledger, a cramped phrasing that sounds, to me, to contain both alacrity and emergency, but I doubt that was the case. And here, in a small plastic frame, are two photos of the students of Higbee in 1933. In the familiar pose of the era, they stand and sit clustered in front of a small stucco building, labeled the Plaza School; the photograph was taken by their teacher, Annabelle Loftis. One shows sixteen students; the other, thirteen. (They were evidently taken on different days—and the label says one may have been taken in 1934; the other was Easter 1933, and reveals a pile of eggs before the gathered children.) The pupils' names are recorded in pen on the back, and, to my delight, I find three Ridennoures—Betty Jo and her two brothers, Ben and Lawrence. While I'm still gazing at the faces, trying to picture them and this dusty-looking building back in the fields I just drove through, the nineteenth-century walls still standing, the sky dry and sere in those drought-fraught years, the museum attendant introduces me to an elderly woman wearing a volunteer's name tag. She is Mrs. Tillie Autry; she grew up in the Purgatoire Valley and remembers Higbee very well. We sit together and visit in a row of wooden chairs, evidently salvaged from a La Junta school auditorium some years past. She is a petite, trim woman, with a friendly but poised face; she wears a lovely sapphire and diamond wedding ring that fits loosely on her slender finger.

Tillie Autry tells me she was born a Ballou. Her mother had been raised in Higbee; she was a Richards, a daughter, I later realize, of one of the original settlers of the tiny town—twenty-eight-year-old William and fifteen-year-old Manuelita, married in 1866. Her father's people were from Kansas, but her grandparents had settled with their children in the nineteenth century in the Sunflower Valley, near Trinidad. In 1900, her parents bought a ranch along the Purgatoire where Plum Canyon meets Chacuaco Creek. (Later I study the map carefully and find the spot. As the crow flies, this looks to be eight or ten miles south—and just a tiny bit west—of the track site. It must have been a lovely ranch location, a side canyon of the Purgatoire, with Chacuaco a real stream, not just a seasonal wash in a dry canyon.) Later, she and her husband bought a ranch across the river from her parents. Yes, she says, she knew the dinosaur track site very well. It was the ford they all used to cross the river until the bridge was built down by Higbee. When was that, I ask her. She looks thoughtful and closes her eyes, and I wonder whether she is revisiting scenes of the construction work or memories of earlier river crossings, as she works to recover the date. She opens her eyes. "It must have been about 1918," she says. It's only now I realize she's even older than I think.

"And, if I may ask, when were you born?" I ask.

"1912." She smiles. "We called it Rock Crossing," she continues; it was the reliable ford, except for times of very high water. "That was the way we always came in to town," she explains. "My dad always called those the Elephant Tracks."

She tells me a bit more about Higbee. It had a hotel, a garage adjacent to a dance hall, a general store. There were about six families in the town (this explains, I think, how tiny the school is). I ask whether it was just a grade school, or whether they went to high school there as well.

"Well," she says, tilting her head slightly, for this is a noteworthy detail. "I went to St. Scholastica Academy in Kansas City."

Five, six hundred miles away, a big-city boarding school for a young rural woman in the 1920s. I think, they must have had some money; more importantly, education was something her family valued. They drove her there, a two- or three-day trip, most likely, and then returned to pick her up for vacations. Yes, she said, you could take the train back then, but her parents made the trip by car. I'm beginning to realize that the woman sitting beside me, white-haired and well-postured, has had a life remarkable as well as long. I don't know enough to know what I should want to ask her, what I should glean from the near-century of her life. She's just a little younger than my grandparents would have been, rural Oklahoma people—my grandfather walked across France in World War I and came home to marry my grandmother the day after she turned sixteen. Mrs. Autry married an Oklahoma man at age eighteen, in 1930, just in time for the Depression. Oh, yes, she tells me, she remembers dust storms in the valley.

"Sometimes people would wet material and put it over the windows, to keep out the dust, but we never did that." The storms in Otero County weren't as severe as those farther south, around the town of Kim. There, she says, lots of people lost their fields, but "It wasn't that bad here," since this was ranch land and hadn't been plowed up for wheat. Much later, in 1948, Mrs. Autry moved in to La Junta, so that her children—five daughters and two sons—could attend high school in town. "We stayed in town throughout the week, and then went and worked on the ranch on weekends." Only in the 1980s, after her husband's death, did she sell their ranch out in the canyon country just south of the Purgatoire.

Later, back home, I study again the maps of wind erosion and review the records of the relief efforts. By the mid-thirties, cattle were starving and suffocating throughout the region; in eastern Colorado rainfall was 45 percent below normal. "The government paid us a dollar a head," Mrs. Autry said of their cattle, "and took them all up and shot them." Her language suggests the emotional damage of the experience; the animals weren't "put down," or some other euphemism. This was destruction, not even a full step ahead of environmental and economic collapse. The Emergency Cattle Purchase Program eventually spent over one and a half million dollars in Colorado. By the decade's end, National Grasslands were trying to reclaim the failed wheat fields from blowout and drift. I think, they lost the cattle, but they kept, and kept on, the land. It could, of course, have turned out differently.

Nothing is left of the town where her grandmother grew up. I'd been imagining the place as a rural community, spread out along the Higbee Road, but she said that's not right: the town and its few businesses were clustered right on Highway 109, before you reach the bridge across the Purgatoire. An obelisk now stands near the road, erected of local stone and holding an iron plaque commemorating the centennial of the founding and listing the male settlers: Higbee, Smith, Richards, Jones, Elkins, Carson, Nelson. The memorial is set behind a sturdy barbed-wire fence, so I have to use binoculars to make out the words. It looks as though the remnants of a picnic shelter stand behind it, but this is most emphatically private land, and even the horse in the next field is kept out, watching from behind another fence. "Did the town burn?" I asked Mrs. Autry. "Was there a fire?"

"No," she said. "They just tore it down."

As the cool, moist morning brightens slightly, I've descended maybe two hundred feet into Vogel Canyon, and, even at noon, a still time of the day, it is full of birds. In shady places the earth is still damp from yesterday's heavy rain, and in the willows along the wash I can see how high flash floodwaters can race, lacing grass and dead branches like remnants of fencing two or three feet above the ground. A few pools linger here, and frog song joins bird call to fill the canyon's intimate space with aural ephemera. This has been an easy hike, and my malingering foot, shod in sturdy boots, hasn't registered any complaints.

Of course, the easy trail means the place is quite accessible, and even though no one else is visible, there are fresh footprints, boot tracks laid down since yesterday's cloudbursts. Along the northern wall, several overhangs shelter rock art, though a few spots are badly damaged by vandalism. "Danny R.L. 6/12/04" smirks in black marker. Several round scars in sandstone show where someone has shot at the cliff, and I wonder, spitefully, if the bullets ever ricochet to hit the Dannys or Dicks in the face. Still, beneath the contemporary trash, one can see a few carved human forms, and two figures that resemble birdmen, with curved, birdlike heads and torsos that look like crooked wings resting atop tall, stick-figure legs. Zigzag lines like snake tracks in sandy soil. Circles. A rectangular shape with vertical bars is high on a cliff marked with vertical streaks of whitewash from some bird's perch, a marvelous conjunction of form and formalism.

From the rim to canyon floor and back, I make a quick list of the day's bird sightings: a female Say's phoebe, feeding her nest of young; an ash-throated flycatcher; pinyon jays nattering in the trees; two prairie falcons coasting over the cliff top; a canyon wren at the deep, still spring against the cliff; mockingbirds, lark sparrows, western kingbirds. Descendants of dinosaurs, moving quickly through the overcast light and shadows of rock.

And among the petroglyphs are three-toed footprints, carved like crane or turkey feet. Smaller than my hand, if my hand could reach that high, they're aligned in perfect verticality. They hang in the abstract plane of vision; they seem to lead nowhere. They're time darkened, marked with the desert patina that shows long exposure to bright sun and dry air. They could be allosaur feet, stepping up toward the land long since eroded from above, or toward the distant matter of the stars. "The path up and down is one and the same," said Heraclitus, even though the journey back is always a different unfolding of moments, just as other and other waters flow on. A kestrel lands on the cliff above the spring and turns to watch me watch him, while I stand still as the sun moves past noon, on a day in late June that is just barely perceptibly shorter than the one before, while, beyond these near cliffs, the river moves silt toward the east, and while the phoebe, relieved that I'm no longer trying to find her nest, flips her wings, deposits a bug, and moves off—all of us caught in the day's stride of becoming and disappearing.

The Shannon Creek Eagles

Topography displays no favorites; North's as near as West.
More delicate than the historians' are the map-makers'
colors.

Elizabeth Bishop

I.

Maps preserve for us a schematic of the useful, of the significant. From the careful rendering my brother once made of an intersection in Bellingham, with each street bending like an arm of Shiva in a confusion of possible directions, to the topo quad I'll carry, sheathed in plastic, as we hike the back county of the Cascades next August, a map encodes what is in terms of what is *needful* information. Some, of course, are transient, the quick scrawl on scrap paper, showing the way to the library, or the store, or the nearest ATM. But maps can be beautiful, reverent, conveying aesthetic delight. I'm always pleased—and a bit surprised—to walk into a room and find one on the wall, both totemic and decorative. "Legends," we call the explanatory codes accompanying our maps; the word suggests the mythic, narrative power inherent in a place that has been traveled through enough—even if only once!—for one to chart.

If an eagle were to map the landscape—imagine for a minute that one would—what kind of image would emerge? I know, this is a flight of fancy, full of wild conjecture, but that's part of the attraction. Eagles have great visual acuity, they're long lived and rather intelligent birds, so setting aside for the moment their probable poor skills in draftsmanship, let's try to intuit what would matter, what would figure, if an eagle laid out a clean, clear rendering of the world below.

First, the scrawl, the hasty draft of the neighborhood. It's springtime, breeding season, so the focal point will be the *nest site*. Immediately surrounding the nest and its supportive tree, the *breeding territory* stretches, defined space that the parents will defend against intruders. Beyond the *territory* extends the *home range*, habitat the birds will frequent, but not defend, in their search for food. Some eagles migrate seasonally, so there may be flyways as connectors between the summer's home range and the wintering grounds. Winter habitat requires open water, sheltered perching and roosting locations—again, tall trees, the former near the water, which is, of course, the source of food. Others remain throughout the year in the same general area; for them the *communal winter perch* may be within the home range. All these must figure in the conceptual world of the eagle.

Maps sometimes display "historic range," or "former range," in contrast to "current range" a juxtaposition that reveals wildlife's disappearance from the land. Here the maps mark memories, little color-floods or hatch-mark patterns that depict shadows of former being cast across the page. *That was then,* they gesture; *this is now.* Although once bald eagles nested in nearly all the contiguous forty-eight states (excepting, records suggest, only Rhode Island and Vermont), by the early 1980s they bred in only thirty-one, and the prairie regions were not among these. North and South Dakota, Nebraska, Kansas— these four states are a thick blank stripe on the map from that decade I have open on my desk, with Oklahoma following right behind, home to fewer than a dozen breeding pairs. Because of the many large reservoirs sprawled along Great Plains rivers, birds sometimes gathered to winter near the open water—as they still do at the River Pond area on the Big Blue, only half a dozen miles from my house—but breeding eagles had been extirpated from this, their homeland. Hunting, habitat destruction, and poisoning; these signatures of civilization emptied the former range of their white-headed habitants. By nature, I'm a melancholy sort, given to thoughts of loss and diminishment, and so I worry over these disappearances. As I enter middle age and survey the years I've spent making this prairie landscape home, what I've done and how I've failed, I feel this urge to chart out what I've seen and learned about the lifeways of the prairie landscape. Today I'm drawn to the totemic power of eagles, the charismatic splendor of their bodies perched in stately patience, or the muscled flight as they pass by, intent on arriving somewhere.

So I've been reading. Armchair naturalist, books spread across the desk and floor, I've learned that in the early years of white settlement they likely nested along the major prairie river waterways of the state. In May of 1843, Audubon sighted nesting pairs near the Missouri River, between the present towns of Kansas City and St. Joseph, Missouri. It would have been a sinuous, meandering landscape then, with numerous creeks and smaller rivers joining the Missouri, and the land is still marked with old crescent lakes and wetlands from former channels, though as a metropolitan area surrounded with agriculture, the topography has greatly changed, with marshes drained and water channels straightened behind flood control levies. A decade after Audubon's journey through the region, the current town site of Lecompton was initially named for the bird. Two explorers, D. Rodrigue and A. G. Boone, moving through the Kansas River valley in 1854—a time when early Kansas settlement was linked to the national struggle over slavery—saw an eagle leave its nest in a large sycamore tree and named the place Bald Eagle, though the name was soon changed. Tiny Lecompton, home today to fewer than seven hundred residents, was once the political center for proslavery forces in Kansas Territory: from 1855 to 1857 it was the seat of the "bogus legislature," the site of the drafting of the Lecompton Constitution, which would have guaranteed slavery, until the constitution's defeat in 1857. At one point during the "bleeding Kansas" period of unrest and struggle, the town's population swelled to five thousand. Writing a history of its early years, in 1934 M. F. Sherar recalled that "many bald eagles rested on several immense sycamore trees, some on the south and some on the north, and here they made their home and raised their young until Lecompton took on city airs and some wanton creature shot them."

The map I want to shape today, the one I'm trying to cajole you into imagining with me, reverses—or corrects—that sad schematic of former and current range, for bald eagles have come back to breed in Kansas. In 1989 a pair first began to nest at Clinton Reservoir, roughly ninety minutes' drive east, and they've been returning ever since. I love this fact: that's the year I first arrived in Kansas, surprised to have found a job here, of all places, and determined to make a good life, to make a home. Throughout the state, seventeen active nests are now known, and more young birds are maturing in the region, likely to pair up and establish their own territories somewhere nearby. I'm becoming acquainted with a couple that has settled, so to speak, in my own home range, twenty miles north of town. For the second year in a row, this particular pair has been in residence along Shannon Creek, on Tuttle Creek Reservoir; this is the second spring I've come, periodically, to gaze across a field and watch as they rear their young.

II.

They could hardly have picked a more propitious place. Here, where their huge nest presides, Shannon Creek curves toward the reservoir, with riparian woods abutting the floodplain, seasonal mud flats and wetlands, and agricultural fields and fallow meadow. A line of tall, dead trees marks where the impounded waters rose in the last epic flood, in 1993, and left the standing dead like lakeshore sentries. Nesting trees, high, strong branches for perching, more sheltered trees for roosts—all these are within easy travel to the lake and its supply of fish and fowl.

Best of all, they're on federal land. Elsewhere, in the more populous East, people have destroyed nests and nest trees in an attempt to keep the birds from establishing themselves in areas slated for development. In Florida, a developer is said to have urged a construction worker to bulldoze a nest tree; despite the obvious gash in the trunk and the calm, still weather at the time, he later suggested the wind must have blown it down. Also in Florida, a nest tree was mysteriously felled with a chainsaw just days before the eggs were due to hatch. But this lakeside habitat is held by the U.S. Army Corps of Engineers and leased to the Kansas Department of Wildlife and Parks, who quickly set up barrier tape and assigned U.S. Fish and Wildlife biologists and rangers to protect the birds from molestation. When I first arrive, markers are clearly in place warning against trespassers; we must set up spotting scopes in the gravel road and focus clear across a field. Even from behind this buffer of distance, the sitting eagle knows she's being watched. She stares intently back, gaze focused, it seems, right through the scope itself to where I stoop to see. This is a little unnerving, like the moment in the Rilke poem where the statue turns to regard—and judge—the viewer. In the translation: "You must change your life." But that's what I'm here for already, really, to change myself through what I take the time to see; I want my chosen home range to mark me, make me richer for having crossed and recrossed its intimate topography. For having stayed here long enough to see this change, and count it as a blessing.

The route there takes me along gorgeous upland prairie country. I drive north of town along Highway 13 and head east across the dam, then north again where 13 parallels Cedar Creek. Then west and north along Carnahan Road, past land that was once considered for federal acquisition as a national park, though communication with the landowner wasn't handled well. According to the story I've heard, when Stuart Udall stepped out of a helicopter on the upland hills, he was met by a rancher with a gun and told to leave. Not far from there is the old Carnahan community church, where one fiercely sweltering July day I sat and watched two of my graduate students get married, the bride flushing crimson from the neckline of her gown, up along her chest and throat, into her face, until finally she stood sobbing, briefly, from the heat of her joy. The road continues north and east, crossing McIntyre Creek, where one winter a snowy owl fetched up, blown down from the north, and where it likely starved, not knowing how to hunt so far from tundra; past Otter Creek, where I glimpsed the only black squirrel I've seen in Kansas, though they're said to congregate in a city park in Marysville, near the Nebraska border; past Booth Creek and

Booth Creek Road, where a few years ago, when I was married, we considered buying a nineteenth-century farmhouse with a barn, a young orchard, and lots of land still carrying native grass. At last the road leaves Carnahan Creek and crosses Highway 16, to meet and follow Shannon Creek north to its entrance into the reservoir, the impounded waters of the Big Blue River.

Nesting eagles have rather specific site requirements, so rather than a simple "X", let's sketch a little legend to indicate something of the necessary texture or depth that the eagle pair would likely note. In all but truly treeless habitats (the desert Southwest, for example, where they build cliff nests), eagles nest in very tall trees. In woodlands they prefer old growth stands, where the most ancient trees tower over the lower canopy, and openings along lakes and rivers allow easy access by flight. Until recent years, the majority of successful breeding pairs resided in forested regions, and they showed a preference for white pine, Douglas fir, ponderosa pine, Sitka spruce, and lodgepole pine. These species, however, aren't exactly plentiful in prairie landscapes, and here deciduous trees of impressive size are favored. The Shannon Creek eagles have chosen a dead bur oak and built their nest in its high, dry, robust limbs. Again, I think it's a good choice: oak will last, maintaining its tensile strength long after the tree has died. In this, it's unlike cottonwood, another large tree that's much more common along these creeks and waterways. Most often, eagles nest in live trees, high up, but with a few live branches extending above the nest's wide ledge. I wonder whether this compromise—the tallest tree here is a deceased deciduous—should be noted. Perhaps a little icon denoting type of tree should accompany whatever we choose to indicate the nest itself. The bleached, bark-free trunk gleams like scoured bone, like sunlit limestone, lending itself to the human mind's desire for abstraction and delineation.

Eagles make the largest nests of any bird in North America. Very old ones—used repeatedly through consecutive seasons—can weigh as much as a car and measure the size of a small dorm room: 8½ X 8½ X 12 feet are the dimensions of a very old nest recorded in Ohio in the first quarter of the twentieth century. These structures become part of the landscape for other creatures: there are records of owls—especially great horneds—making use of abandoned eagle nests and sometimes nesting in the lower reaches of still-active aeries. There is even a single report of an eagle incubating the egg of a great horned owl in a nest in Florida. If undisturbed, bald eagles will return each year to such favored sites, each time rebuilding ramparts around the top, lining the nesting cup with grasses, moss, soft down. Arthur Cleveland Bent, writing in 1937, described a nest he found in the winter of 1924–1925, in Florida: "it rested on several branches and was made of large sticks and rubbish, with a lot of green and dry pine needles and Spanish moss in the flat top; in the center was a pretty little hollow, 20 inches in diameter and 4 or 5 inches deep, lined with the soft gray moss and small pine needles, in which the eggs were partially buried." Another that he found in 1911, in South Carolina, "was deeply lined in the center, up to the level top, with soft grasses, Spanish moss, and feathers." Some eagles top the edges of their nests with fresh leafy branches, "not for use as part of the structure or lining of the nest," Mark Stalmaster wrote in 1987, "but as a sort of decoration on top. The birds often replace the adornments in an apparent effort to maintain a green or fresh appearance." I suppose there could be an adaptive strategy at work here—bright, live leaves will indicate that the nest is active and intruders should look elsewhere—but I like the idea that "adornment" and "fresh appearance" might have aesthetic value for the birds. I imagine a kind of cross between architectural gargoyles warding off bad spirits and new wildflowers set about to brighten the home.

Some birds will build, and even maintain, second homes in the same territory, generally called *alternate nests*. This seems to be a different activity from that of wrens, for example, among whom the male offers his mate two different sites so she may make a selection (a sweet gesture, of which Chaucer's Wife of Bath would surely approve). Instead, eagles may, in alternate years, occupy one or the other of these nests; they may be keeping them at the ready, in case an egg clutch fails or a nest is destroyed by violent weather. They may simply treat them as ostentatious production, signaling that this particular territory is large and actively inhabited by vigorous and healthy birds. Dan Mulhern, a Fish and Wildlife biologist in Kansas, reports that a pair at Perry Reservoir, east and north of Topeka, are "more architecturally active than others" currently nesting in the state. These birds had three or four nests at the ready, all at once, and the biologists were kept guessing for some time which the pair would choose as home for the season. I tell this to my friend Dorian, who is amazed that she and her husband own two different houses, in two rather distant states. She sends me an e-mail describing her discomfort. "You can't nest in two different places, can you?" she writes. "Well, actually . . ." I begin, smiling as I type. The birds at Shannon Creek don't seem to have any alternate nests, however. Perhaps they're young, just starting out—this is only their second year of active breeding here, after all. And, so far, there isn't any competition, no need to display their effective presence to would-be interlopers. One spring day we spy a juvenile bird soaring nearby, perhaps an adolescent from last year's brood, but no other adults seem interested in challenging this pair.

It isn't known which bird actually chooses each nesting site—the male or the female. In 1932, Francis H. Herrick recorded a female who lost two mates, and each time found a new one while overwintering at communal feeding grounds. In each instance, the remarried widow brought the new male to her previous territory. Over fifty years later, two other scientists observed females "defending territories and attempting to attract mates," so there's a good chance it is usually the female who chooses the location, though both sexes work together to construct the nest itself. Both sexes also incubate the eggs, though the female spends much more time doing so than her mate.

Also important features in site selection are good perches—generally tall, dead trees near to the nest, which afford an excellent view of the territory. Of these there are plenty for the Shannon Creek eagles, since a pale-bodied line of flood-killed trees defines the former highest reaches of the lake. On the hill behind the creek is a stand mostly of cedar, offering good roost sites for the night, with shelter from weather, though the brooding bird won't leave the nest in case of rain or springtime hail. She'll stay put, and slightly spread her wings to shelter the young beneath her.

III.

No one knows where these particular birds originated. Neither of the pair is banded, so we know they didn't fledge at any of the earlier active nests that have been monitored throughout the state. They are not, for example, offspring of the carefully observed pair that established themselves at the Clinton Reservoir on the Wakarusa River. That couple arrived in March of 1989 and were reported by two men who spotted the nest in a dead tree where Rock Creek joins the reservoir from the southwest. The birds have been breeding quite successfully ever since. They have a considerably higher-than-average number of three-chick nests, with ten of the past fifteen years producing three fledged eaglets; in three other years they fledged two, and twice they fledged only one. So far, they've successfully parented thirty-eight young, only four of whom are among the nine known mortalities of Kansas-born eagles. (One of these, at the age of two and a half, was shot—probably by "some wanton creature"—along the Verdigris River in Oklahoma. The cause of death of the other three is unknown, though their remains were found ranging from their natal Clinton Reservoir to the Elk River, two counties north of Oklahoma. One was also found in Garden City, Missouri, west and north of the Lake of the Ozarks region. Thus I've plotted, across the central plains, the mapped pattern, though not the meaning, of their deaths.)

The second-oldest (though not continually successful) nest in the state is a real anomaly for bald eagle behavior. It stands in western Kansas, above the subtle, buffy-colored shortgrass prairie of Hodgeman County (now largely converted to agriculture), and it was first noted in 1990, when the pair fledged one chick. Unlike all the other nest sites in Kansas, this one is not placed along a major river or lake; it's near a small, spring-fed pond, where the land more nearly resembles golden eagle habitat. The Hodgeman County eagles nested successfully, usually raising two chicks per year, until 1994, when a storm knocked the nest from the tree before that year's three chicks had fully fledged. While the three survived the season, in subsequent years the parents made no attempt to nest for seven or eight years, until they were again noticed on the nest. This year they are raising two chicks.

A very interesting pair is nesting on Hillsdale Reservoir, south and a little west of Kansas City. This pair's pedigree is very well known, as both are identifiable by leg bands. The male is from the first Clinton Reservoir nest of 1989. After he and his brother were fledged, they were both trapped by Mike Lockhart, a Fish and Wildlife biologist based at the time at Rocky Flats, Colorado, who came specifically to band and examine the young eagles. Since the birds had already left the nest, he used carrion as bait, with a female eagle decoy nearby in order to draw the youngsters' attention to the food. He tried this same method the subsequent year, but for the third group of fledglings, in 1991, he had to resort to a different technique, a fish bait snare. For this he slit a fish and stuffed it with Styrofoam so it would float, affixed two heavy-gauge loops of fish line, and waited, ready to tighten the snare, until the young birds landed on the bait. The whole enterprise must have meant lots of tedious waiting, even if, in the end, it was successful. Ever since, the biologists have sent climbers up into nesting trees in order to band the birds before they can fly, a process that takes a few hours at most, whereas live trapping can stretch over a period of several days.

The female of the Hillsdale pair hatched in the Sutton Avian Research Center in Bartlesville, Oklahoma, and she was fledged at a hacking tower in east central Oklahoma near the Eufaula Reservoir. This couple set a new record for successful parenting; they managed to breed earlier than usual for bald eagles. Sexual maturity is thought to coincide with adult feather plumage, which arrives in the fourth year. Frequently birds don't breed successfully until the fifth year, and the first year's eggs are often infertile, but in 1993 these young birds raised their first offspring, a single chick who fledged during late June. The male parent was four years old; the female was only three. They've been breeding ever since, consistently fledging two chicks every year.

From what I can tell, the return of eagles to Kansas has revealed the birds to be opportunistic and flexible not only in their feeding patterns, which is true of bald eagles in general, but also in establishing their lifeways. "Opportunistic" can have negative connotations, especially when talking about feeding habits. Carrion eating, prey stealing: these kinds of strategies earned the disdain of early naturalists, who claimed the bald eagle's character was weak, unworthy to be our national symbol. But Kansas eagles show a creativity, a kind of plucky adaptability, that I think is quite admirable. Here they are, thriving: the unusually young family at Hillsdale, the culturally different birds in Hodgeman County, the clever settlers at Shannon Creek.

In the national imagination, Kansas is known best, perhaps, for severe weather—those tornadoes you see on postcards in our highway gift shops, those memories of watching wind-whipped Dorothy, in grainy black-and-white, locked out of the storm cellar where the rest of her family has repaired to safety. Or from my own childhood, an ice-clad landscape glittering and sharp, mile after mile as my parents drove us through the state to visit relatives in Oklahoma. It's not surprising that rough weather has demolished eagle nests on occasion. The storm in Hodgeman County that knocked three eaglets to the ground seems to have discouraged the pair, as they made no attempt to nest again for several years, but they've now rebuilt and are again raising young out in the dryland plains. Similarly, a small tornado destroyed a nest at Norton Lake in 2001, killing two of the three just-banded fledglings, and the next year the parents made no attempt to nest again. But in time they may; over the years they've successfully fledged eleven young, and like the Hodgeman County birds, they may regain their confidence. This vulnerability to storm damage comes, ironically, from what I consider the birds' clever flexibility. Although most eagles prefer live trees for nesting, the majority of nests in Kansas are in snags near artificial reservoirs, trees killed when the waters were first impounded in the last half-century. This risky preference may change in future decades, as the dead trees rot and disappear. The most virulent period of dam construction seems to have passed. "Wild, scenic" rivers are again considered desirable, and eagles nesting along open river corridors in the state may select more traditional, live-tree nest sites.

These are cheering stories, in contrast to the pervasive narrative of habitat destruction, population crashes, extinctions. We're all familiar with the legacy of World War II's chemical warfare against the insects, and the plight of the bald eagle kept the shame of this history before our eyes, until finally in June 1972, the EPA banned the domestic use of DDT. But as one reads the details of eagle parenthood, these facts take on greater affective power. DDT and its metabolite, DDE, function insidiously within the body of the mother bird. Their effect, of course, is to disrupt calcium metabolism, preventing the calcium in the bird's bloodstream from laying down the necessary shell layer, resulting in eggs that, in some cases, are thin enough to see through and are doomed to break beneath the weight of the attentive brooding bird. It's easy, I think, to imagine the distress of the parents, whose assiduous presence on their nest would crush the very eggs they meant to shelter. If DDT poisoning is severe, no eggshell at all will form, only a flexible membrane, and the disastrous emergence of eggs-without-eggshells must have seemed surreal and devastating to a nesting pair. I picture them calling, their piteous chirps, and moving to the alternate nest, only to be met again with failure. Konrad Lorenz, after years of his studies with graylag geese, assures us that birds are quite emotional beings—persons, as he says. I don't know whether birds dream, but it is not difficult to believe they found their lives, in the heightened, quickening season of breeding, nightmarish and desperate.

IV.

On a clear, warm day in mid-May, with puffy clouds overhead and temperatures at about eighty degrees, the Fish and Wildlife team head out to Shannon Creek to band this year's young. It is a happy outing, unlike, I imagine, the last years of Charles Broley's grim documentation of eagle extirpation in Florida. From 1939 to 1959, he spent the winter nesting season traveling the state, climbing tall trees and banding eaglets. From 1946 to 1958, the number of young he found to band dropped from 150 to only 2; in the latter year, he wrote in *Audubon* magazine that he was certain "that about 80 percent of the Florida bald eagles are sterile." From the first heady years, in his early retirement, when he decided not to entrust the task to local boys and instead ascended by himself to those aeries, until his death in a grass fire in 1959, he watched the dramatic diminution of eagles.

But this team, as it assembles, is cheerful and confident. Two biologists meet with others from the Army Corps of Engineers in the small parking lot at the Corps headquarters by Tuttle

Creek Reservoir's dam, to carpool and caravan up to Shannon Creek. The scientists joke and chat among themselves, talking about the orphaned baby bobcat that seems to have imprinted on Pat, a biologist stationed at the Milford Reservoir west of Manhattan, and they swap stories about misidentified "eagles" that people have claimed to see—vultures and hawks, mostly. Then Joel and Cheri Brinker arrive; they're the climbing specialists in this operation. Joel owns a tree-care business in town and has participated in a number of interesting projects over the years, including trimming the historic Louis Vieux Elm— a national champion tree at the time—when it was struck by lightning several years ago.

In a variety of vehicles—some state-owned pickups, a late-model station wagon packed with climbing equipment, an SUV—we head out. From Shannon Creek Road we pull into a gravel road along the wildlife area in the lake's flood plain, and then bounce across a fallow field to park a short distance from the tree. As we exit the cars, one of the parents circles overhead, calling its weak-voiced complaint. I think briefly that if this were a television commercial—extolling the toughness of the trucks, or the flexibility of the SUV, say—the producers would surely insist on dubbing in a red-tailed hawk's call, since the eagle's cry is pretty unimpressive. Arthur Cleveland Bent is even more emphatic on the topic of the eagle's call. He declares, "The voice of the bald eagle seems to me to be ridiculously weak and insignificant, more of a squeal than a scream, quite unbecoming a bird of its size and strength." (Bent was also among those who believed the bird's behavior was ungentlemanly and ignoble. William Bartram thought the same. He called the bird "an execrable tyrant," saying, "he supports his assumed dignity and grandeur by rapine and violence.") But on this spring day, in the clear, softening light of late afternoon, I find the scene touching and affecting. The parent—the assumption seems to be that it's most likely the female—loops around the nest tree and a nearby perching tree with her powerful, slow flight, crying out in distress. As she passes nearby, the thick curve of her bill and the brilliance of her head feathers mark the moment with her wildness, while her voice endears her, hinting at what seems surely to be emotional vulnerability.

By now several people have joined us. A large family, landowners from across the road, have ambled across the open field, chatting interestedly among themselves and greeting the scientists. Again, I think how this is in marked contrast to the attitude one reads of in the arid high plains, where ranchers and wool-growers poison and shoot eagles (mostly golden, but also bald), calling them, Bruce Bean writes in 1996, "damn government crows," and where wildlife officials working to protect the birds receive threats of violence. Here, a friendly, relaxed group of observers mill about the vehicles while the biologists take their equipment to set up in a hemlock thicket at the tree's base, and the climber readies for his ascent. A lithe and wiry man, he pulls on a helmet and some climbing gear, and sets purposefully to work.

First, he shoots a lead line high into the tree with a very large slingshot. This is not immediately successful: once or twice the weighted end wraps itself around a branch and must be carefully unwound, the way I've sometimes coaxed the line back down after an unsuccessful attempt to place a bear bag while backpacking. A couple of shots are too low, reaching a limb that doesn't appear sturdy enough. On the fifth shot, the line is just where Joel wants it, and he ties the heavy, climbing rope to the lead and pulls it up and over. Then quickly, athletically, he pulls himself up a distance of perhaps seventy feet, and stands on the branch just below the nest. He looks wiry and atavistic, a man ascended high into the trees.

The eaglets peer at him over the edge. They are clearly visible, even without binoculars, and they look curious and alert while Joel examines various spots to clip himself to the nest in order to make that last ascent. When he actually takes hold of the nest and prepares to enter, however, the nearest bird spreads wings in a threat display and hisses with an open bill, while Joel speaks softly and calmly about his intentions to join them there. I can't hear what he's saying, only that he's talking to the birds, engaging them soothingly, and then in a quick, smooth movement, he is inside. Neither bird has leapt from the nest, and that's exactly what the team has hoped. They need to time these procedures carefully, waiting until the chicks are six weeks old, so their legs are adult sized and ready for the band, but much beyond that the birds are likely to try to fly, even if they're not quite ready.

"If they're not far from fledging," Dan explains, "they'll bail out of the nest." One year at Glen Elder Reservoir, the team had their timing off by a few days, and a young eaglet jumped out of the nest and glided neatly—and, for him, probably giddily—down to the water's surface, where the biologists reached him with their boat and easily scooped him up. Learning to take off from a tall thicket of hemlock or other undergrowth wouldn't be ideal for the eaglets, so "bailing out" is to be avoided. "This looks good," Dan says. "These birds are right at six weeks—we think the first hatch date was April 2." Incubation is usually thirty-five days, so these eggs must have been laid in late February, while the landscape around the lake was anything but springlike.

I look through my binoculars at the helmeted, fair-haired tree surgeon sitting in the nest with the two eaglets. He shows them his gloved hands; he shows them the cloth bag in which they'll be lowered to the scientists below. He's still talking to them, and I wish I could hear what he was saying. Without too much trouble, as it looks to us below, he gets one bagged and lowers it slowly, and then we are all permitted to come closer, to watch the biologists band and measure the birds, one by one. I look around for the parent, realizing I haven't heard her for a while, but she doesn't seem to be in sight.

The first bird is declared to be a female, based on her wing and other body measurements. Female eagles are larger than their mates. She is banded eaglet 7A, and Mike, who holds her while Dan applies the band, asks if any of us would like to touch the bird. I hadn't thought I'd actually be touching the eaglets, nor sitting on a dead log splashed with whitewash right beneath the massive nest. We crossed the open ground and came into such close conjunction with these wild, returning lives, and I'm still a little breathless with the unlikeliness of it all.

I reach out and stroke the bird. Her flight feathers are smooth and dark, while her chest is covered with very soft, gray, downy feathers that look quite ashen and scruffy, almost curly. The top of her head has rough, white-tipped feathers, fuzzy to touch. She watches Mike, watches me, with bright, alert eyes, but she seems calm and unafraid. She was the one who earlier tried to scare Joel away with her spread-winged threat posture; now she blinks and gazes at the people watching her so intently. I want to name her, call her something more familiar and personal than 7A, but I feel a flush of foolishness, as though I'd frame her in cliché or caricature. Throughout my thinking about eagles, I've felt pulled between conflicting diction—the passive-voiced and understated language of survey and study, masking in dispassion the scientists' eager attention to the charismatic birds, and the personifying admiration and delight I feel (we all feel today, surely) for the individuals who embody each statistic, here before our eyes. I shift back and forth, like someone standing with weight on one leg, then the other, trying not to fidget so much that I'll scare the birds away.

Then, after several of us have touched the eaglet and returned to our positions around the study group's periphery, she is hoisted back to the nest, and her sibling is lowered. He is a male, slightly smaller, but the scientists believe he is a couple of days older, rendering the size difference less pronounced than it would have been if his sister had hatched first. From above, Joel reports what the birds have been feeding on.

"Turtles," he calls down. "Lots of turtle shells. And they've been eating drum." And then he asks us to step away so he can rappel down from the high aerie.

I've never heard local fish called drum, but that is Joel's report, and the biologists and I duly note it down. I've shifted weight once more, I realize, and in the scrutiny of my attention the individual diet of these birds merges into the pattern typical for lakeshore diets: bald eagles eat a lot of fish. They scavenge dead fish, steal fish from ospreys (raptors still sometimes called "fish hawks"), and catch their own if no ospreys are around to maraud. When I ask, Dan tells me that these birds are remarkably "clean," based on some blood analysis. They don't appear to be plagued with PCB or heavy metal poisoning like many birds who nest around the Great Lakes in the upper Midwest. Banders in Michigan have found deformed eaglets with crossed bills and club feet, and a wildlife health clinic in Michigan names the poisoned birds it receives after rock stars dead of drug overdoses. The Great Lakes eagles, of course, do not in-dulge in recreational drug use; instead, as the chemical poisons move through the food chain, stored in animals' fat tissues, they biomagnify, or concentrate the contamination level. The eagles, in a symbolic irony, are at the top of this rising spiral. Unlike the waters farther north, our reservoirs are plagued with agricultural runoff, not residue from heavy industry, and I worry about the potential effects of atrazine, a herbicide that concentrates in the reservoir periodically, according to the growing season. It's a weed-killer that is known to cause sexual deformities in frogs and prostate cancer in humans, but as we can see, the Shannon Creek pair are breeding just fine.

The Kansas scientists were especially interested in the diet of the Hodgeman County eagles, and their written reports list a great variety of food: common carp, bullhead, unidentified catfish, green-winged teal, American coot, great blue heron, ring-necked pheasant, red-tailed hawk, black-tailed prairie dog, yellow-faced pocket gopher, black-tailed jackrabbit, eastern cottontail. The published article included Linnaean nomenclature, but I think the common names show plenty of specificity: red-of-tail and yellow-of-face.

V.

By mid-November, the sun has decreased its angle in the sky and slants across the landscape. Places grow more intimate, I think, in this winter light; shadows cast lengtheningly across the land, even in bright, mid-afternoon sunlight, while the sky hangs blue and golden like a breath held before exhaling. It has been a bleak week, and it ends abruptly with news that an acquaintance—a bright, friendly woman, and an occasional dinner guest in my home—has been found dead in her rural house, the victim of a murder. Brutal, wanton. And as yet unexplained, though her ex-husband, a colleague of mine, has been picked up for questioning. We don't know it yet, but in the next two years, he'll be convicted, the dark shadow of the murder laid at his feet. But now, it's all uncertainty, the recoil of shock and disbelief.

Today, though work and its confining cares have kept me indoors for most of the autumn, I suddenly feel I have to have wind in my face, and so Dave and I head east to the lake. We park well below the dam, and stroll through the woods that mark the former river flow. In the mild air, a few trees still hold leaves, fading into yellowed green, and cormorants sun themselves on snags out in the placid water. Great mounds of gravel line the path, in preparation for new campground development. Next year, or the next, these relict riparian woods will be gone, carved and whittled into RV sites. The day is breezy, cool, but bright, and my body moves across this managed landscape feeling anemic and incredulous.

When we reach the shore, we scan the sandy margin—the old riverbank—where once Dave found a perfect, Paleo-Indian spear point. I see feathers, bits of shell and driftwood, smooth wet sand. We scare up a couple of wood ducks. Lifting my gaze, I search the trees for perching eagles, though it may be a few weeks before they begin to gather for the winter. Instead, I find a fine, dark, chocolate-colored hawk, a dark-phase redtail, sitting calmly in a tree. It watches us intently, though it never tenses toward flight.

But then, wheeling slowly from beyond the dam, I see another large bird. It's an eagle, a juvenile, brown underneath with patchy flecks of white, like snow fallen on raw, open ground. It circles, slowly, while we watch, and I am sure it must be one of the two fledged up north of the lake, near Shannon Creek. My lungs keep breathing in the November air, my eyes follow the eagle's flight overhead. The bird is joined in the sky above our heads by an adult, head and tail brilliant in the sun, and we sit together on a fallen log, watching the air above, the lake below, all poised for further change and flux. Whether we will it, plan it, brace ourselves against it, or find ourselves suddenly surrounded by it, here is change. And what does it feel like? As yet, we can hardly tell.

Bones of Fear

There's a photograph by Kevin Carter I can't shake from memory, part of the traveling Pulitzer Prize–winning exhibit from a few years ago. The scene is drought-stricken Africa, Sudan, 1994; a young child, robbed of any specific age by emaciation, can no longer hold up her—or his—heavy head and lies folded on the ground, face down. Her legs are tiny, bent twigs instead of flesh. She seems to wear a white necklace of some sort, but nothing else. The viewer—me, you, millions of us—can tell that the child is near death; so, too, can a vulture that is standing nearby, waiting for a meal that it knows cannot be long off. Its posture seems alert and just tensed, as if it is about to take a hop closer, then another.

This image is one that comes to mind when I think the word *vulture*. It gives the imagination a terrible shiver, the premonition of personal disappearance. It is the sublime in its most terrible form, without a single hint of beauty mixed in. But there are less horrifying thoughts of vultures. I've seen them roost together in Appalachia, in winter, far, far, from the world of drought or famine, where they fill a leafless oak tree with their dark, companionable forms. Where I live in Kansas, the birds leave for the winter, and their return to the skies each spring makes nearly visible the air's thermals lifting from the sun-warmed earth. They soar like our dreams of flight, perfect in their lofted gliding, searching for opportunity.

I'm thinking of vultures because I'm thinking of condors. And I'm thinking of condors because I'm thinking of teratorns, enormous birds of the Americas, that, like so many of the larger animals of the Pleistocene, did not survive to join us in the current age. The remains of more than a hundred individuals have been found in the archival tar pits at La Brea, California, and several subspecies must have ranged through time and place before there were any humans around to look upward in word-sputtering wonder. Perhaps the largest of these was one found in Argentina, with a wingspan of about twenty-three feet. Twenty-three feet: that's the distance from my bedroom to the kitchen, as I disbelievingly pace out the hallway's unprotecting length. Other fossils have been found from Brazil to Oregon; the leg bone of one found in the Willamette River Valley was so robust that it was reportedly mistaken at first for that of an elk. The most commonly found subspecies, *Teratornis merriami*, wasn't quite such a giant, but its wingspan of twelve feet is still an amazement. The shadow it must have cast as it landed to feed, or the flap and swoosh as it lifted, heavily, into flight! It must have been a thunderous bird, a thunderbird.

Teratorns were close relatives of storks and vultures, and are sometimes considered the ancestors of condors. The Pleistocene landscape, with its ground sloths, mammoths, mastodons, giant beavers, and other large mammals who lived their distant lives and died, must have sometimes reeked with substantial carrion. A huge condor could make a good living in such an animate world. But some researchers think that at least a few subspecies may have been only occasional, opportunistic scavengers. Because their bills were more like those of eagles and their legs were longer than those of modern condors, they may have taken live prey, even stalking and pursuing it on the ground. The thought of it makes me feel shrinkingly vulnerable as I think of the few times in my life that a bird of significant size has flown unexpectedly near, so I could hear the sound of the wing beats, the feathers in the air just overhead—pelicans, sandhill cranes, once, even, as I stood blinking in Rhone Delta sunlight and the remains of jet lag, a stork in southern France, heading to its bristling stick nest and four young. I imagine a great bird swooping overhead as I work outdoors—turning the compost, say, or picking herbs from the tiny garden out front.

Or, far from home, as I rest in a long walk from somewhere to somewhere else.

Throughout the Pleistocene, and even back to the world before, the Miocene, the great birds roamed over these continents, falling occasionally into mud or other suitable substrate, then becoming birds of the ground only, utterly still. *Teratornis merriami* presumably disappeared from the skies over the Americas some eight thousand to ten thousand years ago, though some researchers speculate that, like the twentieth-century California condor, isolated populations might have held on in Mexico and the American Southwest into even more recent times. We can begin to imagine their presence with a snippet of written history: During the Corps of Discovery expedition, William Clark once spotted a California condor near what the men called Cape Disappointment, eating the carcass of a whale. Or we can turn to the realm of oral history: The Jicarilla Apache, in the late nineteenth century, told ethnographers about Giant Eagle, a fearsome bird that came from the sky to carry people away to its enormous nest. A young boy managed to kill it through archery skill and careful cunning. At the time, the Apache storytellers referred to an astonishingly large wing kept at Taos Pueblo, the presence of which, they insisted, was clear proof of the story's truth. I wonder what became of that talisman, exhibit, reliquary. Folklorist Adrienne Mayor points out that remains of raptors from the end of the Pleistocene have, indeed, been found in desert caves in the Southwest, and she describes a petroglyph that depicts a giant bird standing erect and holding what looks like a human figure, waving little stick arms and legs in an effort to break free. Perhaps in concordance with the Jicarilla tale, the image shows a scattering of dots near the bird's feet—eggs, she suggests, from the aerial predator's bone-strewn nests? If so, they're images of the unborn and extinct—a visual representation of life unbegun and uncontinued.

In the 1930s, the local people of Charcos, Mexico, would sometimes grind up fossilized bones—they called them *huesos de espanto*, or "bones of fear"—to boil together with special plants. The resulting potion was said to protect against fright and panic—from the bones of monsters and the flourishing earth would come extrahuman courage. In a modern lab, the bones were examined and determined to be mastodon, truly monsters from another age. Farther north, the Navajo spoke of Giant Vulture, who proclaimed, "Whenever Monsters are killed and decay, we . . . will be present as scavengers." The great creatures of the last era were plenty large to cast their shadows deep, deep, within the psyche, to feather forth in cultural tale and image, figure and form. Alexander von Humboldt wrote, after seeing images of what appeared to be mastodons in the twelfth- or thirteen-century Codex Borgia: "Did their traditions reach back to the time when America was still inhabited by these gigantic animals, whose petrified skeletons are [today] found buried?"

This is the very question I keep tracking, across landscapes and literature, and I think the answer must be yes. Some of the tales of water monsters and thunderbirds surely incorporate the real, physical presence of great birds of the world, not merely great creations of the imagination. Steve Mizrach claims that the thunderbird is a true cross-cultural element of Native American mythology, at least across North America. In this, it may be supposed, I think, to function like those DNA markers, tiny mutations in the great double helix of the genome, that date human arrival at one continent or another: Africa to South Asia, to Australia; Africa to the Levant, to Europe. And, sometime, though precisely when still eludes us, even farther, to the Americas. In this metaphor, I take symbol, or mythic figure, as a marker of the cultural journey into the world of figuration, of representation and understanding. But, as with any symbol, I am certain that it has its feet somewhere in the dirt, in the palpable, phenomenal, world. *The natural object is always the adequate symbol.*

In the mid-eighteenth century, a French missionary named Father de Charlevoix learned a tale about Great Elk, a story the Abenaki living east of the Great Lakes told about ancient times. Great Elk (whom the Iroquois knew as Big Elk) was tall enough to stride through the tremendous, eight-foot snowdrifts of the Canadian winters, and its hide was extraordinarily tough. He had "a peculiar, prehensile 'extra arm' extending from its upper body," which, Adrienne Mayor says, "sounds decidedly elephantine." There are a number of these legends from tribal peoples that lift imagistic hints of megafauna from the world before: Huron people told of a monster that had a horn so hard it could puncture even solid stone. From the Algonquins they could—by trading, I suppose, though I don't have any idea what would be an appropriate barter price—sometimes get pieces of it, with its supernatural power. The Creek people made amulets of horn from strange creatures that lurked in bogs or watering holes, and the mound-building cultures, like the Adena of the Ohio Valley, included fossilized morsels of mammoth ivory in the great burial mounds they built in their deciduous homeland. The Cherokees, from farther south, called the Ohio Valley Ukténa, "the land of the horned water monsters"—huge beasts that were enemies of Tlanuhwa, the mythic thunderbirds of the Tennessee River. And an elderly chief, either Wyandot or Iroquois—his identity lost through the imprecision of written history—told the Irish trader George Morgan in the 1760s about the Great Buffalo, terrifying animals that attacked the people until the Great Spirit killed them all with lighting and thunder, leaving only their bones gathered about the sulfur springs at Big Bone Lick, just south of the Ohio River—the very bones that eighteenth-century Europeans and colonists collected with enthusiastic wonder, shipping the specimens off to Philadelphia, London, and Paris. All the beasts were destroyed, said the chief, except for one pair, which were both "shut up in yonder mountain, ready to let loose again should the occasion require." Thomas Jefferson, in *Notes on the State of Virginia*, recounted a Delaware legend about "tremendous animals [that] came to the Bigbone licks, and began an universal destruction of the bear, deer, elks, buffaloes, and other animals" on whom the people depended. Again, divine intervention in the form of lightning bolts destroyed the monstrous herd, "except the big bull . . . [who] bounded over the Ohio, over the Wabash, the Illinois, and finally over the great lakes, where he is living at this day."

Jefferson loved this story, as do I. I imagine him at Monticello, or, later, in the fledgling capital, corresponding with the other renaissance men of the age, wondering about the marvels yet undiscovered farther west. He'd be seated at a handsome wooden desk or table, unfurling line after line of elegant, now nearly alien script, arguing, inquiring, speculating. He wrote in 1799: "In the present interior of our continent there is surely space and range enough for elephants and lions, if in that climate they could subsist, and for mammoths. . . . Our entire ignorance of the immense country to the West and Northwest, and of its contents, does not authorise us to say what it does not contain." So he wrote urgently, hopefully, to Lewis and Clark, directing them to be on the watch for these animals throughout their expedition. When the Corps returned without having seen mammoths in the West, he had both men (at his own expense—not the young government's) collect bones from the Lick along the Ohio River.

For nearly half a century, the site had been easily found by interested explorers. In October 1786, General Samuel Parsons described it as "a resort of all species of beast in that country. A stream of brackish water runs through the land, which is soft clay." In May 1765, George Croghan described "a fine timbered clear wood. We came to a large road which the Buffaloes have beaten, spacious enough for two waggons to go abreast, and heading straight into the Lick." In 1766, Captain Harry Gordon wrote, "The beaten Roads from all quarters to it easily conducted us, they resemble those to an Inland Village where Cattle go to and fro a large Common. . . . [The] Mud being of a Salty Quality is greedily lick'd by Buffaloe, Elk, and Deer, who come from distant parts, in great Numbers for this purpose."

Yet by the early nineteenth century, many of the bones were already gone, collected by various explorers and entrepreneurs. Clark wrote regretfully to Jefferson in 1807, "The Lick has been pillaged so frequently that but few valuable bones are to [be] found entire." I think his word choice is interesting, since he, too, was sent to "pillage" the ground, carting away the bones for study and display far distant, and without the kind of detail-clutching attention to the site itself that we'd expect today. Some of the enormous fossils were already in the hands of George Louis Leclerc de Buffon and his anatomist-assistant Louis Jean-Marie Daubenton, who nonetheless conceived a "theory of degeneracy" in the new world, explaining that all beings—animals as well as humans—were stunted and diminished by the cold, damp climate across the Atlantic. "In this state of abandon," Buffon wrote in *Histoire Naturelle*, "everything languishes, decays, stifles. The air and earth, weighed down by the moist and poisonous vapors, cannot purify themselves, nor profit from the influence of the star of life. The sun vainly pours down its liveliest rays on this cold mass, which is incapable of responding to its ardor." In *Notes on the State of Virginia*, Jefferson responded—ahem—hotly, writing that the great mammoth bones alone should have disabused Buffon of such buffoonery. Like others of the time, he believed the mastodon to be a carnivore because of the conical protrusions on the teeth, while the mammoth was surely a herbivore. It was a terrible predator to imagine, a meat eater as tall as a house, with enormous tusks and bones the size of furniture.

"But to whatever animal we ascribe these remains," he insisted, "it is certain such a one has existed in America, and that it has been the largest of all terrestrial beings. It should have sufficed to have rescued the earth it inhabited, and the atmosphere it breathed, from the imputation of impotence in the conception and nourishment of animal life on a large scale." He ridiculed Buffon's notion that "nature is less active, less en-

ergetic on one side of the globe than she is on the other. As if,"
Jefferson nearly snorted, "both sides were not warmed by the
same genial sun."

Across the swath of centuries, I try to glimpse the astonishing assemblage along the river: the sulfur springs, the roads
beaten by buffaloes, the great bones protruding from the muck
and, evidently, sitting about like fantastic sculptures in an open
parkland, there by the untamed Ohio River. I wonder what the
birdsong might have been—probably not the forest-loving
whippoorwills that I miss so much from nights lying awake in
Appalachian forests. Sedge wrens, maybe, fussing and blus-
tering all day long. When I visit in high summer, the modern
park is filled with the RV crowd, who can play miniature golf or
swim in a cement-lined pool in the campground. Down by the
Licks proper, there's a nicely made diorama, with model mammoths, bison, and a giant ground sloth; a couple of facsimile
turkey vultures perch on the fallen beasts, as if interrupted in
their feeding.

Just after sunup and a quick cup of coffee from the camp
stove, I leave the tent and walk downhill along a neatly mowed,
grassy pathway through the woods. A few black raspberries
are ripe, but only a few in the thorny edges between trees and
sunlight, and I know I'm the first person to walk this way on
this particular morning in July, since spider webs hang undisturbed across the trail every few yards or so. They catch and
smear against my glasses as I head toward the low-lying bot-
tomlands, the site of the old Licks. The wetlands are mostly
gone now, filled in, I've been told by the young park anthropologist, with heavy sedimentation due to nearby Cincinnati's
urban sprawl and general deforestation. But he's showed me
where to push through a screen of hemlock, sumac, and sting-

ing nettle, to stand beside an active spring. The hidden pool is narrow, perhaps three times the length of my galley-style kitchen floor back home, and has a milky, mineral hue; it certainly doesn't bubble and flow. It's framed with mud, bespeckled with deer tracks, and then, like matting within the frame, a border of algae at the water's edge. I stare hard at the water by my boots, and all I see in motion are tiny, rat-tailed maggot larvae, waving their frondlike bodies in the neat, persistent rhythm of decay.

Late July, it was a long, slow slog to Conundrum Hot Springs, high in Colorado's Maroon Bells-Snowmass Wilderness. Flatlanders in our first day of altitude, we dragged ourselves slowly up and up, along nearly nine miles of trail to the tent sites at something over eleven thousand feet. Along the way flies tormented us, biting our arms, our necks, and especially the backs of our legs where we couldn't reach to smack them dead. When they'd land on my forearms, I'd watch them bend their little faces down almost delicately, like tiny bats, to pierce the skin and draw blood. Then, still walking, I'd smash them and leave their corpses on my skin as warnings to their kinfolks, but, I have to admit, the sight of the vanquished never seemed to result in much deterrence.

A summer afternoon rainstorm quickly turned to hail, and thunder bounced down the surrounding high peaks while my friend Gina and I counted the seconds, calculating the lightning's distance. We sat together beneath a tarp strung up between two trees and watched the hailstones collect and melt. Then as the clouds eroded into ragged wisps, and patches of late, blue sky broke through, we headed to the springs, carrying a plastic Nalgene bottle of red wine, some cheddar cheese, and partially pack-pulverized crackers. Leaning back nearly neck deep in the slowly bubbling pool, we could look out over the valley—miles of trees and rocky slides, the nearby snowfields and bare granite, the darkening distance where another intervening fold of uplift finally closed off the view. With the rain well over and the air continuing to clear, we soaked awhile and watched a marmot schlump his stocky body to a smaller pool to begin sipping the minerals and salts. He was busy, hurrying over the rocks, and I thought it unlikely that, in that stony setting, he'd leave so much as a paw print to mark his passing. No bones. No mucky depth. In the clear water, only a tiny film of sediment and algae settled on my loafing flesh.

I remember as a child, hiking in a small group of family and close friends, how complete and utter was the invasion of a storm in the alpine tundra of stonecrop and granite boulders. As the thunder cleaved open the world around us, we hurried to get down below tree line. What was I at the time? Nine? Ten, maybe? I knew the danger of verticality, of being taller than the surrounding features of the landscape, a little mammalian lightning rod attracting destruction from above. And so, while the adults walked briskly, I trotted ahead, crouching beside each glacially placed boulder until they caught up, and then I raced ahead to my next defensive position. I don't remember anything about the rest of the descent, how we must have slowed and caught our breath partway down, among the far greater verticality of pines and aspens. But I recall the feeling, and how, two decades later, I once sat electrically awake, the old tent leaking from its seams, while just outside those flimsy walls the tall pines of New Mexico's Frijoles Canyon were sheeted in downpour and rocked by wind. Not far away a tree crashed down in a branch-ripping spasm of cosmogonic power.

I sat wrapped in my sleeping bag and suffused by near-panic, waiting for daylight.

Panic is a Western name for a universal sensation, drawn from the mythological figure of Pan, that god of both inner and exterior wildness. "Pan was thought to frequent mountains, caves, and lonely places, and sounds heard or fears experienced in such places came to be attributed to him," the *Oxford English Dictionary* reminds us, calmly, as if crossing its legs. But Pan is also everywhere, universal, cosmic, even. Panic can suggest the sudden rise of visceral, unreasonable fear from deep within the psyche, or it can suggest the staggering realization of one's infinitely vulnerable and fragile position in the vastness of unruled being. I think the thunderbird must have served a very similar function in pan-Indian mythology. At one level, it is an allegorical presence of the precipitative world: it's the figure that augurs both rainfall and firestorm. But if you gaze out farther along those broad, multifeathered wings, you may catch glimpses of the world's more general cyclicality: joy to fear, presence to absence, life to death. The dark bird can furl or fold its enormous wings, and somehow the world will change.

In 1705, in Columbia County, New York, some of the first skeletal remains of mammoths and mastodons came to the amazed attention of the colonists. First it was the teeth, enormous grinders weighing over four pounds, and then great bones that must, the gentlemen who examined them deduced, have belonged to prediluvian giants. Joseph Dudley, governor of Massachusetts, mused in a letter to his friend Cotton Mather about this unknown, towering creature "for whom the Flood only could prepare a funeral; and without doubt he waded as long as he could to keep his head above the clouds, but must at length be confounded with all other creatures, and the new sediment after the flood gave him the depth we now find." The Puritan poet Edward Taylor read a description of the discovery in *The Boston News Letter*; he copied sections of this notice into his diary and later wrote an account of a visit that some of the bones made to his own home: a few travelers "brot to my house and shewed me another *Tooth* of the monster buried at Claverack."

Taylor began (but never finished) a poem about the enormous beast, which he also supposed must be a Biblical giant destroyed by the Flood, and he compared it to various other giants of mythology, both Christian and pagan. Yet the poem effuses wonder at "the glorious acts of Nature" and God whom all must "adore" for the variety and glory of His created world and its play on all the senses, such as the myriad sounds of the wind:

By all her Bagpipes, Virginalls and Harps
The Wing'd musicians of the Woods imparts,
Yea, and harsh notes from rugged Organs roar,
Displaying to us also natures store.

The prologue, which contains these lines, shows Taylor at his best in the poem, I think. In imagination, he recrosses the ocean back to his birthland, Britain, the home of the legendary Dun Cow of Dunsmore Heath, slain, it was said, by Guy of Warwick. (The "cow" was reputedly a savage animal, twelve feet tall and dangerously tusked; some scholars suggest it may have been inspired by mammoth bones, puzzlements to the fourteenth-century Britons, so this literary allusion seems even more intricately linked to the Claverack giant than Taylor himself intended.) He lists and considers wonders throughout the world, from Hercules and Antaeus to Goliath, and from an enormous oyster shell to a tremendous tree.

Most interesting, though, is another local rarity, one that scholars have not been able to substantiate. It seems that in the same year the bones were unearthed at Claverack, New York, a peculiar mushroom bloom took place, unprecedented in both form and proportion. They grew

With Humane Heads, Cheeks, Brows and Chin and Nose,
Adorned with Curious Lace like Ruffled towers
On womens heads, and Wigs long in Curld flowers
Of mushrum matter . . .

These figurating fungi "oft rose in a night / And stanck if broken," serving as a cautionary sign to the men and women who wore those towering wigs that "Nature's not blinde / That Checks them thus." So Taylor combined his excitement at the bones as natural curiosity, his literate word-hoard of mythological wonders (he had an extensive personal library for the time, 192 volumes), and his certainty that the world was an image of God Himself, allowing the poet "To set mine Eyes on thy bright selfe to view / As in a looking glass."

Taylor both loved and distrusted the very stories he laid out, bound neatly in rhyming couplets. He warned that

Stories [are] unkinde to us . . . because
They fog them with their metaphorick laws
That by Rhetorick steps such Strides oft take
That a Molehil do a mountain make.

And yet he can't resist them: "But yet we do conclude that by such Stories / Something there did appear of Natures glory."

The poem peters out, growing stale and workmanlike as it "describe[s]" the giant as he must have been, thighs like pillars, eyes like suns. But "something there did appear" in the opening section, the sense of Taylor himself gazing over the ground, at marvels of the New World that hint at other ages in ways that the educated minister strains to read. Yet his translation spells out the subtext in Hebraic letters, gesturing toward distant scrolls from desert places, stories from the Mesopotamian world of flock, and grove, and temple built on the mount. He was of the generation of writers who looked about them at the hardwood forests, the undammed rivers where Atlantic salmon still spawned, and called the place a howling desert. He's best known, of course, for finished, meditational poems like "Upon Wedlock and the Death of Children." In this tightly metaphorical lyric, he initially thanks God for taking something "of mine," as two of his children, little "flowers," die; but later he cries out in less measured and less figurative couplets. "Oh!" he says, in the stricken voice of a man who has watched his children die before his eyes, "The torture, Vomit, screechings, groans; / And six weeks fever would pierce hearts like stones."

One accounting for the swift, widespread extinctions that marked the opening of the Holocene is Paul Martin's view that Clovis people, flourishing across the Americas some 13,000 years ago, were expert hunters dedicated to the pursuit of big game. Resolutely and skillfully, they targeted the charismatic megafauna of the age, some thirty-five genera of large animals—the mammoths, mastodons, ground sloths, archaic bison, various bears, deer, stag moose, shrub and musk ox, saiga, camel . . . it's quite a list of prey. Sequestered behind the impassible wall of northern ice, these beasts animated a landscape that had always held only nonhumans as predators. When the hunters came, Martin argues, they cut through the unprepared populations like a knife through fat, decimating and fracturing the breeding communities. In a matter of a few centuries—perhaps no more than five hundred years—the favored prey was wiped out through "overkill." Other species dependent on the grazers and browsers followed quickly into disappearance. For a time, scavengers (those teratorns, I think, those condors and giant vultures) would have become familiars of the human hunters, vying for the downed prey as eagles and ospreys will tussle over one another's catch. In this overkill model of that transitional time, the ground must been littered with kill sites, with carrion waiting for the great birds from above. But soon, feast would have turned to famine, and the other large animals—predators as well as scavengers—would leave nothing but their bones behind.

It's easy to see parallels between that world and this one, the cusp between ice age and what author Brian Fagan has called "the long summer" of the Holocene. Indeed, researchers have pointed out that Martin offered his hypothesis in 1967—just half a decade after Rachel Carson's *Silent Spring* and three years before the first Earth Day, so the collective imagination was primed to believe that we—or our Clovis-age forebears—were likely to have decimated the animal community of the Americas; we were still doing much the same thing. And in an irony unfolding today, the vigilant attempt to bring California condors back from the obsidian blade edge of extinction is fraught with today's hunters in the desert Southwest, not far from the important Clovis sites.

The dramatic, even desperate attempt to pluck the condors from the jaws of death began in the 1980s: by 1982, only twenty-two individuals were left in the world. In the arid, isolated cliff-

and-canyon country where a few still lived wild in Southern California, the birds were methodically trapped and removed from their last hold. Following several years of an intensive captive breeding program, releases to the wild began, first in Arizona in 1996 and then, symbolically, marvelously, to the Grand Canyon in 2003. One spring morning in 2005, I joined a large party assembled in northern Arizona, along the base of the Vermillion Cliffs, to watch the release of the latest group of fledglings—five of them. Their arrival clearly elicited some interest among the resident adult community, and high above us, as we peered through spotting scopes and binoculars, the birds flew about, welcoming or examining the new arrivals. On the ground, we seemed disappointingly far from the release site— I, at least, had imagined we'd be much closer. But in the desert springtime morning, it was easy to shake off disappointment, like just a bit of dust on one's sleeve.

Four wild-hatched chicks now live in the Kaibab Plateau area. And of the five who were released to bright, clear skies that morning on the first of March, all but one are reported to be "doing fine in the wild." One has died; the researchers attribute the cause of death to starvation, a fact I find deeply poignant, given the cultural image of scavenger birds and human famine. But the returning birds face other hazards beyond hunger, coyotes, or eagles: the expert hunters in the region today wield not fluted points of obsidian or flint, but lead shot, often left in deer carcasses. The feeding birds take in deadly levels of this poison and must be evacuated to receive emergency treatment. They undergo chelation, a chemical process in which some binding agent is introduced to the bloodstream, allowing the deadly lead to form an ionic bond to the chelator instead of the body; it can then be naturally excreted, and the animal may recover. I'm struck that the derivation of the word seems like a little fractal figure of the bird itself: it comes from the Greek *chelè*, or claw.

This is all high-level management, twenty-first-century life support efforts to save not only the life of a single bird—a California condor may live for up to sixty years—but, obviously, to resuscitate the species, the collectivity of its evolutionary presence on this earth. Up from that almost-impossibly tiny band of 22, the world condor population is, as I write, 273 individuals, with the wild birds now living in four distinct regions in Southern California, Baja California, and northern Arizona. Their imprint on the Southwest is delicate, tenuous, still utterly uncertain. But there they are. Amazingly, the day before the release of new young, two adults swooped past the car as we drove along the highway to our own staging ground, a cheap motel called—I am not making this up—the Ancestor Inn.

The overkill hypothesis for the Pleistocene extinctions in the Americas is under attack these days. Donald Grayson and David Meltzer have painstakingly analyzed all the known archaeological sites where evidence of both people and now-extinct Pleistocene mammals have been found in conjunction; there are only seventy-six of these, they report. Of these, only fourteen clearly reveal that the humans were predators—big game hunters who brought down the animals in question. And these are very species specific: twelve were mammoths; the other two were mastodons. The researchers conclude—convincingly, I think—that the physical evidence simply cannot support the kind of blitzkrieg pattern of concentrated hunting that would have been necessary to fold all those giant beasts into the dust of extinction.

So what was it?

As if there were ever one, clear answer. Simplicity is desirable, in both aesthetics and practical life, but so often what we really must negotiate is complexity, rich and dismaying. This is, of course, the view of the ecologist: everything is connected to everything. And it is what oppresses the psyche, sometimes, as the sleeping self tries to tease out what is the matter, what is lurking over there in the shadows, like some large bird hopping about the margin of full awareness?

Yes, there was climate change, the rapid and sustained warming that ushered in the Holocene. But there had been periods of warming before, throughout the long ages of ice. Oddly enough, the Holocene is marked by far less variability, far less change, than the preceding hundreds of thousands of years. Perhaps climate change, coupled with the arrival of hunters?

And what else arrived with the hunters?

If teratorns and giant vultures might have been, as I think of them, "familiars" of the first Paleo-Indians to enter the Americas, the first Americans had other familiars as well. Researchers have drawn on ancient mitochondrial DNA samples to show that the domesticated dog came from Beringia into the New World, along with its people, as early as 13,500 years before the present. As Stuart Fiedel describes, the presence of dogs in the company of the first migrant people to cross the land bridge helps explain many difficulties in the rapid expanse of Clovis culture across the broad landscape. They helped protect against the oversized predators—the dire wolves, the saber-tooth cats, the massive short-faced bears, even larger (and more devotedly carnivorous) than grizzlies. They likely served as pack animals, carrying anything from tired, whining children to surplus food, to firewood. And in lean times, or in extreme environments (such as the initial hypothesized route between the Cordilleran and Laurentide ice sheets), they may have been butchered for meat.

The DNA evidence points to five separate female animals who must have made the journey, members of "the ancestral pack." As Fiedel points out, this is an interesting parallel to similar findings among humans—our own mitochondrial DNA in the Americas shows five separate lineages. He imagines "the original Paleo-Indian group" as perhaps 150 people. If one abstracts from later Plains Indian models, they might have "begun the 1200-mile trek through the corridor with some 900 dogs in tow," he writes. Even if they butchered some of their animals for food, at a rate of one dog per week, "there would have been almost 400 dogs still alive by the time they saw their first mammoth at the southern end of the corridor." His outline invites much imagination: the spare, bare backdrop of an epic journey; the fur-clad figures of the hardy migrants; the abrupt, alert posture of the dogs as they first catch the scent of a new future.

From the Internet I download a series of photographs: California condors at Big Sur, feeding on a beached whale. The whale is a rusty-colored, mottled lump on the beach, and it looks very much like a weathered boulder, the reddish-orange, rounded rock of the Colorado Plateau, the very landscape to which many of the condors are now returning. In a closeup, you can see the birds have ripped off the whale's skin along the lower jaw: they reach their bare, snaky necks into the animal's mouth to feed. I think they're eating its tongue.

Also available on the Internet is a gluttonous offering of stories about avian flu. The slaughter of poultry in Asia. The speculation (as yet unrealized) about transmission by migrating birds. The specter of a pandemic, the social upheaval and death toll likely should the virus make its leap to humans and sweep through the United States. We're reminded that the 1918 influenza pandemic was a bird flu; it has been called the worst infectious disease outbreak in history. And that was in an age before air travel, before the tightly woven tissue of globalization.

How keen these various ironies seem. The national press prints suggestions to prepare for the coming plague: stockpile food and water, be ready to remove your children from school, expect disruption of public services. It's true: an inopportune mutation could kill so many of us, the devastation would be a cataclysmic lightning bolt, a thunderclap, a firestorm, and the world would become, to the bereaved and bewildered survivors, unrecognizable. Meanwhile, those 273 individual birds in the Southwest hang on by little more than a claw, above the abyss of disappearance.

Ross MacPhee suggests something similar happened in those last few hundred years of the Pleistocene. The hunters were brave and resourceful, but they were only human. They were not some tidal wave of stone-tipped slaughter; they couldn't decimate several million megafauna in just a few centuries, he argues. But what if they were hosts to something else that could? The people and their dogs could easily have carried diseases from Europe to which the New World mammals had no inherited immunity. A "hyperdisease" could move from its accustomed host into the new horizons of a range of species. Such an epidemic, joined with the increasing pressures of hunting and climate change, could have visited the very disruption and death we now imagine for ourselves on the existent animal communities of some twelve thousand years ago.

How fragile we seem to feel: how *endangered*. In my town, local authorities are preparing a strategy should avian flu become a hyperdisease, an emerging virus that brings us down like medieval Europeans under the Black Death, like the Arawak under smallpox. Despite published reports to the contrary, the planning document repeats the *fear* that migratory birds may spread the disease as an already-established *fact*, although to date, the source of outbreaks is not wild birds but industrial poultry farms. The authors use telling phrases like *attack rate* rather than *infection rate*, putting that number at 25 percent of the local population. It's difficult, even for men and women in suits, meeting in air-conditioned rooms, to keep the deep-seated viscerality of fear well fenced within the domesticated landscape of data and rationality. That fear is ancient stuff, far older than mammoth bones; it stood up with us long, long ago, and moved with us across the edible, changeable landscape of the ice-gripped world; it found ways to body forth in myth and image, in the rumble of symbol deep in the imagination. Look out, it warns us sometimes. Look out: something dreadful and dangerous, and far larger than you, is about to come winging in. Listen: can you hear it, even now?

Aspects

It appears that mastodonts (and in fact mammoths, too) did not make the same strong impression on prehistoric American artists as mammoths made on Eurasian artists.

Gary Haynes

First it was a picture in a book. The ostensible "Moab Mastodon": a petroglyph in black and white with a man's white-sleeved arm stretched in almost surrealist fashion beneath it, delicately pinching a pen between thumb and finger, just beneath the trunk, to indicate scale. I almost expected the caption to be a quotation from Magritte, "*Çeci n'est pas une pipe.*" But instead there's a note from the researcher, describing the figure. "It appears to have three or four toes, a large trunk, and a hump on its back. This is one of four so-called mastodons that I have seen," he explains. After examining hundreds of bighorn sheep and snakes, some dogs or coyotes, a few birds, I was transfixed by this addition to the depicted animal kingdom in the rock art of the desert Southwest. The book, a nearly oversized volume that already carried an air of importance even when it sat closed on my desk, seemed larger still.

A mastodon? This would have to be far, far older than most of the rock art I'd seen, dating to the uncertain age of Paleo-Indians, the hunter-gatherers who traveled the world long before the cultivation of corn, the construction of cliff villages, the painting and carving left by the Fremont or Ancestral Puebloan residents of the Great Basin landscape. It would be an artistic link, an open-air depiction of a vanished menagerie, the "charismatic megafauna" that roamed the American West in a world that had remained unpeopled until—well, *sometime*. The archaeologists are still debating, with some friction, just when and how Europeans first entered the distant, ice-gripped lands, but it was long, long ago, longer than the once-told tale of ten thousand years, across the Bering land bridge. A link was made earlier, of course, through the relict remains of hunting technology, when archaeologists in the mid-1920s began discussing large spear points associated with the bones of extinct mammals, but since the actual workers, the hired excavators, had moved the pieces before the assemblage could be examined and photographed in situ, it wasn't until the early 1930s that clear, irrefutable proof was unearthed and recorded. Here, as in Europe, people had hunted the great Pleistocene mammals with beautiful, fluted stone-tipped spears. And right here, in eastern Utah, was a plein-air petroglyph, pecked and abraded into the reddish rock, that may have recorded the cultural encounter with those ancient animals: the contemplation, the transference of the inner image to the hard and so hardly yielding face of stone.

The image, it turns out, was first reported in the scientific literature in 1935. An article in *The Scientific Monthly* reported that the author, Byron Cummings (from the University of Arizona), had first heard of it in 1924 from a resident of Moab, but he didn't visit the site until a decade later. "That this pictograph is genuine seems entirely plausible to me," he wrote, noting, "Were it the work of some itinerant cowboy or other person wishing to establish a hoax it does not seem he would have deliberately placed the figure in a position where the likelihood of its discovery would be so remote." Unwittingly, however, Cummings diminished the likelihood that later researchers would be able to test and date the image's plausibility with new techniques: he chalked the animal heavily so it would stand out nicely in the photographs. And it does, at that. It's a fascinating figure, quite unlike the high-shouldered, dome-headed mammoths rendered in European cave art. In fact, it corresponds pretty well to a description of the mastodon's body profile, for, says paleontologist Gary Haynes, "*Mammut* [mastodont or mastodon] was a heavyset animal, with a deep chest, relatively short legs, a long back and wide pelvis, and a head oriented . . . nearly horizontal and without the doming seen in *Mammuthus* [mammoth]." Cummings, though he claims the carving "is designed to be an elephant or mastodon," doesn't even consider the possibility that the rendered mammal might be a mammoth. Nor does he comment on the fact that the image appears to lack tusks, one of the most striking features of European depictions of mammoths. I wonder a little about this, as I gaze at the animal's profile.

I decide that I have to see it for myself.

I know that it's on the south bank of the Colorado River; I know that it's a few miles outside Moab, "off on a side canyon," according to one source. But specific directions are hard to come by. And I can appreciate this. In the years since it was first photographed, the petroglyph has been used for target practice: two bullet holes are clearly visible in a photo from the 1970s, and a third has appeared in the decades since. A researcher at the Center for Desert Archaeology tells me that a group of "well-meaning, but misguided" Boy Scouts recently "refreshed" the image by repecking the form in the stone. So it's understandable that I can't find directions posted in someone's blog on the Web, or in a brochure prepared by the Moab Visitors' Bureau.

But I receive a tip from another researcher and rock art enthusiast, who directs me to a rare book and manuscript collection. It seems he's checked my "credentials" online before responding to my e-mail query. "You seem to be who you say you are," he remarks. And, though he won't tell me directly, he has pointed me in the right direction. "If you are a diligent researcher, you'll be rewarded," he says, enjoying his virtual position as a cryptic oracle, I think, speaking to me through the portals of e-mail. So I spend a couple of days of library work trying to be diligent, surveying manuscript holdings, leafing through decades-old folders. After several hours of this indoor questing, I'm provisioned with a fairly approximate idea of how to get there.

Dave has brought his GPS unit and wants to plot the precise location for us; he's also brought his best (and heaviest) camera, firmly latched atop a monopod that, with a linguistic nod to the poetry of William Carlos Williams, we call "the moveable foot." I've brought apples and granola bars, water bottles and a notebook. Two notebooks, actually. And now we're standing in front of the petroglyph, in the chilly air of early spring, but the sunlight on sandstone looks exuberantly warm and bright. Of course, it's we who are exuberant, triumphant. We shout aloud, having canvassed the landscape along the river, following the field notes I gleaned from earlier researchers, and imagining the world as we see it this early March morning as a point on a line stretching back through innumerable moments, little

Zeno arrow points in a temporal arc, to the day someone stood in this precise location, tool kit spread out on the ground, and began to carve. Connectivity is what we're after, the thrill of the senses as we gaze across this tiny distance, a foot or two of dry desert air, at the figuration in the stone. And if it really offers the relict, stylized glimpse of an animal icon of the ice age, time's arrow will cross distances unmeasurable by any of the tools we have at hand.

Other visitors must have felt some other versions of connective need, but of an aggressive, self-assertive sort: those divots in the stone where someone blasted away with a shotgun surely count as assertion of self—and maybe some kind of vision— on the varnished rind of stone. Around the canyon's bend, not far away, are the names and dates that present twentieth-century graffiti; and I write several of these in my notebook, peevishly, as if I could attach to the owners of those names some little voodoo prick of shame. But even peevishness can't really distract me from the inner dance of enzymes that discovery has unleashed inside me: delight is visceral, flooding the body with the chemical map of where and how my own neural network lit up from being here.

And much later, going over my notes, I'll try to recover the sequence of images we passed in pursuit of this particular petroglyph. Mine is a literate imagination, most enlivened by the urge to tell, to describe, to share with the palpable pulse of words tumbling from my mouth or crawling across the page beneath my hand, or, as right now, clicking their way beneath my fingers, transformed from the neural activity I can only believe is their source within my self, into the verbal trails and traces with which I'll gesture outward. I feel I'm a conduit: the world's impressions somehow translated into what we call *expression*. I recall the slant of the slope we climbed, the shelf of stone like another, older riverbed above the road and actual river that we'd left below. In recollection, I call back the other images—the lizard figures, the two-headed sheep. I remember the bear—I recall, that is, its body, re-membering the legs, like inverted pyramids, with four toes underneath: it's a body-in-profile balanced atop what look almost like footprints seen from above. It is modernity; it is also prehistoric. The visual abstraction of the bear steps down from memory onto the screen that's glowing, itself a decaying metaphor, suggesting a white, blank page.

I wish I could recapture the moment when it first came into view—and the adrenalin flush with which my body answered; I wish, in recollection, I could return to the person I was then. Already, I'm diminished, by time and work and distance. I've quarreled with a dear friend, I've missed an important deadline. I'm imperceptibly but irrefutably closer to my own dim horizon. But if I could only show you, make manifest before your own surprised, perhaps skeptical eyes. It was a portrait, chipped by some anonymous and vanished hand. The animal was poised as if in motion, lifting its flexible trunk above its back.

The sun shone on my shoulders, on my back.

Dave and I had found the image, and, elated, we called out to one another across the illuminated landscape.

I wonder quite a bit about Haynes's assertion that the mammoths and mastodons did not make "a strong impression" on the Paleo-Indians who shared their landscape. It may be true. But it's also possible that few remains of such ancient art exist to show us whatever did impress those hunter-gatherers. One could argue that *caves* were not impressive to their creative and symbolic thinking, and without the shelter of deep decorated galleries, whatever images the ice age artists left on the landscape were far more prone to erosion and disappearance. And, indeed, this part of the world lacks the deep karst formations, the hidden caverns that preserve image, and a whiff of time past, deep within southern Europe's river valleys. This particular spot is marvelously placed, on a sheltered slant of rock, against a dark, impressive patina on the sandstone's surface; it's neatly, cleverly protected from the direct assault of rain or wind. Maybe, ten or twelve thousand years ago, the culture was more mobile and favored portable art in more mutable forms.

There is a written record of the next place I want to see, to seek out traces of mastodons or mammoths. In Bown's Canyon, roughly thirty-seven thousand years' worth of geologic activity can be read from the various soil terraces you can still see, in slope or stairstep form, lifting from the lowest point where an intermittent stream flows south and east to join a great meandering curve in the ancient riverway, the Colorado. Stratigraphic studies from the 1980s elucidate what went on between the high sandstone walls—Navajo sandstone atop Kayenta sandstone in this particular part of the landscape. Alluvial deposition, aeolian deposition. The researchers in the field spent weeks here, in this specific *where*, sampling the soil, learning *what*, and *when*, and *how*—water or wind, accumulation or loss. Loess, dust. Mollisoles, prairie soils. Fossil pollen. And, amazingly, fossil dung, some three hundred cubic meters of it preserved in a remote, most unusual cave in a sunbaked portion of the Colorado Plateau.

When I first found mention of the fossil dung, I couldn't resist some scatological humor. And neither, evidently, could the researchers. The site itself is called Bechan Cave, which means, in Navajo, "really big poo." While the scat of many animals—rabbits, rodents, mountain sheep, extinct shrub ox, and Shasta ground sloth—over several millennia lies in the sheltered alcove, what's most intriguing is the presence of mammoth dung, lots of it, accumulated over a period of about thirty-five hundred years, most of it twelve to thirteen thousand years before the present. Ancient ordure; Pleistocene spoor! Imagine it, I told myself, and tried. Tried hard. So I read the published papers, the painstaking description of the mammoths' diet (mostly grasses and sedges), the identification process (measurement of a few intact boluses, description of the similarity to modern elephant dung). I studied maps, trying to figure out just where the cave was located, and how I might get there. But it looked impossibly remote, a two- or three-day hike over slickrock mesa from the termination of the nearest (no doubt rough) jeep track of a road I could locate in my atlas-gazetteer. Not a venture I wanted to strike out on, on my own.

So I called Larry Agenbroad, one of the lead researchers from the team who initially excavated the cave two decades ago.

"Oh," he told me. "I first got there by boat, through the Park Service. That's your best bet. They were very helpful. Call the Park Service in Page."

When I do, I reach John Spence, a botanist by training who seems to know a great deal about everything in the area surrounding Lake Powell. He's a veteran in a system that shuffles nearly itinerant personnel from place to place; he's worked at Glen Canyon National Recreation Area for a decade and a half, longer than nearly anyone else in the office.

"Could you come in October?" he asks. "We'll be doing some sampling of water holdings along that canyon and could make a combined trip. It's a great time to get out; the weather should be really pleasant by then. We'll go by boat, and then it's an easy hike up canyon from the water's edge."

I cast aside the image of myself limping in summer heat across a slickrock mesa, loaded with about fifty pounds of water and squinting at a map, wondering whether I've come one canyon too far before I make the precipitous drop into the riparian channel. "We'll go by boat," he said. "October," he said. I try to sound vaguely professional on the phone, but I know I've failed. I could almost be squealing, I'm so pleased.

I step out of the motel into blinkingly brilliant desert light, the first week in October. Page is expanding, and the early morning pulses with the sound of construction of a new building across the highway—another motel, most likely, from the look of it. Just down the road, past a tract of open desert and the grocery store, is the headquarters building for Glen Canyon National Recreation Area. I arrive, dump my pack to the floor, and meet the Park Service scientists with whom I'll travel to the cave. They're friendly, welcoming, and running a little late, so I'll have time to sit in the Natural Resources office suite and read a brand new dissertation on the dung of the extinct shrub ox, another in the menagerie of vanished Pleistocene beasts that once ranged and grazed the landscape here. Mark Anderson and Jesse Granete will be traveling farther up Bowns Canyon for their sampling trip; John and I will head off to a side canyon for the visit to Bechan. Then, after they all drop me at Hall's Landing to catch the Park Service plane back to Page, Jesse and Mark will head to nearby Iceberg Canyon to investigate its suitability as a nursery pond for native trout species. That's the plan John describes to me quickly. Jesse heads to the grocery store to buy supplies for the two-day trip; Mark is no-where to be seen; and before leaving me to read the dissertation, "The Extinct Shrub-Ox (*Euceratherium collinum*) and Its Late Quaternary Environment on the Colorado Plateau," John chats with me about his research on plant species left over from the Pleistocene throughout the Colorado Plateau region.

"There's lots of patterns in the landscape today of things that shouldn't be there," he says. In nearby Cow Canyon, bigtooth maple persists at nearly lake level; if you look, you can find wild rose, maybe smooth sumac, various kinds of rushes. *Aurelia spikenard* grows there too, he tells me; it's a kind of climbing shrub. Some of these populate the fragile verdure of the hanging gardens, *encampments*, I think, of plant life that cluster up along the cliffs where water exits the more porous Navajo lime-stone at its conjunction with the less permeable Kayenta layers. It's a geological irony, the placement of these periodic springs and seeps: Navajo sandstone was laid down in more arid conditions, sometime in the Jurassic Period of the Mesozoic Era. Kayenta was a riparian deposit, likely laid down in a river delta or flood-plain environment, holding once-slick particles of shale or clay, and today those are the stony layers that won't transmit the water farther down so it must run laterally, resulting in these high-up seeps, watering holes for plant life that dangles up above the canyon floor. Kayenta's called an aquiclude; it's a word whose consonants in the mouth echo the sharp, sheer cliffs whose vertical reach presents the text of ancient change.

In his recent research, John has focused on Pleistocene relict species, those improbable hangers-on despite the odds, despite both the stuttered variability and the baseline certainty of change. In Zion Canyon, he tells me, there are Douglas fir trees clinging to north-facing alcoves; they could trace their genealogy back to the age of ice, if anyone pursued such family trees. I think of the clusters of aspen and Douglas fir I saw growing elsewhere on the plateau, in the days last spring when I camped in snow on the Shonto Plateau above Tsegi Canyon, just west of the Navajo town of Kayenta. When the snowstorm quit, I hiked down into the dampened niches of the canyon, listening to the steady drip and rush of water, marveling at the ephemeral falls that seemed to measure the cliff's height, bead by bead of tumbling snowmelt. I stood beneath a Douglas fir, much smaller than the trees I know from the Pacific Northwest, and breathed in its wet-needle scent. But no, John tells me, that's a little different. The altitude's much higher there—it's some seventy-four hundred feet—so the presence of the relict species isn't quite so surprising as it is along Glen Canyon, perhaps thirty-five hundred feet lower.

Shortly after lunch, we're ready to go. We drive down to the launch site and load the Silver Bullet, the Park Service boat that will take us seventy or eighty miles upstream to reach our intended side canyons. On a quiet, nearly deserted dock (it is no longer the high season for visitors), I manage to dump the entire plastic cask of our drinking water, lifting it by the handle on the lid rather than those on the sides. Ice cubes skitter across the dock while I sputter mortified apologies. But just a quick trip up the hill replenishes it, and we finish stowing gear behind and within the little cabin, and Mark takes the captain's wheel, and soon we're motoring smoothly away. The early afternoon light, postequinoctial, floods all the visible space in the world: the circumferential sky, the bright expanse of lake. This landscape seems utterly unmediated, unmodulated by shade or vegetation. Sky meets stone; stone meets lake. It's quite breezy, so wind meets water, too, raising a ruffled nap of waves across the surface. The Silver Bullet's metal hull meets water and wind and gleams in this autumnal sunlight; as we pull from the no-wake zone, Mark increases speed, raises his voice, and talks about his work and research on the lake.

After completion of the Glen Canyon Dam, it took nearly twenty years for the reservoir to fill to capacity. But in the past half decade, a severe drought has gripped the region, and the lake level dropped nearly a hundred and fifty feet below what they call, with a pleasant half-rhyme, "full pool." Following last spring's increased rainfall, the level has crept back up, but it's still about a hundred feet shy of capacity. We're surrounded by the image of all that missing water: from the surface extends a pale, calcite crust, a bathtub ring, the scientists joke. It's a perfect, alabaster shadow of the lowered lake, bone-white below the unsubmerged, warmer shades of reddish-dun. The men discuss the drought a little: the summer just past was the hottest on record for the town of Page, with a good week and a half of temperatures above 105 degrees. "And the record high temp ever is 108," John says. No doubt about it: things are warming up.

All the sandstone visible along Lake Powell belongs to what's called the Glen Canyon formation: Navajo atop Kayenta atop Wingate. Mark points out places where the Kayenta layer has slipped and collapsed under the wet presence of the lake. We zoom past visible jumbles of tumbled rock, which, he says, spread out way below the surface in submerged fans of rubble and silt. I'm reminded of the alluvial studies of Bown's Canyon, and the way the researchers traced the periodic changes of the surface soils that dress the bones of bedrock. Aggradation and degradation are the published terminology. At first, I think this must be stream channel–specific vocabulary, dealing with fluvial deposition and down-cutting stream action. But it turns out that the language extends to lake and ocean dynamics, too. And, once, I find *aggradation* (a word my spellchecker doesn't even recognize and my tongue wants to humanize, to transform into the more gregarious-sounding *aggregation*), referring to the impossibly slow abrading of mountains, the eonic process by which they are at last brought down.

In the boat's cabin, leaning against the port-side window, I am quiet as the sun drops and the light slants past Jurassic sandstone. The men are discussing where to spend the night; they want a sheltered spot because of the wind but as near as possible to the canyon mouth for tomorrow's hike. The Rincon, they decide, and I study the location on my map, but I can't see how it is a box canyon, the only translation I know for that Spanish word. I see an elongated hill, an oval mesa of uneroded stone, around which two arms of impounded waters reach. We slow and approach the north cove's narrow beach, to cast anchor, and hurry in the dusk to make supper.

Later, John and Mark sit up awhile on the shore, debating the nature of knowledge. Faith, says Mark, pertains as well to science's acceptance of the data, even the daily barrage of sense impressions, as it does to religion's acceptance of dogma or doctrine. "I make a leap of faith, and accept that what I see is real," he says. "I'm in my own universe, and it's a leap of faith to make connection."

John won't agree. "No, no," he insists. "I'm in a community of others who've similarly tested and examined the data, and they've come to similar conclusions. I'm not alone in this, I'm not inventing the nature of the world."

Several yards away, I lie in my sleeping bag, listening. Aside from the clear sound of human voices, there's hardly any noise at all: no slap of waves on the protected strand, no coyotes, no owls. Occasionally I hear the gulp of carp beside the boat, looking for castoffs from dinner: bits of salad, salmon, and pasta.

Finally I call out in the dark. "You're arguing with Descartes," I tell John. "Mark thinks an Evil Demon might be deceiving him." I get up, come to sit closer. It's more than a two-way debate now. There's no campfire, no moon, but in the mild breeze we sit up awhile longer, talking.

"You know how 'theory' means something different in scientific discussions from how it's used more widely? You guys're doing the same thing that creationists do—you're using 'faith' as if it is a broad, generic meaning. But that's not right. It has to have a different nuance for religious belief."

"A new perspective!" says Jesse. He has spread out his bag on a flat spot, a little ways from the sloped-sand agora of the beach. But he still doesn't enter in the conversation. I think to myself, he's heard this talk play out many times before.

"Watch out," says John. "Mark was a philosophy major before he turned to science." And pretty soon I realize Mark's also Leibnitz, not just Descartes, and if John might try to Socratize him, badger him with questions, he might shake some gaps in this credo, but he doesn't. I want to make some point about the difference between *leaping* into faith—a deliberate submission of reason—and *standing still*, accepting the validity of reason, but all I can think of is Emily Dickinson, who is perhaps not the best example with which to convince the assembled scientists. And I'm getting very, very tired. I'm thickly inarticulate.

It's a dark night—still no moon—and so I give up and go back to lie in my bag, where intermittent gusts of wind flap the fabric into my face, and sand moves not quite imperceptibly around me, changing the beach in ways I won't be able to see come morning.

In full sunlight, we're anchored up against a slope of boulders that lifts some three hundred feet above the surface of the water. Jesse points out a flat spot, maybe twenty feet above the boat, where the crew camped once when the lake was higher. With the Silver Bullet tied securely to two of the large boulders, we load packs for the day hike: raincoats, since the possibility of thunderstorms is forecast; lunch; a full complement of water-testing and insect-sampling equipment for Mark and Jesse. In a wetter time, this inlet of the lake would be met by a plunging waterfall around the corner from the slope we climb, but the stream itself is intermittent, and once up in the higher elevation of the canyon's channel we move from isolated pool to pool, traveling on rock or rough grass between these green spots cupped within the sandstone walls.

The scientists are watching for invasive plant species. Escaped from landscaped lawns in the region, ravenna grass and pampas grass have begun to take hold in the Grand Canyon, and they're worried the aliens may have arrived here, too. Sure enough, we spot some stands in among the indigenous reeds and grasses. John also points out wire grass, *Juncus balticus*, a reed that was established in these canyons in the Pleistocene and has remained in some protected pockets. The stems sprawl sideways under their own weight, or under the force of wind, and I think that it looks as though some very large beast has been lying there, the way the tallgrass back home looks after deer have bedded down, overnight, perhaps, or in the quiet resting of midday. John also shows me *Potamogeton natans*, a beautiful small-leafed plant that hangs, lotuslike, in the still waters of these remnant pools. Floating pondweed, another relict from the ice age plant community.

By 11:00 we've parted from Mark and Jesse; they will hike another five or six miles up canyon to reach distant springs and pools for their sampling project before returning to the boat. John and I make our leisurely way to an eastern side arm of the canyon to reach the cave. It's clouded up, and occasionally a few sprinkles, wind driven, pelt us as we climb. The air is much cooler, and I wonder whether we'll see the thunderstorms that were predicted—a chance of them, anyway—on the boat radio. John pauses to rest and readjust his boots, which are stiff and new and have been bothering him, but I press ahead, eager to see the cave.

I round another headland to my right, pass through a small cluster of stream-level cottonwoods, and there it is, up on the slope, just where the bare expanse of Kayenta stone meets the terraced soil of the canyon floor. It's deeply sheltered. To the left, a rounded knee of sandstone rests like a squat pillar, the newel post of some long-gone gate or banister. To the right, the mesa's face of stone extends at a protective angle, throwing the threshold of the cave in shadow. The slope holds a few juniper trees, the gray bristle of ephedra (known widely as Mormon tea) and a few short, blond strands of grass. A bank of soil and fallen rock slopes just beneath the cave's mouth; I stop and gape, and take a few photographs before the final climb up and inside.

A variety of researchers have learned a great deal about what I have been calling, in my mind, the "aspects" of the world in and around Bechan Cave in the late glacial period. "Aspect" I like, because beyond its common usage, indicating "attributes," the word's history in the language specifies both "the point from which one looks; a point of sight or of view," and "the side or surface which fronts or is turned towards any given direction." That is, both the direction of *seeing* and that of *being seen*. The word, in my thinking about it, provides the full circumference of point of view and, in a single noun, connects observer with the world observed. And yet what I'm thinking about is a world that, today, is largely unobservable. It can only be glimpsed and gleaned from hints and remains: the pollen locked in deposition in the depths of lakes and ponds, the buried bones, the rare, improbable fragments of hair and dung. The petroglyph, perhaps, placed on the rockface, facing the river, and whoever might come down that riparian pathway.

Evidently the larger herbivores in the park today are isolated in the side canyons, in fragmented habitat. For deer, at least, it's a difficult, dry crossing over the cliff tops. Once, they'd have followed the riparian corridor, able to move from one side canyon to another. But now that way is closed off by the lake, and the herd numbers are declining. I imagine that would have been the mammoths' and mastodons' passageway across the landscape, too: following the river, leaving the main channel for one after another tributary-niche of graze and browse, and then returning to the river's connective—arterial—course.

Of course, the late Pleistocene world was wetter and cooler. The sheltered valley, then, would have held more deciduous trees and leafy shrubs. And, evidently, a lot more grass, enough to feed beasts that towered above the current herbivores of the desert Southwest. Today, the plant community is known as *blackbrush desert scrub*; twelve thousand years ago it would have been a *sagebrush steppe*. The nearest analog, say the researchers, is found forty miles north, in the Henry Mountains, some four thousand feet higher in elevation. But, John tells me, it's an inexact match. Even there one cannot find quite the same convergence of plant life as that which vanished from the lower plateau.

In the lab, in the 1980s, a research team teased out some traces of that world as it was seen and grazed by mammoths. Up to 95 percent of the dung layer was composed of leaves and culms (the jointed stems or stalks) of grasses. The animals preferred grazing to browsing, evidently, and their environment accommodated this grass-wish. This preference helps indicate to the team that the proboscideans in the region were mammoths, *Mammuthus*, not mastodons, *Mammut*. The latter, some researchers believe, were more frequent browsers than their woolly cousins. And indeed, studies of fossil pollen in the cave's vicinity reveal "unusually high proportions of grass." Some woody-plant material, though, was included in the grazers' diet—twigs of saltbush, sagebrush, water birch, and blue spruce show up in some of the dung, and I wonder whether they're traces of a year of drought or some other ripple of disturbance in the land of grass. Proboscideans: the word itself means, literally, to feed; it draws our mental attention to the surprise that is the animal's trunk, the nose that's also an arm and a hand and that can rip up sheaves of wild grasses, one mouthful after another.

In contrast, another large resident of the region, the shrub ox, was a browser. It seems to have been something like a cross between a musk ox and a mountain goat; it would have been a little smaller than a modern bison. This one is easier for me to imagine since I've watched bison graze, in gregarious numbers, across the Kansas tallgrass, some of the largest tracts of intact prairie left on the continent. I've seen them moving, shaggy and purposeful, across the upland hills, and found them clustered in the riparian gallery woods—oak, mostly, with a little cottonwood. In the mind's eye, it's not a stretch to imagine the alert curve of their horns metamorphosed into the musk ox's differing slope and droop. I imagine the shrub ox's muscular chest, the surprisingly nimble hooves. Another researcher found these beasts neatly reversed the proportions of plant life in their diet: for each shrub ox pellet examined, 95 percent of the plant material consisted of trees and shrubs, with less than 5 percent grass.

Today I call up the image of the lushest rushes and sedges in the canyon, and transpose tallgrass on the scrubby slope, mentally replacing the yucca plant that snagged my ankle, outnumbering the pinch-twigged ephedra shrubs with Indian grass, the bluestems, the turkey-foot tassels of autumn's aspect that add texture and color to the prairie vista. I scrub out the pale, bleached sheet of cheatgrass, an invasive (I think wryly of Aldo Leopold's essay from a half a century ago—"Cheat Takes Over"). And, gazing, I imagine a different profile of the landscape's slope and terraced lap. Not only was it a wetter world, it had more dirt: layers and depths of living soil to flesh out the substrate of Jurassic sandstone. The cliff tops, and the expanse of mesas, might have been almost as starkly bare as the ones I've hiked across these equinoctial seasons, but drop down into the canyons and river valleys and you'll see that the landscape likely hadn't been so deeply carved, marked by that force of degradation.

"It was an aggradated world," I tell myself, trying out the adjective. Aggraded. And indeed, the stratigraphic studies of the cave's environs tell us that the steep slope I scramble up, on all fours, was once a gentler grade, with an uneroded ramp of sand up which the animals could walk to arrive—unlike me: out of breath, panting in the dry, October air—in the sheltered chamber of the cave itself.

From within the cave's mouth, I gaze out at midday. Clouds have muted the colored sandstone of the canyon's opposite wall. Still, the basic shape of sheer, striped cliff abutting a skirt of underlying stone reminds me of the land's configuration some one hundred miles away, that "south bank" of the Colorado where the mastodon petroglyph stands out against the cliff. I realize I've stored up discrete, fragmented experiences, each like a single mark that the mind tries to assemble into a mental map, a presentation of the world I've seen into some larger, grander fact—the almost-glimpsed connective pattern of how each campsite, each hike's destination, plots a tiny portion of the land's advance toward the horizon. And to arrest in memory, in something like certainty, the present moment on an imagined graph of time.

I'm sitting, briefly, in the dry dust and sand drifted along the cave's threshold, but the wind picks up and tosses grit in my eyes, so I stand and head deeper into the chamber. It's big, stretching more than 170 feet into the hillside, with a high ceiling, in places some 30 feet above the floor. Both floor and ceiling slope downward toward the cave's rear wall, so once I've retreated several yards I'm completely out of the wind and the valley vanishes; all I can see through the mouth is the opposing stone cliff. It's pleasant here: quiet, and warmer without the wind chill. Researchers speculate that all the large mammals that entered the cave and left accumulated dung were only sporadic visitors who likely came to seek shelter from severe weather. I think that a blizzard or thunderstorm could rage outside and anyone sheltering there would gaze out at the inclement world and feel comfort and security from within Bechan's vaulted haven. But it's poignant to think of them, too: some of the dung the mammoths left behind dates to just 670 years before the species is believed to have become extinct in North America.

This, then, really is one of their last holdouts.

By now John's joined me, and we sit together at the cave's mouth, having lunch and regarding the valley below. While we're eating, John turns off the closed-circuit radio that occasionally squawks from his belt—it's quite annoying, we agree. For a while then, we're out of the collective, off line and off the chart. Sandwich in hand, he tells me a bit more about the research that's centered on this portion of the park. To our west, along the south bank of the Escalante River, a great deal of Pleistocene material has been found in Fortymile and Willow Canyons, including what's believed to be the entire, intact skeleton of a mammoth that hasn't yet been excavated. A beautiful Folsom point—not quite as old as Clovis, but still at least 10,000 years old, was also discovered. Here at Bechan, the excavations in the 1980s revealed that nomadic hunter-gatherers periodically used the cave between nearly 7,800 and 5,500 years ago—not quite a documented overlap with the Pleistocene mammals, but tantalizingly interesting all the same. Agriculturalists followed the hunters much later. They were in residence in the valley some 2,600 to 2,950 years ago, farming in the post-Pleistocene landscape. Holocenic, I think, trying another adjective. And then I think of Thoreau, hoeing his field at Walden Pond. Like him, the early farmers here were making the ground say "beans" instead of "grass."

From drawings included in the published research on the cave, I realize we're sitting very near the deepest layer of the mammoth dung, some fifteen inches of it.

"Look," I tell John. There's a little bit of black plastic peeking out from the dirt. There are also several large stones, placed to form a neat right angle on the surface of the floor. This must be the covering for the excavation site. I tease him a little, telling him we surely have a duty to see that nothing's amiss there. Shouldn't we poke about a bit, just lift up the top layers of soil? But though he laughs, he's implacable. We're not going to disturb anything, of course. Again, I must imagine the dung mat, the large, slightly squashed boluses I've seen in photographs, placed against sterile white backgrounds. I think, I should roll in this dust, clogging my pores with it, crusting myself in the particles of passing time. I could be rolling in dung dust, a mammal adorning herself, absurdly but gleefully, in the amazing material world. I squat for a moment, just barely tracing my finger along the surface.

On the way back down, I hear the signature birdsong of the contemporary landscape, a canyon wren fluting through the chill air, but I never see the hidden singer in the cliff. Continuing, John and I loaf and linger at some of the canyon's pools. Bright red cardinal flower is in bloom, but not yet gone to seed. We catch a few leopard frogs, an indigenous species that is having trouble along the lake's side canyons; evidently the young don't compete well with invasive crayfish. The wind continues, and as we reach the mesa from which we'll scramble down the bouldered slope back to the waiting boat, John pulls another piece of equipment from somewhere in his pack. Holding it aloft, he tries to clock the wind speed, but as soon as he's ready, the gusts slow down. Time passes, this way, without our scrawny ability to pin it down or hold it in our hands.

I've slowed down, too, poking my boot against loose litter on the slickrock. From a hundred yards away, John calls out, and I hurry over to see what he's found. It's a flint, a tiny arrowhead, pumpkin-colored and no bigger than my thumbnail. I balance it there a moment, atop my left thumb; like my own nails, it's ragged at the tip, the once-sharp point chipped off. Then I place it on the ground and take photographs with my Swiss army knife for scale; the knife is so large in comparison it casts the point in shadow until I nudge it a bit. Red knife, orange flint. Pink ground beneath, and tiny blond strands of dry grass.

The next morning, when the Park Service plane collects me at Bullfrog Landing for a quick flight back to Page, there's another passenger, a scientist who works with rangeland issues in the park. As we fly above the lake, he points out place names, one after another: canyons, mesas, coves. He tells me how bad the roads are, and I think again how fortunate I was to make my trip to Bechan by boat. The sky's reflected blue stands out so markedly against the warm, pale land; the lake itself meanders, an expansion of the ancient river course. The sequence of flooded coves, mile after mile, make the lake resemble an enormous zipper being pulled open, exposing water between the zipper's teeth. I think fleetingly of another petroglyph I visited, to the north and west of here. In Parowan Gap, a notch of land where some ancient, long-dry river carved its course, there's a peculiar figure called the Zipper Glyph. It's said by some to be an astronomical map, a calendrical design that, together with the east-west orientation of the windy gap and old stone cairns outside its narrow cinch, played a role—sometime—in observing the summer solstice.

But in the dry, bright, autumnal light, we fly above the landscape, and I imagine that the zipper figure of the lake has opened beneath me, just a bit. From this height I can see the gradations in color from the water's depth, the shelves and shallows. I watch our tiny plane's shadow moving like an unknown animal, hurrying across the ground.

I think I've seen another petroglyph depicting an extinct, megafaunal beast. In northeastern Arizona, not far from windswept Winslow, one day I hiked down into Chevelon Canyon with two other women, the three of us paid visitors to the private site, though strangers to each other. The owner, a rancher surely beyond retirement age, and his even older ranch hand were wiry, spry, and, once we arrived at the canyon site itself, remarkably trusting and generous. "Close the gate behind you," they cautioned. "But you can stay as long as you want, have lunch down here, take pictures."

The desert rangeland there is flat, expansive, stretching its dusty surface toward the paler, unclouded horizons, and interrupted only by the snow-capped cluster of the San Francisco peaks. The stream itself, like so many in this part of the world, is intermittent, though in that spring of record-high rains, it ran fast and cold. We climbed down a steep staircase and stood in an improbable and wet riparian fold of rock. From a sandbar beach on one side, we could see hundreds upon hundreds of figures, carved into incredibly thick and dark desert varnish. The opposite wall was heavily weathered, scarred and cracked and abraded. In periodic seasons of flood, that panel must be pummeled with debris: uprooted trees from their colonies on sand bars somewhere up the channel; boulders lifted from their tumbled beds below the length of cliffs; the sand itself, insistent, degradational. Overhead, obscured a little by the branches of one such rooted cottonwood, among the deer, the big-horned sheep, the zigs and zags and ladders leaning upward toward the sky, I noticed a peculiar figure. It was large, larger than any of the others in this panel, and it stood in profile, like nearly every rock art animal I've seen. It could, from its position, be gazing downstream, down where the water deepens into a long, still pool, "the swimming hole," the rancher called it. He played there as a youth.

Like the Moab mastodon, this figure was solidly pecked—no outline, it was an image made to be seen clearly, and to last a long time. The creature was four legged, though the front limbs had disappeared behind some other scar to the rock. A roughly level back. No visible tail. The head narrowed to a flexible-looking, drooping nose. Clearly, it wasn't a bear, nor any kind of cervid. A ground sloth? No, they had large, thick tails. A tapir? An extinct, giant tapir? They existed here, certainly; I've seen articles listing the ice age menagerie, and the tapir is known to have roamed what's now northern Arizona. Four toes on the front feet, three on the back, it's a strange beast, and in the literature about late Pleistocene extinctions and early North American hunters, extremely elusive. A mention, a name in a list, but not a featured figure. I haven't found accounts of their bones in trash heaps, not even here, in the earliest-known campsites of what's called the Little Colorado Terrace Culture, which dates to the days when the climate was changing, the very end of the Pleistocene and the dawning of the current age.

I waded into the cold water, trying to get closer. I tried to make out the feet—the two back legs were clear and distinct, but the feet themselves disappeared into the tangled scars of weathered rock. The current was fast and foot-numbingly cold, and powerful enough that I didn't want to wade in too deep; the waters of the current moment hurried past. The other visitors had climbed back to the rim, to eat at the picnic tables under a canopy roof in the shade, but I didn't want to leave the canyon. There was the nose, the shape of the head. There was the hint of an ear. Another step, and I was almost in to mid-thigh, and the water was even deeper just ahead. So reluctantly I turned back, splashed to the tiny beach of the sand bar, and rubbed my pale, numb toes. I wished I could see the figure from another angle—reach the slender tree, perhaps, and climb a few feet higher. So soon after the spring equinox, the tree was leafless, bare bark the same color as the scarred patina of varnish on the cliff.

In ecology, "aspect" can refer to the seasonal changes in the plant community; I must have been sitting in the *pre-vernal* aspect of Chevelon Canyon. I wondered how the day's changing light would change the petroglyph's appearance; I wondered how this maybe-tapir would appear if I were here in midsummer, estival. I pulled out an apple and a notebook, settled down against the granular bed of eroded cliff, and waited for the sun to dry my skin.

In Such a Homecoming

I can still understand my mother's dream of green quiet places and her struggle to reach them. And there were green places. As I think now of my own childhood, I can still feel an abrupt pang that rises not only from the shape of my parents' lives but also from the very disruption of the earth in Southeastern Ohio.

James Wright

I write this far from the quiet, green places in memory, the rumpled foothills of the Appalachian mountains and their plunging ravines where height sloped steeply downward into creek beds and hollows. It's nearly nine hundred miles across the country's midsection, an asphalted journey through former landscapes—the transformed prairies and forests that once fountained from the soil, under skies that dropped gradations of rainfall, moving toward the rain shadow cast by the Rockies' higher peaks. An academic itinerant, I moved west to Kansas to take the job that presented itself and as an adult learned over several seasons to call tallgrass prairie instead of hardwood forest, "home." It's a sense of home I worked hard to build and, after a devastating divorce, to reinhabit on my own terms. During my marriage, I'd imagined the work I was doing to be making a kind of space for my then husband and me to share and flourish in. As the primary breadwinner for many years, I sometimes spoke of "making a clearing" for our lives together. I wanted to lay emotional claim to the territory I'd come to, and though I broke no literal ground, instead coming quickly to value the much-diminished expanse of indigenous grasslands that rippled under every wind, my metaphoric vocabulary drew on motifs of settlement. A friend once told me, "When you moved to Kansas, you really *moved to Kansas*."

That's true, I like to think. I came into the country, and let it come into me. But it's also true that southeast Ohio remains fast in my psychological and emotional landscape, so that the whiff of fallen leaves in a hardwood forest, the damp touch of Ohio Valley humidity beneath my hair, along my neck—these are so deeply familiar, they suggest the intimacy of family, of place-that-is-in-the-blood. But this kind of environmental legacy, this ecological intimacy, this sense of the land as *oikos*, home—it isn't a matter of simple residency, citizenship. It's a complexity, worth teasing apart, or trying to, to see whatever cause and pattern can be found.

"Where are *you* from?" It was the way children establish identities in the brief encounters that occur on family vacations. As the older sister, I answered for us both: my younger brother and me.

"We're from Ohio." A pause. Then, eliciting further conversation. "But ask us where we wish we lived."

The other child was obliging. "Okay. Where *do* you wish you lived?"

"Colorado. We used to live there, but we moved away when I was seven."

I remember this exchange, though I'm not sure where it took place: at the beach, at Nag's Head the year we drove south and east to spend a week in an old-fashioned resort hotel, surely long since torn down for more aggressive development? Or were we actually on the road, perhaps gathered at a motel swimming pool, a Howard Johnson's maybe, somewhere along the interstate on the way west for one of the beloved summers spent, throughout my grade-school years, in the mountains of Colorado, the ostensible paradise we'd left behind?

Because for some time, I adopted my mother's attitude toward our "new home" in southeast Ohio. She was desperately unhappy there, though it would take me years to realize that it was not *because* of Ohio, or even (which I also believed) because of *us*, her children. It was the nearly inexplicable fact that she had somehow taken up residence within the confines of deep, personality-crushing, even physically crippling depression, from which she couldn't emerge. And so our surroundings took on the dark colors of that psychological domesticity of despair, with its clouded windows and dusty staircase to the cold, closed-off second floor. The little hill town where we lived was "culturally deprived," the rivers and streams polluted, the countryside molested by decades of strip mining. I realize now it was far too much like the worst aspects of eastern Oklahoma, the place of her childhood that she'd strived so hard to leave, investing heavily in education as a ticket up and out. So in her frustration, my mother took us to *West Virginia* ("Oh, *Mother!*") to shop for school clothes, since there weren't adequate stores in town. As we drove south along Route 7, we passed coal-fired power plants, appalling in their inhuman belch and roar. And as we headed into the countryside for weekend visits to the various state parks, we'd pass tumbled-down coal tipples, unreclaimed mine sites, and creeks that ran oozing and crusted red or orange with acid mine drainage. Meanwhile, at school, my classmates (peers from Elsewhere, anyway), told West Virginia jokes, with Appalachia as the cultural butt end of every punch line.

But each summer, for a few brief years, our family drove back west and spent weeks in the mountains in a primitive cabin resort where my mother boiled our drinking water, pumped up from the creek in a thick black hose; where we had fires in the stone fireplace even in July; where one morning I awoke and, looking straight out from the cabin's porch, saw fresh snow topping the peak in the distance. In reality, this too, was a ravaged country: the immediate area had been a nineteenth-century mining center, and on a long walk we sometimes took up the canyon we'd come across tipples and shafts and pale, sulfurous slag heaps from the boom-and-bust days of the gold mines. But it was Paradise. My parents fly-fished, my father spent the mornings writing, and my brother and I wandered the aspen-rustling hillsides, learned to read where avalanches had bent or broken the slender trees, visited the astonishing communes of anthills, conglomerates of pine needles and grains of granite. Once, I recall, we found one torn apart by digging—a bear, most likely—and we hurried back to tell about it.

It was, I'm sure, this migrant lifestyle that delayed my own identification with Ohio as home, reinforced by my mother's unhappiness in our hillside house on Grosvenor Street, our disgust with the junky used car lot down the street, the local, unfamiliar accent that said "spatial" when people really meant "special." What was it, finally, that changed my mind? That is, what changed *me* and the myriad subtle, even subliminal emotional whispers that would shift from "there" to "here"?

It's a complicated process, the way in which we learn about our "place" in the world. I don't mean by this primarily one's social position—class or caste, one's ranking in the pecking order that is the economic reality in which a family, figuratively, resides. I mean really, literally, the *place* itself: the lay of the land, the rhythm of its weathers, the precessional change that the seasons bring throughout the year, the march of shadows, drought, and frost across the enduring ground. We all know the fact of Americans' mobility: from a history of immigration, we have settled into an expectation of transience, moving on average every five years or so. Some of this movement is from the apartment or starter home into a larger house, the upward mobility of real estate acquisition. Some of it is the due to the severance of divorce, the rupture and fission of households. But much of it is, indeed, a kind of itinerancy, following a job or a company relocation. That's how we came to Ohio, following my father's career. We joined a university community already seething with the conflict over the Vietnam War. Throughout my time in the public schools, hostility was bristly and virulent between children of local families who'd lived in the area for generations and children of newcomers, whose parents most likely worked for the university. There remained a shadow of colonialism. Appalachia had long been a place removed from the sources of power; it was a land that supplied resources through extractive industry (timber, iron, coal) with very little development of locally controlled wealth. So it was true from the outset, we were outsiders.

The disintegration of my parents' marriage, my mother's moving out of the house—our house—while my brother and I remained with our father; this, of course, figured largely in our emotional lives. It was unusual: my father became the custodial parent, deeply, unceasingly dedicated to the role. For a few years, we remained in the bedrooms where we'd chosen the wallpaper, in the house from which we could *all* walk to school—my brother to East Elementary, me to Athens Middle School, my father to the university campus. We no longer hired the woman from out in the county to come clean house. Instead, a weekly list of chores hung on the refrigerator, and my brother and I were to initial each job as we completed it, choosing and owning the work we did for the household. In those few years, as if in a perplexing modernist novel chapter called, say, "Time Passes," further change unfolded before and around us, which can be elided into the barest of narrative summary: I entered high school; we moved a few miles out of town to the country; my father remarried. But I want to examine what happened when and how I stepped out of the confines that my mother's despair had erected like heavy Victorian drapes. Long before my first semester in the university dorm, or my first apartment, I spent increasing time out of the house, *outside*, in the second- and third-growth forests that had reclaimed southern Ohio from the nineteenth-century attempts at subsistence agriculture on steep clay slopes. One year I was given a tent, another, cross-country skis. I remember heading to the woods, to a particular tree I considered a good location for thought, to write a paper for my high school English class. In college, I took a sociology course that focused on Appalachia. I read Henry Caudill's *Night Comes to the Cumberlands* and learned, with surprise, of indentured servitude's role in the settlement of the region. I learned of Zane's Trace and the Northwest Territory; I read about Simon Kenton in historical novels by Allan W. Eckart, and I even read James Wright's poetry precociously and naively, sometimes sitting out under a large tree. But I believe it was the time spent outdoors, in contact with land itself, under its deciduous canopy of trees, that suggested to me I was not ultimately, irrevocably, an alienated outsider.

Once my father and stepmother moved out to the country, my brother and I had miles and miles to explore. We rode our bicycles five curving miles, the last three all downhill, to the state park at Dow Lake and then turned around for the slow, low-gear grind back up, with each bend in the blacktop road marked by the scent of its foliage: oak leaf, sumac, sycamore. A distance runner, I'd sometimes jog the route as well, returning home elated with exhaustion. On foot, together we wandered into each steep ravine, and, hike by hike, we came across the history of settlement along the watersheds of Peach Ridge. In one hillside pocket, we found the sandstone foundations of a house long since melted away, and, a few hundred yards below, a spot where someone once had set a great ceramic crock, with a hole knocked in its bottom, into the hillside. A slow seep of a spring would have once gathered in a kind of well, but by then the crock was filled with dirt. I imagined the family living there, perhaps daily drawing water faster than the seep could refill the crock. Perhaps, we reasoned, they had a rain barrel, too? We came back with shovels and wrestled the artifact up, out of the clutch of hillside clay. It must have taken us most of an afternoon; it took muscle-knotting effort, and I loved it. The deeper we dug, the sloppier the soil; we knelt in the mud, sat in the mud, pulled mud from within the cavity and around its base. Finally, muddily triumphant, we rolled it uphill to the ridge-top road, and on along the quarter-mile to home. My stepmother recognized its worth instantly, and with a flourish of enthusiasm made it a planter, to keep things alive and blooming near the house.

One winter day, layered in long johns and boots, my brother and I headed miles away, along a deeply cut ravine that met up with another such side valley and then opened into a tiny flat spot with the narrow trace of a stream flowing past, just enough level land for two log cabins that still stood there, rotting darkly among the piebald sycamores. From the much-collapsed doorway of one, I stood still and looked straight up, imagining how the hills, day after day, would allow only a segment of sunlight past their steep, austere horizons. Sunlight maybe from ten to three, as in the song about Kentucky's deep valleys and the darkness of poverty. Even farther down that same trickle of stream we found a house of frame construction, with newsprint from the 1940s papering the walls. Beavers had dammed the creek and built their stick mound of a lodge, and we spent time pond side, then and later, hoping for a glimpse of the animals themselves. I knew that formerly the animals had almost disappeared from many American waterway systems, trapped into scarcity for their pelts. It seemed marvelous to know they'd come back here, to homestead where the people had given up and moved out.

Even farther down that hollow the valley widened, opening into a tiny rural community, an actual store (long-since abandoned, of course) with an old tin roof and a rusted sign leaning against the wall. It was summer when we found it. The place was lush and dense with the spider webs that lace together the underbrush, and clotted with the great snarls of greenbrier that take over disturbed land, leaving decades-long legacies of thorn and thicket. The air must have smelled like sassafras, a scent I roll around in my thoughts, as if tasting it now in nostalgic absence, half a continent away. A house and a barn stood nearby, all dating to perhaps the first few decades of the twentieth century. Exploring among the fallen boards, the rusting machinery, the summer-warmed undergrowth of jewelweed and bracken, we startled a large snake, which startled us even more. A copperhead! My brother, urging me to stand back, killed it. And so we'd had a kind of testing far from home, it felt to us then; we had journeyed in, and come through danger, and made our way back safely to tell the tale.

These were the woods adventures of my adolescence and my brother's childhood. They allowed us to step right out the front door into a kind of historic frontier, where we examined the hillsides for bits of history: hidden pathways of old roads, former homesteads, the current communities of maturing hardwood. It's easy to see these as the archetypal enactments they were, and even at the time I knew how performative of inner discoveries our travels were (I was, after all, a reader and writer, even then). When we told the story of the slain snake, I am sure I smiled at the symbolism of it: my brother, deep in the forest, had dispatched the dragon that lived among the ruins, and had saved his sister's life. The fact that neither of us was ever in any real danger made the death of the snake unnecessary, but, an isolated event, it didn't mark my brother as an habitual or senseless killer, not by a long shot. It was mythic imagination, playing out in the landscape where we were growing to maturity, marking us and changing us in the period of our lives that's evolutionarily dedicated to change.

This kind of play is today almost absent from American childhoods. There are soccer leagues and expansive, halogen-lit playing fields; there is concern about predatory adults who may molest or kidnap or kill; and there's less and less land left fallow amidst development. Today, the valley where we found the abandoned store and killed the snake is a small, upscale subdivision, planted with fescue in among the thinned trees, with signs declaring, in lettering that looks well paid for, Private Drive. The hillside where we excavated the crock lies just across the road from a large parcel of land owned privately by out-of-towners as a hunting zone. One recent year, as adults come back to visit, we scorned the braying red-and-black perimeter of tacked-up NO TRESPASSING signs, and trudged, silent and grim, along bush-hogged pathways to the specter of feeding stations, where plastic barrels of corn lay in wait for later, deadly use beneath the shooting platforms riveted into the trees. Though it wasn't yet rifle season (the very reason why we dared to climb over the metal gate that blocked entrance and head into those woods), we could easily picture the men in camouflage, coiled above the bait, waiting. The landscape was in the grip of killers, wealthy and, we felt certain, walking home along the low-grade blacktop, unprincipled.

I'm certainly not the only person who believes that getting outside helps the mind believe in its own good health. The writer Richard Louv openly discusses a nature-deficit disorder that he believes afflicts American children, often in the form of ADHD. But it wasn't just play in the acres and miles that lay in concentric fields of walking distance around our house in the southeast Ohio woods that, I believe, allowed us to "come home" to Ohio in our psyches. One spring break, I took my brother camping in Zaleski State Forest. I think it was the first or second year I owned a car, an ancient black VW bug, as old as I was, anyway, hardly highway safe, but I drove it around the southern part of the state, hoping not to get stopped for any inspection, since the turn signal didn't work. Neither did the horn, come to think of it, and on the passenger side there were holes in the floor large enough to catch glimpses of road rushing beneath. But the car ran, and it was mine, and together he and I piled our gear in the back and drove to a trailhead in hardwood forest for a weekend backpacking trip. It was too early for most wildflowers—trillium and spring beauty would bloom soon, but not yet—and we nearly froze overnight, but despite its spartan minimalism, I think of that trip as the inauguration of decades, later, of camping together.

Another time I signed us up for a "Century Ride," an organized cycling trip to Forked Run State Park, beside the Ohio River. Our entry fee secured room for our gear in the sag wagon and paid for two meals, dinner that night and breakfast the next morning. It was the longest ride either of us had ever made. I was nineteen or twenty, my brother thirteen or fourteen, before he underwent the growth that would, forever after, reverse our roles and leave me following in his athletic wake, trying to keep up. We hung together for much of the ride, though in the social throng of peddlers, we'd sometimes go separate ways and travel in conversation with some other acquaintance. Two of the riders had been our next-door neighbors when we lived in town, owners of a bicycle and outdoors store. Another couple were current neighbors from the country who lived across the hollow. The year before, they'd taught me how to ski cross country, crashing ungainly but elated along forest trails they'd cleared near their place.

We peddled fifty miles that day, over back roads heading south and east. For a brief, alert while we strung out along a state highway but then turned off again, into more quiet miles among trees. The park itself sprawls over a couple of thousand acres, where the Shade River joins the Ohio. It's bottomland: wet and warm and buggy, the air thick with the river's respiration, as well as the trees', and, of course, our own hot panting as we rolled slowly in and leaned the bikes against a sapling. We pitched our tent—my first tent, I realize; it must have been fairly new then—and I lay down to fall instantly asleep.

My little brother, a skinny, smooth-faced boy already developing greater stamina, went swimming in a pond and later stood in line for our dinner and brought mine back to me, where I lay crushed by exertion. That evening, the campground was dotted with wood fires and low voices, interrupted occasionally by the percussion of someone's laughter. And the next morning, after a terrifically caloric breakfast, our stuff stashed in the support van, we headed back up north, fifty miles again, into the hills of our home county.

One year I spent a weekend backpacking with my college roommate, another local girl who'd stayed close to go to school in our hometown. In high school, she and I had hiked together in England's Lake District, constantly cold and wet, hoping each night at the youth hostel we would be able to dry our perpetually sodden gear. I was near-hypothermic the entire time I tramped through Wordsworth's country, and she developed a phenomenal case of blisters and would lance them in the evening in whatever castle or tower-turned-hostel we'd reached for the night, while I watched with horrified interest. Once, we had sat together in the evening's gathering chill beside Loch Ness, wondering what would happen if we actually glimpsed anything unusual out across the water, in the misty distance. We'd crossed Mount Helvelyn's scree-field crust and descended to a little village pub where I ate steak-and-kidney pie and thought it was the most deliciously hot meal possible: Pangloss potpie. So here, we chose a sunny, warm weekend in autumn. With each tree nearly leafless, we moved through extravagant sunlight in southeast Ohio's hilly terrain.

The trail meandered through handsome stands of hardwood, curving in and out of hollows and ravines, but it also crossed through pine plantations that had replaced some former clear-cut. We carried all our water for the weekend; my friend's father, a biologist at the university, studied the effects of acid mine drainage on the invertebrate population, and we considered ourselves forewarned. We had no intention of drinking any water we came across in the injured woods of coal-mining country. At one point the trail crossed a wasteland of tailings: it was hardpan, with hardly any vegetation at all. Water pooled in red and orange, oozy-looking shallows. Wounds, obviously. Unhealed and leaking.

But the trail moved back into forest, and we followed its horizontal saunter across a history of land use: former farms, former roads, sections of variously aged forest. We came upon two young men, tents pitched behind them while they sprawled in the sunlight, eating from an aluminum pot of macaroni and cheese the color of mine drainage. We passed rock outcrops and overhangs cloaked in thick moss and trailing the litter of fallen leaves—season after season of accumulation from the forest's dropped canopy. We ate peanut butter and apple and chocolate. We talked almost incessantly, as young woman do. And that night, we pitched our tent—my tent—alone in the margin of light before dusk, and cooked the utterly unimaginative meal of ramen noodles over her brand new, exquisitely minimalist backpacking stove. It wasn't wilderness, but it was, then, lovely: dark skies above the near-bare branches.

And so, in the contemplation of how I learned to feel at home in southeast Ohio, I've stepped into the pathway of memoir, holding memory's imperfect thumbprint images of a quarter-century ago, when, emerging first into and then from adolescence, I moved across the Appalachian landscape, *a place*, as we say tiredly of those whose lives have taken more than one questionable turn, *with a past*. Somehow the patterns left by earlier eras seemed to me, most often, poignant: the great coke furnace named, as if in purposeful irony, the Hope Furnace, where slag still lies in cast-off piles from the years when old-growth hardwood was turned to charcoal to fuel the iron mills that, for example, made most of the cannonballs for the Civil War. Or the occasional depressions in the forest recognizable as old cellar holes. Sometimes, even in the depth of the returned forest, daffodils still bloom in banks that mark a former walkway, or the spot beneath a window where a woman must have looked outside to see their bright, early-spring flourish.

When, a year ago, I had the opportunity to make a kind of pilgrimage to a tiny stand of tallgrass prairie back in the upland forest country of southeast Ohio, the possibility instantly rose up tinted with the shadows and gilt trim of symbolism. Could this be a kind of circling back, a chance to put worlds together—"my" worlds, that is, of forest and prairie, past and present? It was a chance to come outside again in the middle of my adulthood, to explore the world of my childhood—the *world* itself, not just my narrative footpath through the realm of memory. In such a homecoming, I'd be again on the land, in my skin, coming into the country of the self through the sensory play of place upon person.

Buffalo Beats is a tiny open spot in the hardwood forest, less than an acre of grass and forbs beneath—on that particular day—a dinner platter of blue sky, clear and full of October light. I'd read about this place years before and marveled at it: such a minuscule portion of prairie, a relict of what has been called the prairie peninsula, the fingers of grassland that during warmer, drier cycles in the climate of the distant past, reached this easternmost position in Ohio. It's amusing and rather touching to read the early descriptions of the place in scientific publications. In the mid-1940s, a researcher wrote of "the date of migration and the migration routes of the ancestors of the prairie plants" of such isolated grasslands. Were these personifications invasions from the West, dating to some time before the great glaciation periods, the Illinoisan and Wisconsinian? Or were they later arrivals, come up from Kentucky, like the many rural Appalachians who, mid-twentieth century, left the green hollows for work in Ohio cities? And so, from a distance, across the smooth margin of the desk and the page, I took it as a personal symbol, a kind of mental amulet I carried in imagination instead of on my person.

This prairie enclave is a secret place, defined in part by its fragility, not open to the public though it lies on public land, and it took some work to parlay my way there. But on the day I'm scheduled to visit, I arrive to find that my contact has called in sick, and so another Forest Service employee kindly agrees to make time in her day to take me there. She's not a botanist and she hasn't been to the site very often, but she seems cheerful about the task. After all, it's a beautiful day, and she's glad to put on her boots and head into the field. We drive a few miles along dirt back roads and leave my car, with the fine dust of Kansas still clinging to its hubcaps, to explore the hillside. She's not sure precisely where it is, so we must canvass the area. From a high point, I scan the forest with my binoculars, looking for some pattern of light and shadow, or the pale hint of grass in sunlight.

And it works; I pass her the field glasses, and we agree, that looks like an opening in the forest, on a hill in the near distance. We move through the mild autumn day and step into the clearing; the sunlight catches in the drying grass and looks nearly ethereal. Today I can recognize many of these plants, though I wouldn't have growing up: big bluestem, Indian grass, New Jersey tea, prairie gay-feather. The last, *liatris*, now grows in my front yard beside the mailbox. Yet here we stand in Ohio, in the crisp, sun-warmed smell of hardwood forest, the deciduous sniff of one home, and the dry-stemmed glint and wind-whisper of another. How powerfully smell figures in memory, in emotion, in what we call in animals *territoriality*, the endocrine system laying synaptic and hormonal claim to the world that impinges on us richly, through the portals of our senses.

There was once a footpath that ran here between the little communities of Happy Valley and Utah Ridge to the town of Buchtel. We can see no trace of it among the grasses, though it can, on occasion, be found in the surrounding woods. It dates to a time when people would have walked, often, from home to town or elsewhere in the cycles of their daily business. I think of the various tiny communities—a house or two, or the place I've inwardly named The Store in Snake Hollow—which my brother and I rediscovered in our cozy adventures, fanning out from home, and the possible paths we must have retraced along ridge and ravine. Today, arriving at the opening in the forest, we're ringed mostly by oaks, living palings that mark the encroaching perimeter of the forest. I stand in the center of the circle of grass and turn slowly, looking up, looking all around. I sit down, grass reaching just over my head, and the forest disappears. I stand again, and the prairie instantly shrinks, domesticated by vertical perspective.

This little holdout of tallgrass has, indeed, held on—researchers say the soil records a grassland community that existed here at least some thirteen thousand years ago. It's a tiny portion of the Pleistocene world once grazed and ranged by the vanished animals that lived south of the ice sheet: the giant ground sloth, stag moose, musk ox, mammoth and mastodon, and perhaps, in some nearby lowland swamp, the preposterously giant beaver the size of a bear, called *Castoroides ohioensis*. I like the possibility of these distant beaver kin existing somewhere close by; I like the fact that the first remains of a *Castoroides* lodge ever found was also in Ohio, along the Beaver River in the western part of the state. I think of the beaver lodge my brother and I found along the little creek two ravines away from home; I think as well of the beaver dam that broke one summer on the Colorado stream we lived near, and how the resultant flood amazed us with its force and stagnant smell. And in the flood of memory, of worlds converging within me as well as without, I stand still in this, the middle of my life, and see again my little brother in his blue-striped shirt, standing beside me, or already moving off ahead.

The Kingdom

It's the first night on the trail. We got a late start, my brother, his girlfriend, and I, and we huffed our way steeply up through an old clear-cut and then through mature forest before crossing some invisible line into designated wilderness. We're hurrying, hardly pausing to admire the wildflowers or taste the berries along the way, sweating to make it before dark to Hope Lake, the first possible campsite along this section of the Pacific Crest Trail. We'll be out a week, and the packs are heavy with provisions.

But when we reach the lake, we have to stop and reconnoiter. There are already two parties assembled here. One has pitched a couple of cheap tents right beside the water (not, we note scornfully, the required one hundred feet from shore), with an illegal campfire sending surly smoke slowly from its scar in the grass; two hoodlum-looking teenagers slouch in the clearing. The other party, a group of four, isn't camping. They are a middle-aged father, his young son, and two men who look to be in their early twenties; they are having a tense conversation with the scruffy teenagers from, as we say in the language of political struggles, "the other camp." Hudson, Dawn, and I stand still to catch our breath and watch the little drama.

The father and his group have been doing trail restoration work all day, carrying heavy saws and picks and shovels. They evidently left their other gear stashed in the woods by the pond, and now, they say, it's missing. The hoodlums deny knowing anything about it, but none of us believes them. They also say a ranger was there earlier in the day and told them their fire was fine so long as they made sure it was out before they left. We don't believe this, either.

"Would you mind staying for a few minutes?" the father quietly asks my burly brother. And so we become International Observers, there along the Pacific Crest Trail. We stand quietly, the air stiff with tension and our own drying sweat.

One of the hoodlums finally confesses—"My friend took your stuff, okay? I'll try to find it for you"—and he plunges theatrically into the underbrush. His initial efforts retrieve a backpack, a flashlight, and not much else. The little boy's pack is missing, as is the father's sleeping bag. Two more hoodlums arrive and mill ineffectually about. A man of perhaps thirty-five or forty appears—he seems to be the leader of their outlaw gang—and declares repeatedly that he had *no idea* what the boys had been up to; he'd just brought them for a fishing trip and to show them the wilderness. I stand beside him, tell him, brightly, that this is a teaching opportunity he can take advantage of, though in truth I wouldn't trust him further than I can spit—which, after the hot, quick climb, might not be much farther than my own boots. The young men from the father's party also search, and they have greater success than the sullen louts: the father's sleeping bag is located and the son's pack, though a few items are still missing.

"I can't find my Ninja Turtle!" the boy says. (He is perhaps ten.)

"Oh," I say to the Head Hood, as if he will share in my indignation. "For shame. Stealing from a child." He sputters a bit, wanting, I suspect, to be mistaken for a better man than he is.

We need to get moving; this peacekeeping mission has taken nearly an hour, and the sun is dropping fast. There's no question of our staying here now, bedfellows (or at least shorefellows) with the shamed and surly riffraff, so it's on with the packs and away we go, at an achingly brisk pace. Perhaps another mile and a half along, according to the map, we'll cross a ridge and hit a small stream. That's our new goal, since we've left Hope behind (I can't resist pointing this out, but we're walking too fast for anyone else to chuckle much).

Turns out it's more than a mile and a half—and it's a very, very small stream. We set up tents in the day's last light, while dried vegetables soak in a water bottle. We're all a little snappish, hungry, and unhappy to have arrived right on the verge of dark, and of course out of sorts about our brush with delinquency. The backpacking stove sputters and gasps and uses too much air, blackening my lightweight cookware with fuel-smelling soot.

But dinner is wonderful. It's Alpine Stew, with vegetables I blanched and dehydrated back home: carrots, peas, potatoes, mushrooms. A powdered cream sauce. A miniature can of chicken. And biscuits, hot and delicious, if unevenly browned because of the disreputable—indeed, delinquent—behavior of the stove. I turn to Hudson and Dawn, and quote Steinbeck to them. "Now each of you kids get a nice flat stick," I say, but this joke falls flat too, even to my ears. Ma Joad is out of place here, and we want to have left the struggle of the social world behind. Hudson and Dawn wash dishes in the dark, scrubbing the soot with wet pine cones; we hang the bear bag, dangling our food high out of reach, and we feel sheltered by the old-growth trees. The air chills quickly with the sun down, and the ground smells moist, fungal, and rich.

We talk briefly about tomorrow—where we'll go, what we might see. What we'll eat. I suggest, "we could have pasta with salmon and nettles. Or pasta with morels." Hudson has packed in a Nalgene bottle of Chardonnay as well; we'll set it to chill in some high-elevation lake, and the wild mushrooms, brought all the way from a riparian woods in eastern Kansas, will plump up in the cold water. We feel communally self-sufficient, with gear and food and excellent company.

I spend a lot of time preparing for these backpacking trips. A lowlander in prairie country, I look forward each year to the time I can spend in the montane West. I spend days dehydrating vegetables as they come ripe in spring and summer—blanched asparagus from the local farmer's market, cut into inch-long pieces and dried. With grated parmesan, egg noodles, and a powdered cream sauce, they're sumptuous. Dozens of straw-berries, sliced and dried, to be soaked in water and served with oatmeal, or in chocolate pudding, or with powdered milk and sugar over biscuits as a kind of shortcake. Dried season-ing from my tiny herb patch on the south side of the house. Young, tender nettles, picked in early spring and quickly dried, which reconstitute like tiny thumbnail-sized spinach leaves. Later, when the local market sells bruised or overripe fruit on hot days, I come home with whole bags of plums, whirl them with honey or a ripe banana in the food processor, and make indestructible, delectable fruit leather. Throughout the spring and early summer, I gather and prepare the food we'll need for trail season—high summer and early fall. Do the descriptions make your mouth water? Maybe not; dried nettles might sound like an eccentric's penance, a way to mortify the flesh. But al-titude and exhilaration make an excellent sauce, and Hudson is likely to carry up real butter; I might have roasted pine nuts tucked in a baggie, too.

Best of all are the morels. I gather these in April, out in the county along the Kansas River. One of Dave's courtship rituals, as I recovered from the emotional damage of an abrupt and crushing divorce, involved bringing me to his family's secret spot, harvesting, cleaning and cooking, and eating the morels together. Part of kinship and community, however stylized or nearly unrecognizable in the commodification of modernity, is still the sharing of food. We watch the trees as spring breathes its southerly winds across the prairie, and as soon as the oak leaves are the size of squirrels' ears we head out to the river bottom, each carrying a knife and a large cloth sack, with pants tucked resolutely into socks in case the ticks are also out this early in the season.

For the contemporary gourmand, mushrooms are attractive because of their low calorie count and absence of fats or cholesterol. For the backpacker, they dry to marvelously light, compact slivers of nutrition, since fresh mushrooms are roughly 90 percent water. And morels concentrate their unmatchable flavor as they dry, ensuring that, weeks or months later, the rehydrated meal will be splendidly savory. Their protein content, I've read, rivals that of spinach or potatoes, two foods well storied for strength (the former) and survival (the latter). Wild morels measure up to 35 percent protein, compared with single-digit percentages for oatmeal or barley bread, the ancient, so-called staff of life. But fungi can also concentrate heavy metals deep in their cellular structure. Along highways where they have been exposed to leaded fuel exhaust, as in Eastern Europe, wild mushrooms are very high in lead; near the disaster site of Chernobyl, radioactive isotopes have tainted the otherwise edible fungi. A fungus is a great recycler; it's not surprising mushrooms should pass along the poisons of modernity, though it's ironic this radioactive legacy should take its form in a literal, living mushroom, not the iconic cloud towering above the ravaged ground.

When we first went hunting for morels together, Dave's daughter Ellen showed me how to slice them right where the waxy stalk disappears like a tiny tunnel into the forest floor. "Look around the base of the really big trees," she taught me. "When you see one, then you'll probably see lots."

And in this miniature forest on the banks of the Kaw, there are, indeed, some really big trees—pale-branched sycamores, canopied bur oaks, and the cottonwoods, clusters of trunks splayed out from their microclimate of moisture and mulch. Morels love the soil near great, old cottonwoods. Along this particular stretch of river, there are several such secret groves in the larger woods. They are the homeland of mushrooms. Mycorrhizal, morels live in symbiosis with tree roots; the fungal filaments extend throughout the smallest rootlets and help them absorb nutrients, while in turn the plant supplies the fungus with sugars. Like animals, mushrooms can't produce their own food through photosynthesis, and so they rely on plants, whether decaying wood or living roots, for their nutrition. In fact, though they occupy their own phylogenetic kingdom, fungi are evolutionarily more closely related to animals than to plants. Researchers theorize that just over a billion years ago, a single-celled ancestor for both fungi and animals diverged from the lineage that would lead to the plant kingdom. Perhaps we could consider only two "kingdoms" from this genetic history: Makers and Eaters. Metaphoric predators and prey. I've read that in the language of some indigenous people in South America, there are two separate verbs that mean "to eat." One is used for eating plants; the other, for meat and mushrooms.

This year our first successful "hunt" was even earlier than usual, as spring seems to come increasingly early to the plains. Dave, Ellen and her teenaged friend Cynthia, and I all headed out one bright afternoon after school. The woods were still bare as we entered the gothic structure of cottonwoods and honeysuckles. The girls, dressed in retro punk-rock, ripped-shirt style, quickly made themselves invisible, urchins in the forest. We heard them for a while, laughing and singing, but then they moved out of range. Perhaps an hour later, as the day waned, Dave and I decided it was time to start working our way back, crashing noisily through bracken and dead branches. At last we emerged, our bags plump with morels; there was Ellen, waiting for us.

But where was Cynthia? We all called, but got no answer.

Now, this is not a vast forest. It is a thick, inviting woods, but it's a hard place, I think, to really get lost in. Dave and I can both yell with impressive force, which we did repeatedly, but for over forty minutes we sought and found no Cynthia. We canvassed the woods again, sweating and breaking underbrush. We honked the car horn. At one point I said to Dave, "There was a pickup parked by that oak when we got here; it's gone now. Should we be worried about that?"

"I'm worried about it, yes," he said.

Then I spoke with Ellen. "Did you girls have a falling-out? Is that why you weren't working together? Is she maybe unhappy or hiding?" No, Ellen didn't think any of those things were true. So then, in imagination, I encountered visions of a kidnapped ragamuffin teenager and our having to call the police, and then her parents. I pictured some dangerous rapist driving her away, over the back roads along the river, to the next county or the next state. But at last she emerged, her own cloth bag slung about her neck, walking quickly in her used, black combat boots. She said she'd never heard us calling, down there in the girth and tangle of the woods.

The role of mushrooms in diet and folklore can be traced far back in the Old World. For millennia, people have used certain forms of fungi as tinder—one in particular, *Fomes fomentaria*, is commonly known as "true tinder bracket." Never having tried it, I suppose it must be a little like the fire starters that intrepid Girl Scouts learn to fashion from readily available materials—a mixture of drier lint and wax from old candle stubs. Knowledge about mushrooms with medicinal properties long predates Alexander Fleming's discovery of the penicillin mold: some have been used to treat arthritis or gout; some were considered aphrodisiacs. Others—the famous fly agaric or *Amanita muscaria*—were poisons used to kill pesky insects. Medieval herbals and Greek natural histories treat delicacies and poisons in their discussions of fungus, but people have known since time immemorial about the hallucinations that some species bring. And fungi have even extended into the iconography of the heraldic world: a few European families included mushrooms in their clans' coats of arms.

In the special collections of my university's library, I poke around for mushrooms in the knowledge and cuisine of earlier centuries. One afternoon, I hold a copy of Platina's *De Honesta Voluptate*, the earliest known cookbook in a native, regional language, first printed in 1462; this particular copy dates to 1487. It's the only book I've ever held that has a wooden cover; there is some insect damage to the boards (and to a few of the pages within). Early in the twentieth century, the volume belonged to Joseph D. Vehling, a scholar and the biographer of Platina; his bookplate shows a grinning skull wearing a white chef's cap. *Mors Coqva*, it says. Death of the cook!

Fortunately the library also has an English translation of the original Italian, and I thumb through. It's clear Platina didn't think much of mushrooms, as he has few words on their culinary preparation, but much to say about their deleterious role in society:

From many examples we learn that the eating of mushrooms is conducive to crime. By this enticing advantage, Agrippa killed Prince Claudius with a mixture of mushrooms and poison. Mushrooms have a cold and damp nature; and on account of this, they possess the force of poison. They grow in leaky soil and sour dirt. . . . They are pale and like the fig tree in color, and those that grew near iron mines and serpents' lairs are thought to be deadly. The dampness also clings, showing as it floats on top of the poisonous kind. I believe I have read that mushrooms are in open regions also, and these are deceptive. For we know in our time acquaintances who have died from them.

By 1770, in Britain, Mrs. Martha Bradley, "late of Bath," held a less judgmental view of mushrooms, including in her book half a dozen recipes and no sociological tracts against the moral repugnance owing to fungi. She groups them with greens, in her discussion of ingredients, and says that in summer, "There are mushrooms from the Hot-beds and from pastures, but the latter are vastly preferable."

In 1829, in Philadelphia, a Mr. Colin Mackenzie published an astonishing volume titled *Mackenzie's five thousand receipts in all the useful and domestic arts: constituting a complete practical library relative to agriculture, bees, bleaching, brewing, calico printing, carving at table, cements, confectionary, cooking . . . By an American Physician.* The first chapter is on metallurgy, not a very tentative introduction to domestic arts, I think. This "complete practical library" is well used, judging by its weakened binding. Tucked inside is an invoice from a Boston bookseller, dating to 1971; the volume cost the library $25. I turn the fragile pages and find two interesting passages. The first is a how-to for the citizen-farmer. "To produce mushrooms. If the water wherein mushrooms have been steeped or washed be poured upon an old bed, or if the broken parts of mushrooms be strewed thereon, there will speedily arise great numbers." The other passage is a recipe for pickling the harvest, storing them in glass jars with cork stoppers, "in a cool place."

The Boston Cookbook of 1883, by Mrs. Mary J. Lincoln, declares that "Mushrooms are considered difficult of digestion. They are a fungous growth, and have a woody odor and a meaty flavor. Unless familiar with the difference between the edible and the poisonous mushrooms it is safer to use the canned mushrooms, or to obtain the fresh at a reliable market. . . . Those with yellow or white fur, and which grow in damp shady places, should be avoided. The good mushrooms spring up in open sunny fields in August and September." Though immigrants coming to Kansas from the eastern states might have found Mr. Mackenzie's printed database invaluable while staking a claim and establishing settlements, Mrs. Lincoln's would not have proved very useful, I'd guess.

In fact, in the first half-century of white settlement in Kansas, nearly all the attention paid to the region's fungi dealt with rusts and smuts injurious to agriculture. Not until 1919 did Elam Bartholomew, a rancher near Stockton, publish a short article on edible species. Appearing in the Transactions of the Kansas Academy of Science, its tone was not one of measured, scholarly objectivity. "When the good Lord staked out the territory of Kansas," he proclaimed, "it pleased Him to hedge it about with such peculiar conditions that we are almost if not entirely free from poisonous species." And of the edible species, there was great bounty. One day in June, he says, he came across so many meadow mushrooms, *Agaricus campestris*, that "I feel safe in saying . . . there could have been gathered a large farm wagonload."

I conclude my little indoor survey and leave the windowless reading room with its green-shade reading lamps, and sign out as I leave. If I hurry, I can spend a few hours outside before nightfall, and I realize that I want very much to go for a walk, out among the "peculiar conditions" beyond the campus lawn.

Such variety, such mystery. One early summer day, walking to work, I pass a perfect ring of white agarics that have sprouted after a rain in a large, grassy lot where a university fraternity intends to build a new house, if they ever raise enough money. It does look magical, this so-called fairy ring, this hoop of mushrooms on the grass-and-clover lawn. Another day Dave shows me a strange, strong-smelling specimen that he has found. It's from the stinkhorn family, and its name is well chosen, for the colorful, finger-sized fungus soon fills the room with a smell like a mixture of rotting meat and sodden compost. I consult a book and find that these stinkhorns have had even more colorful names than the vivid Anglo Saxon: here is *phallus impudicus* or *fungus virilis penis erecta forma*. In a late-nineteenth-century U.S. Department of Agriculture publication I find a drawing of a spotted white stalk with a green cap, similar to our summer stinkhorn (though the cap on our specimen was the unfortunate color of a puffed-cheese curl); it has the common name

"Fetid Wood-witch." The description given is the shortest of all those under discussion: "If this species had not been eaten, it would hardly be necessary to refer to it. It is offensive and dangerous." *Stincan*, I remember, was a strong verb in Old English, inflected *stink, stank, stunk.*

I can't quite believe Dave has brought me this thing. "*Simblum spaerocephalum*," he says cheerfully. But it's a stinkhorn.

It's true that mushrooms, like flowers, are essentially genitalia. Most of the fungus lives unseen in the dark, in the soil or leaf litter. Microscopic filaments, called hyphae, spread through the earth, sometimes throughout several acres. These filaments accumulate to form the *mycelium*, from the Greek *mykes*, or fungus. When two filaments pair, a *primordium* forms, a tiny, nonanimal homunculus, a mushroom in miniature. This is the fruit of the fungus, which will rise from the soil to disperse spores, either through the air or with the aid of insects. The paired filaments must not be of the same sex, though among the fungi there are various numbers of sexes, making literally thousands of pairings possible. Oddly, the books I read refer to various "genders" in each species, which I think shows unscientific inexactness, since, as any sophomore women's studies student will tell you, sex is intrinsic, biological difference, while gender is culturally prescribed behavior. Type, perhaps, and stereotype.

According to biologist Nicholas P. Money, fungi helped change the world early in the planet's cultivation of life on its fragile crust. Half a billion years ago, mycorrhizal fungi spread their thin, pugilistic hyphae through rock, reaming out tiny conduits for water to percolate and breaking down stone into protosoil. There wasn't much humus then, only, he says, "thin sludges derived from cyanobacteria and other simple microorganisms," but the force of the fungi helped make the Earth's earth. Their fossils, dark trails preserved in granite, show how they perforated the hard, unpeopled ground, facilitating the evolution of plants. Eons later, humans stood among the savannah's grasses, and then slowly trailed their way north, and east, and west, across the scattered continents.

I think about the last time we went gathering morels. How companionable it felt; we were a small band of hominids moving through the forest, breaking branches and rustling through the leaves. Occasionally we would make little contact calls to one another, like birds, perhaps, or other primates, being mindful of the story of The Separation of Cynthia from the Group, and not wanting to repeat that particular experience as we gathered food for the evening meal.

Lately, I have been reading an account of the discovery and study of Ötzi, the fifty-three-hundred-year-old mummified corpse found frozen in the Tyrolean Alps. Found by energetic, athletic hikers where he poked out of the rapidly melting ice of retreating glaciers, Ötzi became the object of a power struggle among the Austrian and Italian governments, the central government in Rome, and the local authorities in South Tyrol. At first, they assumed he was a recent corpse, something only decades old, or maybe from the last century. Then, after they ripped and chiseled him out of the ice, they realized they were looking at someone who died long before the rise of nation-states and bungling governments.

In their bickering, the authorities relied on maps that indicated that his body lay on Austrian soil; later surveys, however, determined the exact spot was south of the border, in Italy. Political jockeying and posturing followed until a negotiated agreement called for the study of the corpse by a regional Austrian university at Innsbruck, after which the remains would be returned to the Italian province of South Tyrol. I am interested because I've come across a brief note that the Iceman had carried different sorts of fungus with him—tinder and two dried mushrooms.

"What purpose did they serve?" Dave asks.

"I don't know yet. Maybe it was a kind of talisman. The guys who dug him out of the ice really tore him up—they used a jackhammer that shredded his hips, and maybe tore off his penis. Reconstituted, maybe a nice bolete could serve as a shamanic, prosthetic penis."

Dave dismisses this idea with appropriate scorn, and I return, giggling, to the book. (Further reading discloses that the penis was not torn off—it was only so shrunken and desiccated the scientists hadn't even noticed it in their initial examination of the corpse, and I mirthfully report this, too.)

Despite this bawdy humor at his expense, Ötzi is a deeply appealing character in his multimillennial drama. He lived—and died—at the cusp of two eras: most of his tools are stone and bone, but he also carried an ax cast of nearly pure copper.

The archaeologist Konrad Spindler has suggested a disaster narrative, in which the long-dead man was an Alpine shepherd who had come down from his usual pasturage in the high country to his home village in the valley, perhaps to help with an agricultural harvest. There he fell victim to some kind of attack, during which some of his equipment—arrows in his quiver, his bow—as well as a few of his ribs were broken. Perhaps it was a struggle for land, or personal property, or some other thing thought worth fighting over. In Spindler's story, the man quickly cut wood for a new bow and shafts for twelve new arrows, and then fled to the high country where he could be safe in terrain he knew well. Exhausted and injured, however, he never made it off the pass where he was found more than five thousand years later.

But part of this story is contradicted by biologists' analysis of the botanical samples recovered from his person. He didn't die in early autumn, as the scientists first guessed. It was months earlier. And the ribs showed no signs of healing along their fractured edge, suggesting that they might have been broken after his death, due to some disturbance or compression to the body in the snow and ice. After picking apart material from the man's gut, botanists found einkorn, a domestic crop from early in the age of agriculture, evidently ground up and baked into some kind of flatbread—tiny bits of charcoal attached to the bran showed it had been baked over a conifer fire. Painstaking analysis revealed that he had swallowed lots of pollen from the hop-hornbeam tree, which flowers throughout late spring or summer in valleys lying to the south of the mountain range. The pollen, which must have settled on his water or his food, proves that he came from the south—modern-day Italy—and was heading across the Hauslabjoch ridge, north through the Alps into modern Austria. In that season, crops might be growing in the lower valley of his village, but there was surely snow along the mountain pass.

Not long after that final meal, the man must have collected his belongings and hiked north into the high-country world of snow and stone. He carried excellent gear: a birch-bark container holding embers for fire starting, a leather fanny pack holding flint blades and a drill bit, an awl of bone, a wood-handled retoucher for sharpening stone blades, and the fungal tinder. He had a quiver with arrows and his new, partially carved bow; a flint-bladed dagger with a little grass carrying pouch; a wooden backpack frame. He wore leather boots lined with grass, a fur coat or undercloak, leather leggings tucked into the boots, a fur cap with earflaps, and a water-repellant grass cape.

Most interesting to me, he seems to have had something of a first-aid kit. Those two mushrooms that had early caught my interest, threaded on a leather thong as if for a talisman or ornament, were identified as *Piptoporus betulinus*, commonly known as the razor-strop fungus, a bolete that has antibiotic properties. I nod, reading. One should always be prepared, of course, when heading into the back country. And he wasn't in the flower of youth; he was likely old for his era, in his late forties. There were small tattoos on his lower back, legs, and feet, several corresponding with ancient Chinese acupuncture points. X-rays revealed that he suffered from arthritis, so researchers wondered whether the tattoos, too, were a form of therapy.

As June begins, I find myself thinking of this ancient traveler, this Ötzi. Named for a river valley in the region, the Ötztal, he represents a largely inaccessible part of our prehistory in Europe. He is a man of his time and his place, in ways that far exceed what we usually mean by that phrase, and his body preserves tiny material emblems of a world that has largely vanished into our unconscious, or perhaps into unrecognized vestiges of language or belief. All winter I've suffered a foot injury that threatens to keep me off the trail this summer, though it's also likely I'll heal just enough to decide I can risk it, and so load up both equipment and desire and head northwest. Maybe that's one reason I feel such tenderness for Ötzi, for his individual humanity—and mortality—wrapped and buried deep within the wonder of his age.

He died in violence and far from home. Recently, researchers trained a CAT scan on his bones and found what killed him—a stone arrowhead lodged in his left shoulder. He was shot in the back by someone who had likely tracked him there after an earlier meeting—small cuts are still visible on his right hand and wrist that might have been made as he raised his arm to protect himself against attack, perhaps from a hatchet. These wounds had begun to close, so we know he survived the initial altercation for at least a day or so. But someone found him, there in the high country. Someone stood above him, as he must have lain bleeding, and pulled out the shaft, leaving the arrowhead in place. Perhaps their eyes met, briefly, so that Ötzi knew who killed him, just before he bled to death.

I am—I hardly need to say this—no longer young, though it's also hard to convince myself of that on days when I dream of joining my brother among the Pacific Northwest peaks. The mountains hide among their jags and folds so may unexpecteds; they embody a kind of solitude, but I'm thinking today, it's good not to be traveling alone.

The meal together by the lake.

The shared moment at the pass.

The view—*oh*, we say to one another, voices small in the sky's dome that hardly covers us, *come look*—from here.

The Scribe in the Woods

Would you know more, or what?

This is a refrain that surfaces, at intervals I'm not schooled enough to recognize in the Old Icelandic meters, throughout an early-thirteenth-century poem called, a little mysteriously, *The Prose Edda*. I say mysteriously because no one seems to know the derivation of the title; it may refer to Oddi, an estate where the poet, Snorri Sturluson, studied as a young man under the care of his foster father. What a lovely place name it is. I think, if I ever own property in northern latitudes (though that's not very likely), I should name the place "Edda." But in some contexts the word means "great grandmother," a translation that scholars find irrelevant to this admittedly very masculine composition, though, if you let your mind wander enough, gazing out the window, you can almost convince yourself the name fits. Or "Edda" may be derived from a word containing the eth symbol, "óðr." This thick little word means soul, mind, or perhaps poetic gift. Should we choose among these meanings? Did Snorri himself, that dead, far-distant author, engage in a little meaningful punning and wordplay? Ægir, a character in *The Edda*, complains that kennings and figurative language can obscure things. More reticently, but with similar conclusion, a contemporary scholar muses: "It is more prudent to leave the question open."

But I'm getting ahead of myself. *The Edda* recounts Old Norse mythology, tales of the world's formation and the early doings of the gods and giants and other beings that shared the world with humans. It's a link to the storied past of northern Germanic peoples, separated from us by hundreds of years and significant language changes; it offers glimpses of the landscape they inhabited, at least as they conceived it and themselves within it. The Edda contains distant worlds. *Would you know more, or what?*

Gylfi, a Swedish king, wishes to understand the power of the gods, and he undertakes a journey to their home and stronghold, Asgarðr. Disguised as Gangleri (Wayworn), he asks his questions, and from three great personages (High, Equally High, and Third), he receives answers. I read them all in a prose translation.

The gods hold court, he learns, by the ash Yggdrasil. "The ash is the best and greatest of all trees," Equally High tells him and promptly launches into a mythic geography lesson. "Its branches spread out over the whole world and reach up over heaven. The tree is held in position by three roots that spread far out." These roots reach toward different realms of existence—one extends to the gods, the Æsir, one to the frost ogres who dwell in a dangerous territory containing a spring, called Mímir, "in which is hidden wisdom and understanding." The third root, continues Equally High in his description of the realms of existence, "is in the sky, and under that root is the very sacred spring called the Spring of Destiny. There the gods hold their court of justice. The Æsir ride up to that place every day over the bridge Bifröst (Rainbow)."

Yggdrasil is the Cosmic Tree, both the habitat and the regenerative force of the world. "There is a great deal to tell about it," says High One, mildly. "In the branches of the ash sits an eagle, and it is very knowledgeable, and between its eyes sits a hawk called Veðrfölner. A squirrel called Ratatosk springs up and down the ash tree and conveys words of abuse exchanged between the eagle and Niðhögg." Niðhögg is Striker-that-De-stroys, who lives below the well of Hvergelmir and gnaws continually at the third root. Other forces of destruction abrade Yggdrasil, too: four harts eat the shoots and leap through the branches; along with Niðhögg dwell "so many serpents no tongue can count them." In this telling, High One interrupts his own narration to quote another, even older poem:

The ash Yggdrasil
endures more pain
than men perceive,
the hart devours it from above
and the sides of it decay,
Niðhögg is gnawing from below.

Despite affliction, the tree persists. Again, High One quotes poetry:

I know an ash-tree
known as Yggdrasil,
tall and sacred
besprent with white clay,
thence come the dews
that fall in the dales;
it stands ever green
over Urð's spring.

In my study, a wall of books at my back and before me a picture window facing north, opening to a view of hackberry and cedar trees that punctuate and define the yard, I smile to learn that a poetic kenning that Snorri uses to name and honor the world-tree is aldrnara, life-sustainer.

Would you know more, or what?

The footbridge across Thunder Creek was washed out in last October's back-to-back floods. Salvaged pieces of railroad tie lie stacked on the far shore; the banks are still tangled and torn with debris and a logjam provisionally clots the current, an incomplete dam of huge trees washed from clear-cuts farther up the watershed. The trail is closed, with a flimsy barrier tape warning against the dangers of a bridgeless world. But we sidestep the tape and set foot on the nearest of these half-submerged boles and trunks, some a good three feet in diameter, and make our way across the river. "Creek," says the map, but I think it's a river—still swift here, just before it stalls out in the impounded reach of Diablo Reservoir. The water is turquoise blue in the afternoon sun, the color of glacier melt, powdered with stone dust from the heights beyond view. A few of the great logs shift slightly underfoot, but nothing really rolls, and it's a quick, easy crossing to the sand-heaped bank beyond, a width of perhaps forty feet at this broad point. We thrash briefly through nettles and devil's claw, skirt or leap a few more standing pools, and then recover the trail that in former years has led to campsites in the ancient forest spread along this cool, Northern Cascades valley, under cedars, hemlocks, Douglas firs. Once, we stop and file right through the split trunk of a western red cedar, its sides standing like two blocks of sandstone fallen from some slowly shifting cliff. Ephemeral flesh inside the tree, I watch the landscape's demonstration of phenomenology, the world as if paused in its continued play of matter commanding the senses.

We're hot. We're a little cross and cramped from too many hours in the car and we don't tarry long at either log or cedar edifice. Instead, we stride higher into the forest, my brother and his girlfriend pointing out the names of ferns they recognize, exclaiming over the cushy depth of moss, trying to glimpse the creek as it navigates the steeper landscape with whitewater features, waves and chutes that hold their position as the water rushes through, reminding us that time is grander than the casual mind remembers. An hour in, we begin to look for a place to sit and eat a late-day lunch. We pass two designated campsites, empty now, dark green and still beneath the landmark trees, but then push on for a better view of the creek. At last we find it, an open spot poised against a cutbank from the autumn floods, where there are downed trunks to serve as furniture and a handsome view upstream. After damp pita, dry hummus (a disappointing combination), and some salvational dark chocolate, Hudson puts his hat over his eyes to rest for a few moments, and Dawn and I approach the ragged cliff bank and look below to the rocks and thundering creek. We throw in a few sticks that thrash and bob and speed downstream. Then we look at the nearest log, and at each other.

Of course, I have objections. The bank is concave and could crumble beneath us—a tumbling collapse to the stones and frigid current below. But it's too tempting, and we both ignore my concerns, roll the heavy log up to the bank's ragged selvage and cast it over the edge. I jump back and watch as it drops ten or twelve feet to land—on land, at the dry foot of the cliff bank, where it stops quite still, short of the water.

This, too, is disappointing. We'd imagined the log in the current, bucking and splashing down to eventually join the logjam we had illicitly crossed. But by now Hud is fully awake, chuckling, and has snapped a few photographs. He stows the camera in the pack, still smiling.

As we wend back down the way we came, I keep pausing to look up at the trees, so essentially straight in the afternoon air and richly quiet. Hardly any birds. And no other people in this, a kind of double reserve, a closed trail in a preserved, old-growth forest. Up, up, the still trees reach through shadow into sunlight. Here, where the mountain soil is poorer than in lower slopes, they grow slowly, so these enormous trunks must be *very* old—many hundreds of years, certainly. Up, up. And we walk down, to cross again the self-stationed raft of debris; the water has risen since our earlier crossing, with a few wedged logs riding noticeably lower than before. Perhaps that's the normal rhythm of the day, we think, the river's summertime refrain: an evening rise with the warm day's meltwater from above. We cross over on the backs of felled and flood-borne trees and continue through the ancient forest. In an enormous, rotting stump on the slope above the trail, I see notched holes, apertures where the loggers who felled that tree—perhaps a century ago, themselves by now long dead—thrust in a make-shift plank to stand on as they made the downhill cut. "Spring-boards" they were called, like a modern diving board, and I wonder whether they quivered and moved beneath the sawyers' effort, and whether the men, as they finished the cut, leaped off to scramble clear as the great tree came crashing down.

Where the water has slowed in the reservoir's southern-most cove, we stop again and put on suits for a quick dip. Dawn grew up in Michigan and speaks enthusiastically of plunging into northern lakes to swim. This water is very cold, as only snowmelt feels against the body. But the air is warm, and once out, my skin tingles and glows with the sensual delight of the blood's response. Again I dive in and half-swim, half-stagger back and dance briefly on the sand bar as we watch the sun strike the eastern, opposite shore. The perfect horizontal of the lake abuts a low border of willows, before the sharp rise of young mountains and ancient trees. I watch the portion of sunlit water grow narrower, until only the beach and willow leaves shine.

Flood damage marks the landscape throughout the Mt. Baker-Snoqualmie National Forest this year, from fresh scars along the highway, where car-sized boulders closed the road and brought trees sliding from the slope, to the bridges in the back country that, until last October, spanned creeks and streams for trail and road alike. When Hudson and I arrive at the Hildebrand Creek trailhead, bound for Elbow Lake, we find that the bridge across the Nooksack is also gone, buried in a great heap of dead trees and boulders, but a new log, smelling of freshly peeled bark, has been laid across the water several hundred yards downstream. It probably won't stay put in another season of high water but for now it's tidy and sturdy, and it lets us cross over into the Mt. Baker Wilderness, along a gently climbing trail amid so many enormous trees.

In fair weather these forests suggest stillness, endurance that comes from patience rather than violence or struggle. At ground level you can see how the world is made, how the earth grows from the trees as well as they from it. Two hundred feet of fallen trunk, wrapped in a green pelt of moss and lichen long before it flattens and melts into the earth (since that will take centuries), is itself a hillock sprouting hemlock in the canopy's shade. Beneath the repeated, seasonal drumbeats of sapsuckers, a great cedar snag drops a talus-slope of wood chips and dust. And at the base of a vigorous Douglas fir you can climb a foothill that stands well above your height, a sloped collection of duff and humus, stuff sloughed over centuries to form a landscape feature fashioned by the place itself. The trees, I think, are places; they are persons; they are things. But they are also, on a scale I hardly know how to notice, verbs. And while some landscapes, and some weathers, suggest the austerity of the sublime—the abrupt and sudden juxtaposition between sky and ground, stone and earth, now and long ago—I find these northwest forests very different. They blur past and present, like a verb tense that must exist in some languages, but none that I know. They defy my available toolkit of grammatical categorization, and so set me to thinking about transcendence and connection.

I wanted to think about old trees this summer. I'm grateful that my brother takes me into ancient forests, ecosystems he's devoted his career to saving. At night he barks his imitation of a spotted owl (a rare bird he's seen exactly once); by day he pauses patiently while I gaze along the rising line of Douglas firs or try to identify the thrush that's disappearing farther into the shadows. The world registers as a field of forms, but the forms hint at motions behind them, a dance just beyond, or within, the visible realm.

Would you know more, or what?

As we amble upward, we step into a shaft of sunlight. Caught in the illumination, a few wisps of tree—needle? lichen?—sift downward. "Litterfall," I have read, is the name of this slow accumulation of matter—for the biologist, *nutrients*—from the upper reaches to the lower. "Throughfall," a similar process, brings water along each needle and twig. In the resulting "stemflow," rain and fog dissolve additional nutrients along the slender branches in the canopy, all of which will travel through some three hundred feet of forest air to reach the earth. A mature Douglas fir can live a thousand years, holding along its body some thirty pounds of lichens; the tallest ever recorded (after being felled, of course) was 385 feet. These trees, I think, are translative, as, throughout the summer drought, they harvest fog drip, intercepting from the sky as much as eight inches' worth of water. The landscape that was dominated by Douglas fir once stretched five hundred miles along the Northwest coast and covered at least 28 million acres. Much of this is gone now, but there are still marvelous stretches of that forest world, intact and healthy, and Hudson tells me of various efforts to protect not only trees but the realms they build and harbor. We hike a gentle four miles today, through timber both protected and not, till we pitch our tent between two lakes, hang our food from a tall but youthful Douglas fir, and sleep. We lie against the slowly changing earth, while moonlight crosses Elbow Lake from between the darkened wings of evergreen; all night the trees conduct their silent transactions between soil and sky.

"Hwæt!" exclaims the Old English poet, perhaps a man named Cynewulf, sometime in or just before the eighth century, as he begins "The Dream of the Rood." Within several alliterative lines, the great tree in the poet's dream begins to speak, to recount to the dreamer its passion and suffering in holding the crucified Christ against its blood-stained wood. The poem is fascinating on many accounts—its antiquity, of course, and, if you stumble a bit through the Old English vocabulary, the weird, rocking rhythm of the telling. But it's the point of view that seems so striking, so arresting. The poet disappears into his own dream, becomes thrall to the vision of the tree, itself mere matter metamorphosed into everlasting glory through its sympathy with the tortured Christ. In a prose translation, "the best of trees began to speak words."

"It was long ago—I remember it still—that I was hewn down at the wood's edge, taken from my stump. Strong foes seized me there, hewed me to the shape they wished to see, commanded me to lift their criminals." Thus is the tree slaughtered and then enslaved by the slayers of Christ. Yet after his "grievous sorrows," the tree is chosen by God as a beacon for Christian contemplation and awe: "On me God's son suffered a while; therefore I tower now glorious under the heavens," the tree explains.

Folded deep within this Christian dream-vision lies the pattern of Christianity's destruction of the older, pagan world. As the sacred groves of Europe were cut down to silence their inhabiting gods, this tree, too, is felled—and then removed and refashioned. While the tree itself becomes a kind of Christ figure—first pierced with nails, then risen—it holds the power of its original vertical reach.

I'm thinking here of spirituality, the replacement of nature and place-based religions with Christianity's portable teachings of the relationships between God and, specifically, man, embodied through the mortal son of God, all independent of any sacred connection to the living landscape. But of course, there's an alternate, more secular tale laid down in the tree's narration, another version of which Walt Whitman would tell centuries later in "Song of the Redwood Tree." Large, multitudinous, and ebulliently enthusiastic, the American Bard sings a tree's celebration of anthropocentric orthogenesis, an attitude of purposeful evolution whereby the noble trees gladly give way to industry and imperialism. "A chorus of dryads, fading, departing, or hamadryads departing, / A murmuring, fateful, giant voice, out of the earth and sky, / Voice of a mighty dying tree in the redwood forest dense," the poet hears, and translates. "Nor yield we mournfully majestic brothers," says the redwood,

We who have grandly fill'd our time;
With Nature's calm content, with tacit huge delight,
We welcome what we wrought for through the past,
And leave the field for them.

They, of course, are the choppers, the "quick-ear'd teamsters," broad humanity, woman and man, whom Whitman loves to praise: "the true America, heir of the past so grand, / To build a grander future."

When my students read this poem, they shake their heads. They like Whitman far more than they like Thoreau (which surprises me a little), and they feel he has let them down personally with such rhetoric. Andrea, a passionate, outspoken woman, is nearly outraged. "I don't care if he was a man of his time! This is almost disgusting," she exclaims. Another student asks, "So, had he ever been to California?" Had he ever seen a forest of redwoods? Did he know what he was talking about? It's an excellent question. And he hadn't. He'd traveled to the "west" of his age, the Mississippi River, and down to bustling New Orleans, but for him the farther reaches of the American West remained abstractions, symbolic possibilities of democratic vistas. He hadn't ever walked among those particular, tremendous lives.

"[N]ever before did I enjoy so noble an exhilaration of motion," exclaims John Muir in The Mountains of California. He has, following a winter rainstorm, climbed to the top of what he calls a Douglas Spruce. It is one of a clump of like-aged trees, about one hundred feet high, he tells us, "no one of which seemed likely to fall unless the rest fell with it." Here he rests "for hours," while the wind continues to move through the upper reaches of the forest, surveying the countryside around him and glorying in the "storm-streams of air in the mountain woods." He grows philosophical, of course. "We all travel the milky way together," he writes, "trees and men; but it never occurred to me until this storm-day, while swinging in the wind, that trees are travelers, in the ordinary sense. They make many journeys, not extensive ones, it is true; but our own little journeys, away and back again, are only little more than tree-wavings—many of them not so much." This, I think, from a man who walked from Wisconsin to the Gulf of Mexico. This, from a man who fairly towered in the nineteenth century. And I like to think of him perched, that brightening morning as the sun came out above the Sierras, in the needled interstices between the earth and the sky.

I sat on my Horse viewing the prospect around me; endeavoured with the small portion of light & understanding I was furnished with, to feel after the propriety of removing here: being resigned (as I thought) to remove here or any where else, that I could believe was my proper allottment___perhaps I looked for greater clearness, than was in wisdom seen meet to be dispensed to me, and which I hoped I should be furnished with to enable me with cheerfulness to undertake a wearisome Journey to a Strange land, with a tender wife and helpless offspring, over so many terrible mountains, which I have dreaded from the time I crossed them, and often, very often, reflected on since.

A young man named Joseph Gibbons, a Quaker from eastern Pennsylvania, wrote these thoughts in his travel notes in 1804, as he searched in Belmont County, Ohio, for a suitable place to buy for his family; they intended to emigrate from Chester County, east of Lancaster, Pennsylvania. Throughout October, with his father-in-law and a friend, he toured the newly settled lands just west of the Ohio River. It wasn't wild frontier, he wrote, as there were numerous towns and settlements, and there had been no Indian skirmishes for a few years, but the country was still heavily forested around the developing farms and he worried about the difficulty in getting crops and produce to a well-paying market along rough roads. He hoped for "clearness," a Quaker concept based on reflection to discover divine purpose. Perhaps what was difficult for Joseph was that he needed to come to his decision largely by himself; he traveled with two good companions who also intended to relocate, but it was up to him alone to select the land on which his family would settle. Even today, "clearness committees" formed by the Quakers' meetings offer communal "testing and discernment" to help with these kinds of momentous decisions. Such a committee "makes the space for us to deepen our awareness," as a contemporary writer explains. But no such group advised Joseph as he journeyed along the Ohio Valley. His notes sound lonely in their contemplation of the great change this move would mean.

As he traveled, he wrote about the country's timber, soil, crops currently in cultivation, and its establishment of stream-powered mills, with his eye toward both the present and the future prospects. Once, near Short Creek, he rode along "a beautiful level Road through exceeding Rich land___the border of the bank at our right was lined with large trees of various kinds amongst which were a great number of Sycamore trees ___I measured the Stump of one that had blown down & found its Circumference at the height of 3 feet from the Ground was 28 feet___another one was growing & appeared to be perfectly Sound measured 40 feet."

Elsewhere in Gibbons's notes he enumerates the trees that constitute the "extraordinary fine" timber: "White and Black oaks, Red, Spanish, & Chesnut Oaks, Sugar Maple, Hickory, Black & White Walnut___Beech in some places plenty & large, Wild Cherry, Honey & Common Locusts, Pawpaw or Custard tree, black and white Mulberry, very fine Ash, Some Chestnut, but not plenty, a good deal of large Shell bark___Iron tree, Buck-Eye, Elm, Lynn, Gum, Ash Sassafrass___in some place the Cucumber tree & a tree called Mahogony, Crab Apple, Plumb trees, nine bark, Spice, and leather wood bushes." I love these lists of particulars, the common-name specifics that comprise the forest around him. He's describing the great woods, the eastern deciduous world that preceded European contact. Researchers believe that 95 percent of what is now Ohio was once covered with such forest, stippled and perforated with prairie peninsulas and canopy gaps from storm damage. Despite Indian rearrangements of the landscape—farm fields, villages, burned openings to provide grazing land for game—a forest ecosystem once dominated the land east of the Mississippi, now only glimpsed in miniature enclaves, little islets of individual trees rather than wide watersheds of woodland community. One of these remnants still exists in Belmont County, a few miles from the same route that Gibbons took two hundred years ago as he searched for "clearness" and cleared land on which to situate his young family. It's called Dysart Woods, some fifty old-growth acres spread across two ravine slopes separated by a ridge-top county road, where, in 1813, Miles Hart settled to farm. Hart likely knew his neighbor Joseph Gibbons though he leaves no written record of his own first arrival to convert the forest into farm. In 1902, when Henderson Dysart acquired the land, those slopes remained in original forest, and throughout the first half of the twentieth century the Dysart family left the trees uncut.

Today the old white oaks are the hardwood elders of the hillsides, some with diameters of four feet across and heights of 140 feet. I spend an afternoon here, walking a figure-eight trail that loops through both ravines, past large beech and maple on the moister, north-facing slope, past a few great tulip poplars, one fallen just a year ago, another still towering its straight, impressive girth to the heights of the upper canopy. This is a world of colors and odors I love from my youth in southeast Ohio, and the brook that runs over blond sandstone, with autumn leaves already beginning to line the streambed, looks utterly familiar to me: it is homeland. How deeply the senses speak to memory and to the body's recording of its own emotional life. In a sun-warmed forest, the light on the turning maple leaves, the mingling of leaf mold with the dried crispness of beech leaves shed this season, the slight rippling of the shallow creek—all these cohere as I descend into the cupped incline of the ravine, stepping down into personal history, natural history, and the autumnal sense of rich senescence. It's been over a decade since I spent an autumn in the East, and I feel I'm making a sort of pilgrimage, a journey home in search of woodlands and old growth, family and old friends. But despite my years in Appalachia, I'd never seen this tiny patch of original forest, and the poplars and oaks I knew personally were only second or even third growth, trees that had sprouted and flourished early in the twentieth century, in the sudden open sunlight left after the nineteenth century's great spasm of lumbering. These trees in Dysart Woods date much further back: they were small saplings in the seventeenth century.

"I'd give a few pennies to know what was going on in that forest four hundred years ago," says Brian McCarthy, leaning back in his fourth floor office in Porter Hall, where more than twenty years ago I took geology and geography courses. "But we'll probably just never know."

He's the director of the Dysart Woods Research Natural Area; some of his studies focus on dendrochronology and dendroecology, identifying and documenting, as he says, "historical disturbance regimes in forest stands." Pre-Columbian times, he explains, are difficult for ecologists to address. Dendrochronologists can use tree-ring studies going back sixteen hundred years or so for the very oldest extant trees. Since European-American weather records sometimes include only the last century and a half or so, it can be impossible to place radial growth rates found in the trees' core samples against their backdrop of drought and flood, unseasonal frosts, or other tropospheric events.

That is, it's hard to be a student of disturbance.

Paleochronologists, McCarthy continues, can use pollen deposits beginning about a thousand years ago. For his own work in Dysart Woods, the existing tree-ring record can take him only so far—he's studied fire scars, for example, from a 324-year-old white oak that was toppled in a windstorm, and can narrate the sequence of fires in the forest, twenty-seven of them stretching from 1731 to 1881. He has mapped and surveyed the living presence of trees (fourteen different species) and quantified what's called the relative importance value of each species (this is the relative density—how many trees per sampling area—plus the relative basal area [each tree's girth at its base] divided by two). Despite the algebraic equation, I like the term, *relative importance value*, which suggests, I think, community, contribution, and not simply numerical value but contextual appraisal. I imagine it demands, even from the professional researcher who will be evaluated sternly by his peers, some kind of relationship with the subject of study.

But the oaks are dying now in Dysart Woods. That is, as Brian has written, they show "obvious decline symptoms . . . branch dieback, limb loss, mortality." And he tells me, in unguarded conversation, that it makes him sad, sometimes, walking around in those woods. Though white oaks can theoretically reach perhaps six hundred years in age, he speculates, most can't hope to fulfill that potential; their natural life span for these particular forest conditions—soil type, slope aspect, and so on—may be limited to four hundred years or so. Or there could be something else at work that's killing them. A severe drought wracked the Midwest in the late 1980s; the weakened trees may be more easily susceptible to pollutants in the Ohio Valley, like lead or acid rain.

However, a very different danger threatens to literally undermine the old-growth trees in Dysart Woods. Like so much of Appalachia, the surface and the substrate have been legally separated for generations. Even though Ohio University has owned the land since 1967, the mineral rights belong to the Ohio Valley Coal Company, which has filed a permit application to mine the area: longwall mining adjacent to the old-growth plots, with room-and-pillar mining directly beneath the ancient trees. At issue is the Pittsburg Number 8 Coal seam: upper Pennsylvanian and lower Permian formations, the metamorphosed death of ancient, vanished forests, in what geologists call the Dunkard Group.

The mining proposal calls for "rooms" of extracted coal measuring twenty feet wide, with intermittent supporting pillars left in place that are forty-five feet wide and sixty feet long. The "extraction ratio" ranges from 48.1 percent to 52.3 percent. That is, roughly half the coal seam will be removed, several hundred feet below the surface, leaving bleak, artificial chambers within the vein of coal where, if all were to go well, for hundreds of years absolutely nothing would happen. No water would enter, and none, as acid mine drainage, would emerge to bleed across the landscape. An empty stasis would inhabit the catacombs left from the extraction, as if in physical fulfillment of the myth of separation—surface from subsurface, action from result, all carefully suspended in language's conditional mode.

But several experts have testified that the company has no basis for its claim that the forest will not suffer from the operations. As one hydrologist notes, "drily," I think, the company's permit application to the State of Ohio "does not present defendable hydrologic consequences." Two springs lie within the old-growth section of the forest, named in the literature unceremoniously as Springs 151 and 152. Along with others throughout the entire woodland acreage, they have been mapped and marked with orange stakes, for monitoring both before and after mining begins. One lies high on the hillside of the southern plot and drains along a small, stone-shelved seep; you pass it like a stationary sentry on your way downhill, before you've even glimpsed the shapes of the big trees below. Another lies near the creek bed, flooding a tiny marshy opening among the trees, ringed with what local people call swamp maple saplings. I think briefly of the springs beneath Yggdrasil, and the mythic Niðhögg that continually gnaws the cosmic tree but cannot overcome its life-sustaining power.

Brian tells me that the president of the coal company has ceased thinking about the project rationally; for him, it is reduced to a matter of pride and might. "He is the most obstreperous, obnoxious human being you will ever meet," he says. "Within five minutes he will let you know that you are the scum of the earth and he can buy and sell hundreds of people just like you." In the sunlit cinder-block formality of Brian's office, he shakes his head. The man, Brian says, "is willing to spend more money on the litigation than the coal is actually worth." And it seems the strategy of his opponents is, wisely, to slow the process down, to keep appeals stalling his plans until, perhaps, he is no longer part of the equation. He's elderly, says Brian; perhaps they all can wait him out.

I pay another October visit to the woods, this time in mid-morning, and the slope of the hillside I descend is a yellow world of just-fallen autumn leaves, bright color that will last at most another day or two. Thinking of Joseph Gibbons, I measure the girth of the fallen poplar. The tree was perhaps twelve feet around at the time of its fall, less than half the size of the great sycamore blowdown Gibbons measured two hundred years ago. Thinking of Muir, rocked and buoyed in the heights of the fir he'd climbed, I sit securely on the ground, looking out eye level at the half-acre of sun-loving forbs that have shot up in the sudden clearing beneath the canopy gap and that still, in the gentle autumn air, hold their summer leaves. They won't last long before the understory closes over and whatever species is ascendant reclaims the upper sunlight, shading out, again, the ground below. Brian has speculated that maybe the end of the cold phase called the Little Ice Age had something to do with the initial flourishing of white oaks in Dysart Woods. The colder, drier climes that reached their chilly maximum in Europe and North America from roughly 1550 to 1800 might have played some role in the forest ecology that hasn't yet been understood. These oldest oaks were sprouting and taking hold of the hillsides as young saplings during the first decades of the cold spell, before the world endured another shift, though there's no library of temperature recordings to consult for Belmont County in the 1600s to specify these changes. I fold my notes of impressive tree girths—an oak of seventeen-feet circumference, two more at fourteen, another at fourteen and a half—and climb back into sunlight on the ridge top.

Later, I stop at the tiny country grocery in the village of Belmont to buy a cold drink and chat with the woman at the checkout and her only other customer, an elderly man dressed in denim and flannel. I ask them if they think the proposed mine will affect the nearby forest.

"Of course, it will," replies the man. The woman agrees and says that the whole area has been longwalled, destroying her friends' and neighbors' rural wells. "The company will truck in water for you, or pay to have a water line extended, but only for a couple of years. Then you have to pay for it yourself." The man exclaims: "There—did you see that? That was a water truck, just went by. That's what we're talking about. They haul out to my son's place, since they dried up his well." He gestures toward the wall behind the cashier counter, a wall that divides the one-room store from the adjacent house where I presume the owners still live.

"It's just like if I took out all the beams here," the man declares. "The plaster and the ceiling might last awhile, but you know it's going to come down before long. You know it will."

The Lumberman

He stands on a peak and gazes o'er
A forest dim and old;
But naught of its spirit vast and hoar
Can stifle his lust for gold:

Little he cares for the trees that rise
In the forest vast and old:
Each mossy trunk is a logger's prize,
And he measures its worth in gold.

So begins a surprising little poem written by Andrew Gennett, president of the Gennett Lumber Company, sometime around 1910. At least, I think it is surprising, since Gennett himself was a lumberman. Born in 1874 into a merchant-class family in Nashville, by the turn of the century Gennett and his brother, Nat, had entered the timber business, and throughout the first third of the twentieth century they worked the southern hardwood forests, converting old-growth trees and watersheds into speculative commodities, board feet, and, finally, greenbacks if not actual gold coins or bullion. His memoir describes the fall and winter of 1902, spent "examining each poplar tree and each creek and hollow. . . . I think it was there that my love of the woods and the examination of timber first began. While I toiled and sweated over those rough creeks and hollows, I was learning the timber, its size, its quantity, and the way it grew."

I find the poem one afternoon while leafing through the files of the National Forest Service in Asheville, North Carolina. The day before, I hiked a trail along Little Santeetlah Creek, just south of the Tennessee border, passing through Poplar Cove, a steep-sloped portion of the Slickrock Wilderness. Poplar Cove is legendary among environmentalists and forest ecologists. Here, in the heart of the Appalachian plateau, tulip poplars stand like deciduous brontosaurs: thick, old, and very tall. In autumn, the leaves largely fallen, late-day light was still filtered through rain clouds rolling in, the sun dropping lower in the southwestern sky. In the half-lit hollow, I leaned against the still, cool, hardwood bodies, imagining springtime on that rich, deciduous slope. Once, I scrambled several hundred yards from the trail and sank down to sit at the base of one great-boled poplar, out of sight from the trail long enough to eat an apple and drain my water bottle, a tiny mammalian bump on the vegetal world.

The largest trees in Poplar Cove are twenty feet in circumference, braced only by their own girth and strength against the hillside's slope. On a Sunday afternoon, dusk coming on, the parking lot at the trailhead was still nearly full, and the woods echoed with the whoops of children and teenagers. After ninety minutes or so, I left the cove and hiked fast to the ridge top, then struck out along the Jenkins Meadow Trail to see what kind of perspective distance might lend the old-growth cove. For nearly an hour I strode through younger woods—lots of oak and a little hemlock—but never reached the namesake meadow. Instead I turned back, descending again into Poplar Cove along the creek, and imagined returning some other year, pack full of gear, to plumb the wilderness that stretched away into the Smoky Mountains, across the border and into Tennessee. Sometime, I thought, I want to sleep within this green world, miles from road or parking lot, and listen to slight breeze in the poplar leaves, or to rain as it describes, in touch turned to sound, the depths from canopy to leaf mold far below.

But today I'm indoors, looking for details about the thirteen thousand acres of original growth that the Forest Service bought in 1936. Pat Momich, the information specialist at the front desk, is clearly used to fielding queries about the memorial forest. It turns out she wrote the glossy brochure that reproduces Joyce Kilmer's famous little poem "Trees" and summarizes the Forest Service decision to dedicate Poplar Cove as a memorial to the slain poet, fulfilling the request of his World War I battalion. There's an interesting symbolism here—some of the largest old-growth trees in the East were saved to honor a dead poet; my father remarks, when I tell him about Poplar Cove, that it's surprising the power a bad poem can have.

The more questions I ask, the more interested Pat becomes, and at last she invites me upstairs to explore the Depression-era files that document the government's acquisition of the land. As she works quietly in her cubicle next door, I turn pages, trying to piece together the story. In his memoirs, Gennett describes buying the land along Santeetlah Creek in 1926 as a "speculative purchase," even though the company had largely quit speculative buying more than a decade before. "Speculation in mountain lands was becoming more and more difficult," he explains. "But in 1926 the price of swamp timber had gotten so high as to return once more the pressure of furnishing the higher grades of hardwood for the furniture factories and planing mills." Just such high-grade hardwood, the Gennett brothers expected, would be found in their new tract of land. By 1935, they were in negotiation with Ritter Lumber, a company from Ohio, and were eager to sell. "Gennett Lumber Company was in very straitened circumstances," he explains, "and this sale seemed almost to be a matter of life and death to us." Only after the negotiations with Ritter Lumber Company fell through did Gennett approach the U.S. government, and then he did so reluctantly, "thinking that under the present governmental attitude of dislike and hatred toward the capitalist, they would cruise our lands with a view to depressing its price."

Despite his rhymed critique of the lumberman's greed, Gennett remained a devoted capitalist and entrepreneur, a harsh critic of the New Deal and what he called "Mr. Roosevelt's foolish experiments in social justice" as well as the administration's "punishment and persecution of business," even as he maneuvered to take advantage of the young Forest Service's plans to buy "cutover lands" from the lumber companies, following their extraction of timber. His memoir describes in some detail the failure to sell the land to another lumber company and his subsequent deal with the U.S. government; he makes only passing reference to the preservation of the trees in the memorial park. And yet other readers have seen him differently—"by inclination he was an artist" says John Alger in his introduction to Gennett's memoir. "Gennett left the [Joyce Kilmer tract] unlogged because he wished to, because he felt its value to be greater in that state." I try to glimpse this person in the prose of his memoir and in the Forest Service records, but I never see him, neither in his own words nor in the photographs that show him in the forest and along the rivers, a handsome man posing with those he hired to take down the big trees. Instead, his own language almost exclusively covers the terrain of business.

A letter from August 1, 1935, contains the regional forester's endorsement of the purchase, which he sends to the chief of the Forest Service quite enthusiastically. The land, he says, is "some of the finest original growth in the Appalachians. It offers the Government the only opportunity of setting aside an area of original growth, containing coves of very large yellow poplar and red oak. . . . I have no doubt that if the Government does not purchase the tract, it will be sold for immediate logging." And the accompanying documents support this caution; a lengthy "stumpage appraisal" lays out the expected timber value of the land, identifying 56 million board feet of "merchantable saw-timber" and identifying the detailed plan for what today would be called its "harvest," though that term never appears in Gennett's papers.

"Logging and milling will continue for 252 days a year. 7½ million bd. ft. will be cut per year and it is planned to cut the entire stand in 8 years," the appraisal declares, calling for thirty men to work ten-hour days. Based on extensive "timber cruises," the forest is estimated to consist of "19% poplar, 23% red oak, 11% chestnut, 6% birch, 8% basswood, 4% hard maple, 2% soft maple, 1% cherry, 4% buckeye, 7% chestnut oak, 2% ash, and 10% other. The largest poplar tree measured on this tract showed a d.b.h. of 80 inches." This ancestral forest still existed in 1935, when chestnut was still vigorous across the southern mountains; here it's reduced to percentages and lists. "This is one of the last remnants of virgin hardwoods in Western North Carolina," the appraisal continues, "and it is hoped that it may be spared from the havoc of destructive lumbering by government acquisition." But immediately the document moves on to itemize production costs—wages for the men to fell the trees, $2.50/day; feed costs for the oxen teams ($600/year); railroad costs for removal of logs to the mill, including one ton of coal per day at $500, along with seventy-five cents' worth of oil and grease; labor at the mill yard, ranging from

$6/day for the foremen to $2/day for the oiler, the night watch-man, the trimmerman, the utility man, and a few others. In the very document that urges against "the havoc of destructive lumbering," the only method of valuation is the reduction to lumber—the cost outlays and the return the commodity will bring.

Then there are the photographs, where wages and job titles take shape as bearded men dressed in suspenders and slouch hats. Enclosed with the Forest Service supervisor's letter are images of men standing among some of the large trees of the Santeetlah Creek tract and clustered before their canvas tent pitched in the woods. Accompanying Gennett's memoir are men standing on and among the huge logs and brush felled across the Appalachian hillsides; splash dams on the creeks, built to float the logs downriver to the sawmill; logging loco-motives piled with timber and log loaders; and a photo taken from Poplar Cove, the memorial-to-become, that shows men rendered minute, as if inconsequential. They stand in a cluster of poplars so large the black-and-white photograph looks like pictures from the Northwest coast of giant firs and redwoods. Only a few slim, leafed branches indicate that these are decidu-ous trees of the East, while the canopy remains way out of sight, at least a hundred feet above the men's behatted heads.

"I'd love to know what was going on in that forest five hun-dred years ago," Pat tells me, and I think how much her words echo those of Brian McCarthy, thinking about the Little Ice Age in Dysart Woods. Those poplars must have sprouted in a rather extensive clearing, she explains, since they are not shade-lov-ing trees. There must have been, say the ecologists, some dis-turbance—weather or fire, perhaps. But the sheltered cove seems an unlikely place for a massive tornado blowdown. This was good land, not some marginal world of environmental extremes; it was also the heart of the Cherokee homeland.

"I think this would have been a village site," she tells me, "open for farming and homes." There was plenty of water, with the two forks of Santeetlah Creek meeting just below the current parking lot. During the mid-sixteenth century, about the time that DeSoto made his way through the Appalachians not far north and east of Poplar Cove, today's big trees germinated. Had disease wiped out a mountain village, spreading its contagious, deadly reach beyond the actual arrival of Europeans? We know such epidemic decimation took place elsewhere along the East coast, emptying villages and leaving crops untended in the fields, sometimes even convincing the Christian immigrants that God was preparing the New World for them by clearing away the resident devils. If so, the suddenly abandoned land lay ready for the forest's energetic reclamation. I ask her what kinds of archaeological surveys have been conducted there. "There's been some digging," she tells me, "but no one has found any sign of a village." She pauses. "Not yet." We stand together, speculating.

One stanza in "The Lumberman" omits the refrain of gold, and relies, for a moment, on the almost-surprise of slant rhyme, before the poet returns to established form. A small typographical error makes the page seem to me vulnerable, though the man himself remains inaccessible, shaded by cliché and the bulk of his life's work:

The beauty of brook, of bloom, of tree,
The music of bird and wind,
The dreamer of dreams may hear and see,
The Logger is deaf and blind.

The Peace of Ages is torn apart
In the greed of his search for gold,
And he drives his axe to the patient heart
of [sic] the forest dim and old.

Blackwater rivers are filled with tannins, dark as tea if you scoop your hands full and lift the water into the sunlight, dark as coffee if you gaze down at their still, backwater coves and watch where bald cypress and tupelo cast their reflections across the surface, doubling the imagery of tree and leaf. They are filled with dead plant matter, as if they were southern rivers dreaming of northern bogs, as if current and motion longed to just stop, to lie down and gaze at the sky. In our rented canoe, my friend John and I push away from the bank and head downstream on the Black River, beginning a twelve-mile stretch of what's reputed to be one of the most beautiful places for paddling in North Carolina.

But you have to really want to get here. There's very little public access along the Black River, and no local canoe livery. We rented from an outfitter where John lives near Durham and hit the road before daylight to drive south and east, buffeted by passing trucks and aggressive morning commuters, arriving at Henry's Landing shortly after 10:00. Mr. Carlton Henry will, for a fee, provide us with shuttle service from the takeout spot downstream and allow us to put in at the sandy boat landing on his family land—bought by his great, great grandfather in 1886, he tells me. This is still isolated, rural country; there are blueberry farms and a vineyard, and logging trucks still haul timber from the lowland forests. Mr. Henry seems to do a little of this and some of that; he appears a bit worried already that his daughter, getting married next summer, doesn't plan to continue living on the family property. "They'll keep the land," he says, "But they won't live *here*."

But today, I do really want to be here. A few miles downstream are ancient bald cypress trees, and the only way to reach them is by water, since there's no road through the wild wetlands that surround them. What does one call such a community of cypress? A grove? A copse? Both terms seem terrestrial, not riparian, so I think simply, "a swampful of cypress." Mr. Henry says that there are likely to be downed trees along the river from Hurricanes Ivan and Fran, and I wonder whether we'll see any recent storm damage to the ancient trees. They have weathered other hurricanes, centuries of them. In the pen-and-ink drawing I've come across in my reading, they record and reflect both wreckage and perseverance in their gnarled, broken-off forms.

The day is clear and bright after yesterday's heavy rain and seems doubly lovely since rain is forecast to return again tomorrow. In this window of sunny weather, we float on a calm, dark current, watching each bend in the river for backwaters and bays that might harbor the Swampful of Cypress. Where the river curves into a thicket of cypress knees, poison ivy–covered stumps, and, even farther, hummocks of tupelo and flotillas of arrow-shaped weeds, we exclaim to one another that we must have arrived; a sentinel tree stands straight and very tall, though diagnostically flat topped. John sits in the boat and eats an apple and almonds while I clamber over the buttressed base of the tree, wrapping a nylon rope around it to record "diameter at breast height" and watching nervously for snakes. I tie a knot to denote the tree's girth, and then wrap it neatly from elbow to thumb, counting lengths of my forearm: fourteen. At home, with measuring tape, I'll later translate this to just over sixteen feet. The tree looks remarkably healthy, with its own (*her own*, says John, for she's obviously the mother tree) disk-shaped congregation of knees that cluster like thin little Giacometti figures across forty feet of water. A few yards away, another cypress stands straight and tall and obviously old, but not nearly as large in circumference as the mother-leviathan. This one casts a still mirror image of its body, buttress to crown, which our boat skirts as we drift. We're studying an aerial photograph of the river that John has laminated, passing it back and forth between us, but we can't quite place ourselves along the one-dimensional snake shape, black-on-gray like a pictograph, I think, or like a black-and-white photograph of the Great Serpent Mound in Ohio.

The Swampful of Cypress is actually called the Three Sisters, but we don't know what this metaphoric place name gestures toward. Where we stopped for lunch and measurement three large trees—sisters, perhaps?—were clearly visible from the center of the river, but we had rather expected to see more ancient trees before the banks gave way to less remarkable forest. I'm a little disappointed, and I bet John is too, so when another stream, or some side channel, joins the Black River, we poke and pole our way back until the canoe can't go any further. Then I wade well upstream with the rope, measuring cypress trunks and knotting their girth along its tannin-stained length, until John sounds a blast on his whistle to let me know he's been left alone in the boat *quite* long enough, and where am I, anyway, in this trackless swamp? We are lucky: despite the pleasant weather, we've seen almost no mosquitoes, not a single snake, and only a few fishermen tooling slowly about in their motorboats. Once we met a group of four canoes headed upstream, filled with surly adolescent boys and great plastic containers of gear. They seemed to be youths on some Outward Bound excursion that most of them weren't enjoying very much, though one boomed a proud warning about snakes ahead.

Despite the research I've done already, I don't know how to read this landscape, any more than I know how to transcribe our physical experience of the river's course against the visual map, encased in plastic, that we pass back and forth in the boat. The mild autumn day feels deeply exotic, there among palmettos and Spanish moss. Then the landscape shifts, and the feeling of otherness intensifies as we realize that only now are we entering the heart of the swamp, an area called in a paddler's guide "The Narrows." Here the river sheets out in shallows that slip over hard-packed sand, scoured clean of any swamp muck. That's part of what's so surprising: the sand and sky are so bright they seem flushed free of cloud or decay. Yet the sunlit water moves past and among the ancient trees, dozens of them, one broken, hollowed trunk after another. We are surrounded by their knees, which stand like thick shoulderless statues in the current, half-formed, faceless persons lifting from the white sand and darkened water. The boat scrapes aground in the shallows so I step out and wade; the canoe with John still at the stern floats again, and we move in parallel, he steering and paddling and I walking about on the fine-sand bottom, stepping abruptly from depths calf high to thigh high. Once, I find a thin, black shell of a stump, only a couple of inches thick but holding a vanished tree's girth over three feet across, with a neat round pool of river flooding the cavity that was its trunk. I step inside, a woman in water in wood. I stand in water, in wood, and in the very middle of my life.

In the Narrows, we watch carefully for tiny yellow flags tied near eye height that mark the navigable passage through the swamp. These are faded strips of surveyor's tape, almost the same color and shape as the plumes of Spanish moss that dangle from the outstretched limbs above the water, so they seem to disappear at every turn. Once we do travel full circle, recognizing that we shouldn't be moving against the current, but we can't quite see how else to turn. The flags are tenuous, dangling signs.

Here most of the oldest trees have been so broken and hollowed that they can't be dated through dendrochronology, but one cypress with a sound core (doubtless not the oldest in the swamp) was tested several years ago: it was found to be seventeen hundred years old. More than a millennium and a half, nearly two. One's sense of time, of life-time, is nudged from its usual channel. Here, in nutrient-poor waters, old trees grow slowly, as little as one circumferential inch per century. What other lives converged with these matriarchs, one wonders—and then the rhythms of human generations seem to squeeze together like indecipherable rings, a dark blur around the edges of a thousand years. Meanwhile, I look up: the canopy is scalloped with destruction, flat-topped trunks beneath the October sky; empty holes where branches once reached out their horizontal arms; gothic archways at the water's surface where the buttressed roots have rotted out to bare the cavity to the current; snapped trunks that stand wholly open on one side, as if presenting a doorway to some passage just out of sight. *The winds destroy it from above; The heartwood rots from within its sides.* Which way to go? The swamp refuses to answer. The waters slip past, the sun continues to shift downward in the autumn sky, and the trees stand still in the breezeless air, silent and stationary, while we make our choices and propel ourselves forward. At last we're back in the river, a real channel that suggests linearity, direction, the physical image of the journey in or out. Young tupelo branches shade green palmetto along the bank; once, from a shaded, sheltered bend, wood ducks startle up from the water and head noisily elsewhere. A kingfisher scolds from up ahead.

Suddenly, before I have any idea what has happened, the boat has tipped and we're both in the water, well over our heads, gasping at one another while we travel downstream with surprising speed. But the boat seems almost to right itself, though it's full of water, and I check it for backpack, dry bag, water bottles while John treads water in the river, waiting for one of the paddles to float toward him, and then comes ashore. Are we all right? We are. It's cold, but manageable. Did we lose anything? One of the maps, still in a zip-lock bag, has floated away, and the rope has sunk to the bottom with its record of the five tree-girths I marked with knots. I have only the memory of fourteen forearms' length for the mother-leviathan, a few miles upstream.

From here on, the passage out is frequently blocked with downed trees, several with still-leafy branches, obvious casualties of Fran and Ivan. More than once we must portage the canoe through snarls of greenbrier; when the thicket is too impenetrable, we climb out of the boat and float it, empty, over a submerged log before, wet and cold, we crawl back in and continue downstream, past tupelo and shade-splashed bark.

It's very nearly dark by the time we finally reach the takeout spot and haul our wet selves up the concrete ramp, hoist the canoe atop the car, and think about changing into something dry. An old man chats with us as he removes his fishing boat; he's clearly surprised to hear we paddled all the way from Henry's Landing. "It's a mess in there," he says flatly. Later, the young man who rented us the canoe will ask about the storm damage. It sounds as though he's been involved in volunteer clearing efforts before, since, to my fascination, he can speak knowledgeably about the importance of using soy-based bar chain oil to avoid polluting the water while wielding a chain saw from a boat in midstream, an image I have a hard time keeping in focus.

In 1773, during his famous journey through the American Southeast, William Bartram passed through country I imagine must have been similar to the wild stretch of the Black River. He had much to say about it. With his characteristic enthusiasm, he declared the cypress to be

in the first order of North American trees. Its majestic stature is surprising; and on approaching it, we are struck with a kind of awe, at beholding the stateliness of the trunk, lifting its cumbrous top towards the skies, and casting a wide shade upon the ground, as a dark intervening cloud, which, for a time, excludes the rays of the sun. The delicacy of its colour and texture of its leaves, exceed every thing in vegetation. It generally grows in the water, or in low flat lands, near the banks of great rivers and lakes, that are covered, great part of the year, with two or three feet depth of water; and that part of the trunk which is subject to be under water, and four or five feet higher up, is greatly enlarged by prodigious buttresses, or pilasters, which, in full grown trees, project out on every side, to such a distance, that several men might easily hide themselves in the hollows between. Each pilaster terminates under ground, in a very large, strong, serpentine root, which strikes off, and branches every way, just under the surface of the earth: and from these roots grow woody cones, called cypress knees, four, five, and six feet high, and from six to eighteen inches and two feet in diameter at their bases. The large ones are hollow, and serve very well for beehives; a small space of the tree itself is hollow, nearly as high as the buttresses already mentioned. From this place, the tree, as it were, takes another beginning, forming a grand straight column eighty or ninety feet high, when it divides every way around into an extensive flat horizontal top, like an umbrella, where eagles have their secure nests, and cranes and storks their temporary resting places; and what adds to the magnificence of their appearance is the streamers of long moss that hang from the lofty limbs and float in the winds.

Bartram passed through a century or more before the timber companies of the Southeast would turn their attention to lumber extraction from swamps and rivers. In his time, agriculture—the plantation culture developing in the South—was the source of clearing. Slaves were the source of labor. "When the planters fell these mighty trees," he continued, "they raise a stage round them, as high as to reach above the buttresses; on this stage, eight or ten negroes ascend with their axes, and fall to work round its trunk. I have seen trunks of these trees that would measure eight, ten, and twelve feet in diameter, for forty and fifty feet straight shaft."

I have not seen such trees, not here, but I can imagine them, inhabitants of former worlds, bridging with their bodies the impossible gap between what has passed and what is, reaching through realms—earth, water, air. "Pilaster," writes Bartram. "Buttress." Room and pillar. Root and canopy. So we name and describe their architectural importance, the embodiment of trees that hold up, and hold together, the disparate and multisectioned world.

So the imagination has leaped again, across time and distance, taking me outside myself, beyond myself. Isn't this what we want, when we reach toward the spiritual realms that seem to lie both within and beyond us? Isn't this what we want on our best days when we rise up and turn our faces outward? The world offers innumerable bridges from the inner to the outer realms, avenues of transcendence or narrow passages from one mode of being to another. Gaze up. Gaze back.

There's a snippet of ninth-century Irish poetry, called "The Scribe in the Woods," that I read once in translation. Seamus Heaney describes it as "another glimpse of nature through the rinsed eyes of Celtic Christianity":

A wall of forest looms above
and sweetly the blackbird sings;
all the birds make melody
over me and my books and things.

Would you know more, or what?

Selected Bibliography

Setting Forth in Their Footprints

Heidegger, Martin. *Off the Beaten Track*. Edited and translated by Julian Young and Kenneth Haynes. Cambridge: Cambridge University Press, 2002.

Jolly, Alison. *Lucy's Legacy: Sex and Intelligence in Human Evolution*. Cambridge MA: Harvard University Press, 1999.

Lynch, John, and Louise Barrett. *Walking with Cave Men: Eye to Eye with Your Ancestors*. New York: DK Publishing, 2003.

Pfeiffer, Friedrich, and Teresa Zielinska. *Walking: Biological and Technological Aspects*. International Centre for Mechanical Sciences, Courses and Lectures no. 467. New York: Springer Wien, 2004.

Memory's Hills

Burling, Robbins. *The Talking Ape: How Language Evolved*. New York: Oxford University Press, 2005.

Christos, George. *Memory and Dreams: The Creative Human Mind*. New Brunswick NJ: Rutgers University Press, 2003.

Crownfield, David R. "Consciousness and the Voices of the Gods: An Essay Review." *Journal of the American Academy of Religion* 46, no. 2 (June 1978): 193–202.

Jaynes, Julian. *The Origin of Consciousness in the Breakdown of the Bicameral Mind*. Boston: Houghton Mifflin, 1976.

Kroster, Paula H., and G. R. Kroster. "The Life Style of El Tajín." *American Antiquity* 38, no. 2 (1973): 199–205.

Saraceni, Jessica E. "Redating Serpent Mound." *Archaeology* 49, no. 6 (November/December 1996).

Schacter, Daniel, and Elaine Scarry, eds. *Memory, Brain, and Belief.* Cambridge MA: Harvard University Press, 2000.

Cold Meditations

Barfield, Owen. *Poetic Diction: A Study in Meaning.* With afterword by the author. Middletown CT: Wesleyan University Press, 1973.

Givón, T., ed. *The Evolution of Language Out of Pre-language.* Amsterdam and Philadelphia: J. Benjamins Publishing, 2002.

Heaney, Seamus, trans. *Beowulf: A Verse Translation*, edited by Daniel Donoghue. New York: W.W. Norton, 2002.

Li, Charles N. "Missing Links, Issues and Hypotheses in the Evolutionary Origin of Language." In *The Evolution of Language Out of Pre-language*, edited by T. Givón, 83–106. Amsterdam and Philadelphia: J. Benjamins Publishing, 2002.

Oppenheimer, Stephen. *Out of Eden: The Peopling of the World.* London: Constable, 2003.

Quammen, David. *Monster of God: The Man-eating Predator in the Jungles of History and the Mind.* New York: W.W. Norton, 2003.

Tolkien, J. R. R. *Beowulf, the Monsters and the Critics.* Folcroft PA: Folcroft Press, 1969.

Walden, Woods

Thoreau, Henry David. *Walden.* Edited by Jeffrey S. Cramer. New Haven: Yale University Press, 2004.

Cañonicity

Balge-Crozier, Marjorie. "The Sublime Landscapes of Georgia O'Keeffe." In *Georgia O'Keeffe: Visions of the Sublime*, edited by Joseph Czestochowski, 103–11. Memphis: The Torch Press, 2004.

Baudrillard, Jean. *Simulacra and Simulation*. Translated by Sheila Faria Glaser. Ann Arbor: University of Michigan Press, 1994.

Czestochowski, Joseph, ed. *Georgia O'Keeffe: Visions of the Sublime*. Memphis: The Torch Press, 2004.

Fine, Ruth, and Barbara Buhler Lynes, eds. *O'Keeffe on Paper*. Washington DC: National Gallery of Art, 2000.

Fine, Ruth, and Elizabeth Glassman. "Thoughts without Words: O'Keeffe in Context." In *O'Keeffe on Paper*, edited by Ruth Fine and Barbara Buhler Lynes, 13–36. Washington DC: National Gallery of Art, 2000.

Flores, Dan. *Caprock Canyonlands*. Austin: University of Texas Press, 1990.

———. *Horizontal Yellow: Nature and History in the Near Southwest*. Albuquerque: University of New Mexico Press, 1999.

Guy, Duane, ed. *The Story of Palo Duro Canyon*. Canyon TX: Panhandle Plains Historical Society, 1979.

Hartley, Marsden. *Adventures in the Arts*. New York: Boni and Liveright, 1921.

Lewis, Jo Ann. "The Art That Went from Boon to Bust: O'Keeffe or Not O'Keeffe." *Washington Post*, December 3, 1999.

———. "Collector Strikes Out with O'Keeffe." *Washington Post*, December 18, 1999.

———. "The Curious Case of the Spurious O'Keeffes." *Washington Post*, August 6, 2000.

Lynes, Barbara Buhler. *Georgia O'Keeffe: Catalogue Raisonné.* Vol. I. New Haven: Yale University Press, 1999.

Mathews, William A. *The Geologic Story of Palo Duro Canyon.* Bureau of Economic Geology Guidebook no. 8. Austin: University of Texas, 1983.

O'Keeffe, Georgia. *Georgia O'Keeffe.* New York: Viking Press, 1976.

―――. Sketchbook, 1905–1906. Georgia O'Keeffe Museum Research Center, Santa Fe, New Mexico.

―――. *Georgia O'Keeffe: Canyon Suite.* Introduction by Barbara Bloemink. New York: George Braziller, in association with Kemper Museum of Contemporary Art and Design, 1995.

Paul, Steve, Mike McGraw, Alice Thorson, and Loring Leifer. Georgia O'Keeffe series of articles. *Kansas City Star,* 1999–2006.

Peters, Sarah Whitaker. *Becoming O'Keeffe: The Early Years.* New York: Abbeville Press, 1994.

Reynolds, Gretchen. "Did Georgia O'Keeffe Really Create This Collection of O'Keeffes?" *New York Times,* March 7, 2000.

Robinson, Roxana. *Georgia O'Keeffe: A Life.* Hanover NH: University Press of New England, 1989.

Rosenfeld, Paul. *Port of New York.* 1924. Reprint, Champagne-Urbana: University of Illinois Press, 1961.

Salazar, E. "SF Man Says No One Will Tell Story of O'Keeffe Collaboration." *Albuquerque Journal North,* February 13, 2000.

Udall, Sharyn R. "Nature after God: Waterfalls in the American Modernist Imagination." In *Georgia O'Keeffe: Visions of the Sublime,* edited by Joseph Czestochowski, 53–61. Memphis: The Torch Press, 2004.

―――. *O'Keeffe and Texas.* San Antonio TX: The Marion Koogler Art Museum and Harry N. Abrams, 1998.

Wilmerding, John. "Georgia O'Keeffe and the American Landscape Tradition." In *Georgia O'Keeffe: Visions of the Sublime*, edited by Joseph Czestochowski, 13–19. Memphis: The Torch Press, 2004.

In the Mind's Eye

Fox, William L. *Mapping the Empty: Eight Artists and Nevada*. Reno: University of Nevada Press, 1999.

Lewis-Williams, David. *The Mind in the Cave: Consciousness and the Origins of Art*. London: Thames and Hudson, 2002.

Patterson, Alex. *A Field Guide to Rock Art Symbols of the Greater Southwest*. Boulder CO: Johnson Books, 1992.

Whitely, David S. *A Guide to Rock Art Sites: Southern California and Southern Nevada*. Missoula MT: Mountain Press Publishing, 2001.

Here the Animal

Bahn, Paul. *The Cambridge Illustrated History of Prehistoric Art*. Cambridge: Cambridge University Press, 1998.

——— and Jean Vertut. *Journey through the Ice Age*. Berkeley: University of California Press, 1997.

Brassai. *Conversations with Picasso*. Translated by Jane Marie Todd. Chicago: University of Chicago Press, 1999.

Chauvet, Jean-Marie, Eliette Brunel Deschamps, and Christian Hillaire. *Dawn of Art: The Chauvet Cave*. New York: Harry Abrams, 1996.

Clottes, Jean. *Chauvet Cave: The Art of Earliest Times*. Salt Lake City: University of Utah Press, 2003.

Dissanayake, Ellen. *Art and Intimacy: How the Arts Began*. Seattle: University of Washington Press, 2000.

Dubos, Rene. *So Human an Animal*. New York: Scribner, 1968.

Johnson, Paul. *Art: A New History*. New York: HarperCollins, 2003.

La Descente

Simmonet, Robert. "Approvisionnement en silex au paleolithique superieur; deplacements et caracteristiques physionomiques des paysages, l'exemple des Pyrenees centrales." In *Pyrenees Prehistoriques: arts et societes*, Actes du 118e congres national des societes historiques et scientifiques sous la direction de Henri Delporte et Jean Clottes, 117–28. Paris: editions du CTHS, 1996.

————. "Les techniques de representation dans la grotte ornee de Labastide (Hautes-Pyrenees)." In *Pyrenees Prehistoriques: arts et societes*, 341–52. Paris: editions du CTHS, 1996.

In Situ

Abbey, Edward. *Desert Solitaire: A Season in the Wilderness*. Salt Lake City: Peregrine Smith, 1981.

Billman, Brian, Patricia M. Lambert, and Banks L. Leonard. "Cannibalism, Warfare, and Drought in the Mesa Verde Region during the 12th Century AD." *American Antiquity* 65, no. 1 (2000): 145–78.

Coulam, Nancy J., and Alan R. Schroedl. "Early Archaic Clay Figurines from Cowboy and Walters Caves in Southeastern Utah." *KIVA* 61, no. 4 (1996): 401–12.

Dissanayeke, Ellen. "Chimera, Spandrel, or Adaptation: Conceptualizing Art in Human Adaptation." *Human Nature* 6 (1995): 99–117.

Dongoske, Kurt, Debra L. Martin, and T. J. Ferguson. "Critique of the Claim of Cannibalism at Cowboy Wash." *American Antiquity* 65, no. 1 (2000): 179–90.

Gombrich, Ernst. *The Story of Art*. London: Phaidon, 1950.

Lewis-Williams, David. *The Mind in the Cave: Consciousness and the Origins of Art*. London: Thames and Hudson, 2002.

Schafsmaa, Polly. "Trance and Transformation in the Canyons: Shamanism and Early Rock Art on the Colorado Plateau" (brochure). Washington DC: National Park Service, U.S. Dept. of the Interior. http://www.nps.gov/cany/horseshoe.

Slifer, Dennis. *Guide to Rock Art of the Utah Region*. Santa Fe NM: Ancient City Press, 2000.

Tipps, Betsy L. "Barrier Canyon Rock Art Dating." In *The Archaeology of Canyonlands National Park*. Washington DC: National Park Service, U.S. Department of the Interior, 35–45. http://www.nps.gov/cany/horseshoe.

Turner, Christy G., II, and Jacqueline A. *Man Corn: Cannibalism and Violence in the Prehistoric American Southwest*. Salt Lake City: University of Utah Press, 1999.

Fragments

Bishop, Elizabeth. "The Map." In *The Complete Poems 1927–1979*. New York: Farrar, Straus, Giroux, 1983.

Comanche National Grassland Picket Wire Canyonlands Management Plan. USDA Forest Service, 1994.

Hurt, R. Douglas. *The Agricultural History of the Dust Bowl*. Chicago: Nelson Hall, 1981.

Kahn, Charles H., trans. *The Art and Thought of Heraclitus: An Edition of the Fragments with Translation and Commentary*. Cambridge: Cambridge University Press, 1979.

Lockley, Martin G., Barbara J. Fillmore, and Lori Marquardt.

Dinosaur Lake: The Story of the Purgatoire Valley Dinosaur Tracksite Area. Special Publication no. 40. Denver: Colorado Geological Survey, 1997.

———, Karen J. Houck, and Nancy K. Prince. "North America's Largest Dinosaur Trackway Site: Implications for Morrison Formation Paleoecology." *Geological Society of America Bulletin* 97 (October 1986): 1163–76.

MacClary, J. S. "Dinosaur Trails of Purgatory." *Scientific American* 158 (February 1938): 72.

———. "Footprints in Colorado." *Life* 1, no. 6 (1936): 5.

———. "Mysterious Steps in Purgatory." *Natural History* 43 (1939): 128.

Sternberg, Charles. *The Life of a Fossil Hunter.* Introduction by Henry Fairfield Osborn. New York: H. Holt and Co., 1909.

———. *The Story of the Past: Or the Romance of Science.* Boston: Sherman, French & Co., 1911.

Wooster, Donald. *Dust Bowl: The Southern Plains in the 1930s.* New York: Oxford University Press, 1979.

The Shannon Creek Eagles

Beans, Bruce E. *Eagle's Plume: Preserving the Life and Habitat of America's Bald Eagle.* New York: Scribner, 1996.

Bent, Arthur Cleveland. *Life Histories of North American Birds, Part I.* New York: Dover Publications, 1961.

Buehler, David A. "Bald Eagle." In *The Birds of North America,* no. 506. Ithaca NY: Cornell Laboratory of Ornithology and the Academy of Natural Sciences, 2000.

Johnsgard, Paul. *Hawks, Eagles, and Falcons of North America.* 1990. Reprint, Washington DC: Smithsonian Institution Press, 2001.

Levenson, Howard, and James W. Bee. "Bald Eagle Use of

Kansas River Riparian Habitat in Northeastern Kansas." *Kansas Ornithological Society Bulletin* 31, no. 4 (1980): 28–38.

Lorenz, Konrad. *On Aggression.* Translated by Marjorie Kerr Wilson. New York: Harcourt, Brace & World, 1966.

Mulhern, Daniel W., Michael A. Watkins, M. Alan Jenkins, and Steve K Sherrod. "Successful Nesting by a Pair of Bald Eagles at Ages Three and Four." *Journal of Raptor Research* 28, no. 2 (1994): 113–14.

Stalmaster, Mark V. *The Bald Eagle.* New York: Universe Books, 1987.

Watkins, Michael A., and Daniel W. Mulhern. "Ten Years of Successful Bald Eagle Nesting in Kansas." *Kansas Ornithological Society Bulletin* 50, no. 3 (1949): 29–33.

Bones of Fear

Campbell, Kenneth E. "The World's Largest Flying Bird." *Terra: The Quarterly Magazine of the Natural History Museum of Los Angeles County* 19, no. 2 (fall 1980): 20–23.

"The Description of the Great Bones Dug Up at Claverack on the Banks of Hudsons River, A.D. 1705." Edward Taylor Collection, Beinecke Rare Book and Manuscript Library, Yale University.

Fagan, Brian. *The Long Summer: How Climate Changed Civilization.* New York: Basic Books, 2004.

Fiedel, Stuart J. "Man's Best Friend—Mammoth's Worst Enemy? A Speculative Essay on the Role of Dogs in Paleoindian Colonization and Megafaunal Extinction." *World Archaeology* 37, no. 1 (2005): 11–21.

Grayson, Donald K., and David J. Meltzer. "Clovis Hunting and Large Mammal Extinction: A Critical Review of the Evidence." *Journal of World Prehistory* 16, no. 4 (December 2002): 313–59.

Jefferson, Thomas. *Notes on the State of Virginia*. Edited with an introduction and notes by William Peden. Chapel Hill: University of North Carolina Press, 1955.

Mayor, Adrienne. *Fossil Legends of the First Americans*. Princeton NJ: Princeton University Press, 2005.

Mizrach, Steven. "Thunderbird and Trickster." http://www.fiu.edu/ffimizrachs/thunderbird-and-trickster.html (accessed 2006).

Peregrine Fund official Web site. http//www.peregrinefund.org/default.asp.

Pound, Ezra. *Literary Essays*. Edited with an introduction by T. S. Eliot. Norfolk CT: New Directions, 1954.

Aspects

Davis, Owen K. "Caves As Sources of Biotic Remains in Arid Western North America." *Palaeogeography, Palaeoclimatology, Palaeoecology* 76 (1990): 331–48.

Haynes, Gary. *Mammoths, Mastodonts, and Elephants: Biology, Behavior, and the Fossil Record*. New York: Cambridge University Press, 1991.

Kropf, Manny. "The Extinct Shrub-Ox (Euceratherium collinum) and Its Late Quaternary Environment on the Colorado Plateau." PhD diss., Northern Arizona University, 2005.

Leopold, Aldo. *A Sand County Almanac and Essays Here and There*. New York: Oxford University Press, 1989.

Mead, Jim I., Larry D. Agenbroad, Paul S. Martin, and Owen K. Davis. "The Mammoth and Sloth Dung from Bechan Cave in Southern Utah." *Paleoenvironments: Vertebrates Current Research* 1 (1984): 79–80.

————. "Dung of *Mammuthus* in the Arid Southwest, North America." *Quaternary Research* 25 (1986): 121–27.

"The Moab Mastodon Pictograph." *The Scientific Monthly* 41, no. 4 (October 1935): 378–79.

In Such a Homecoming

Jones, Clive. "Studies in Ohio Floristics—III. Vegetation of Ohio Prairies." *Bulletin of the Torrey Botanical Club* 71, no. 5 (September 1944): 536–48.

Louv, Richard. *Last Child in the Woods: Saving Our Children from Nature-Deficit Disorder.* Chapel Hill NC: Algonquin Books of Chapel Hill, 2005.

Wright, James. *Collected Prose.* Edited by Anne Wright. Ann Arbor: University of Michigan Press, 1983.

The Kingdom

Apicius. *De Re Coquinaria.* N.p., Gryphium, 1541.

Fowler, Brenda. *Iceman: Discovering the Life and Times of a Prehistoric Man Found in an Alpine Glacier.* Chicago: University of Chicago Press, 2000.

Hall, Stephen S. "Last Hours of the Iceman." *National Geographic* (July 2007): 69–81.

Horn, Bruce, Richard Kay, and Dean Abel. *A Guide to Kansas Mushrooms.* Lawrence: University Press of Kansas, 1993.

Lincoln, Mary J. *Mrs. Lincoln's Boston Cook Book: What to Do and What Not to Do in Cooking.* Boston: Little, Brown, 1899.

Mackenzie, Colin. *Mackenzie's Five Thousand Receipts in All the Useful and Domestic Arts: Constituting a Complete Practical Library Relative to Agriculture, Bees, Bleaching, Brewing, Calico Printing, Carving at Table, Cements, Confectionary, Cookery . . . by an American Physician.* Philadelphia: James Kay Jr., and Brother, 1829.

Money, Nicholas P. *Mr. Bloomfield's Orchard: The Mysterious World of Mushrooms, Molds, and Mycologists.* New York: Oxford University Press, 2002.

Platina. *On Right Pleasure and Good Health: A Critical Edition and Translation of De honesta voluptate et valetudine.* Edited and translated by Mary Ella Milham. Tempe AZ: Medieval and Renaissance Texts and Studies, 1998.

Schaechter, Elio. *In the Company of Mushrooms: A Biologist's Tale.* Cambridge MA: Harvard University Press, 1997.

Taylor, Thomas. *Food Products.* Washington DC: U.S. Department of Agriculture, Division of Microscopy, 1894.

The Scribe in the Woods

Bartram, William. *Travels through North and South Carolina, Georgia, East and West Florida.* Charlottesville: University Press of Virginia, 1980.

Bryan, Hal. "An Evaluation of the Effects of Underground Mining on Dysart Woods." Unpublished manuscript, December 2003.

Gennett, Andrew. *Sound Wormy: Memoir of Andrew Gennett.* Edited by Nicole Hayler. Athens: University of Georgia Press, 2007.

Hallberg, Peter. *Old Icelandic Poetry: Eddic Lay and Skaldic Verse.* Lincoln: University of Nebraska Press, 1962.

Lynch, J. Merrill. "Old Growth in Southeastern Westlands." In *Eastern Old Growth Forests: Prospects for Rediscovery and Recovery.* Edited by Mary Byrd Davis, 199–209. Washington DC: Island Press, 1996.

Marino, Gennaro G. "Geotechnical Analysis of Coal Mining and Reclamation Permit D-0360-12-Dysart Woods." Unpublished manuscript, December 2003.

McCarthy, Brian, "Composition, Structure and Dynamics of Dysart Woods, and Old-Growth Mixed Mesophytic Forest of Southeastern Ohio." *Forest Ecology and Management* 140 (2001): 193–213.

Muir, John. *The Mountains of California*. New York: Penguin Viking, 1985.

Morgan Worldwide Mining Consultants. "Expert Opinion on ovcc Permit Application D-0360-12." Unpublished manuscript, December 2003.

Norris, Charles. H. "Expert Report Geology and Hydrology of Issues Related to Appeal of Permit Application for D-0360-12." Unpublished manuscript, December 2003.

Norse, Elliott A., ed. *Ancient Forests of the Pacific Northwest*. Washington DC: Island Press, 1990.

Rubino, Darrin L., and Brian C. McCarthy. "Comparative Analysis of Dendroecological Methods Used to Assess Disturbance Events." *Dendrochronologia* 21, no. 3 (2004): 97–115.

Stahle, David W. "Tree Rings and Ancient Forest History." In *Eastern Old Growth Forests: Prospects for Rediscovery and Recovery*, edited by Mary Byrd Davis, 321–43. Washington DC: Island Press, 1996.

Walker, Joseph, ed. "The Travel Notes of Joseph Gibbons, 1804." *Ohio History* 92 (1983): 96–146.

Yahner, Richard. *Eastern Deciduous Forest: Ecology and Wildlife Conservation*. Minneapolis: University of Minnesota Press, 1995.

Young, Jean I., trans. *The Prose Edda of Snorri Sturluson: Tales from Norse Mythology*. Berkeley: University of California Press, 1964.